Innovative Legal Service Applications

A Guide to Improved Client Services

Lawrence S. Pascoe

AMERICAN BAR ASSOCIATION
Solo, Small Firm and General Practice Division

Cover design by Jill Tedhams/ABA Design

Printed in the United States of America.

26 25 24 23 22 5 4 3 2 1

Library of Congress Cataloging-in-Publication Data

Names: Pascoe, Lawrence S., author. | American Bar Association. Solo, Small Firm and General Practice Division, sponsoring body.

Title: Innovative legal service applications : a guide to improved client services / Lawrence S. Pascoe.

Description: Chicago, Illinois : American Bar Association, [2022] | Includes index. | Summary: "This book is about how lawyers can specifically improve their service to clients which will obtain more business. Besides providing numerous specific innovative legal service applications, this book will discuss the theories and actions to create, implement and evaluate innovative legal service applications. This book will provide a jump start for lawyers to enhance their service to clients by suggesting numerous innovative legal service applications. This book does not just say to listen to your clients and give them what they want. Instead, it will provide applications that lawyers can immediately utilize to improve their quality of service to their clients"--Provided by publisher.

Identifiers: LCCN 2021062382 (print) | LCCN 2021062383 (ebook) | ISBN 9781639051052 (board) | ISBN 9781639051069 (epub)

Subjects: LCSH: Practice of law.

Classification: LCC K120 .P37 2022 (print) | LCC K120 (ebook) | DDC 340.068--dc23/eng/20220325

LC record available at https://lccn.loc.gov/2021062382

LC ebook record available at https://lccn.loc.gov/2021062383

Discounts are available for books ordered in bulk. Special consideration is given to state bars, CLE programs, and other bar-related organizations. Inquire at Book Publishing, ABA Publishing, American Bar Association, 321 N. Clark Street, Chicago, Illinois 60654-7598.

www.shopABA.org

To Carol, my partner in life, without whose support and editing I could not have written this book.

Contents

Chapter 3:

Appendix

PART 1
Introduction

1

Opening Remarks

1.1 Why Should Lawyers Read This Book?

I was a lawyer for over 40 years. During that time, I witnessed changes, some revolutionary, in all areas of the law. There were, however, only minor changes in the way lawyers managed their practices and served their clients. I saw the introduction of lawyer advertising, which had not been legal until the late 1970s. I observed technology improve the efficiency of producing legal documents, doing legal research, and dealing with law firm finances. I watched the internet change how lawyers communicated with each other, clients, and the courts, and how it allowed lawyers to use new ways to promote themselves. But I did not observe too many differences and improvements in how lawyers serviced their clients. Lawyers did not advance their customer service as much as other businesses did in this same 40-year period.

As is well known, competition for legal services has increased since I started practicing. By my calculations, in 1980 there was, on average, one lawyer for every 394 people in the United States. By contrast, in 2020, there was one lawyer for every 250 people. Competition now also comes from many non-lawyers who are providing services previously done only by lawyers. There is also now a large number of self-represented people. Rather than vying for clients with improved products, as other businesses have done, most lawyers have opted to obtain clients by using advertising and other forms of promotional marketing. These lawyers base their advertising mostly on touting that they do everything, their years of experience, and how great they are. This advertising gives little value to clients. Rather than relying on promotional marketing to persuade prospective clients to retain them, lawyers should significantly improve the quality of their service. The reliance on promotional marketing rather than product improvement to obtain business diminishes the legal profession and is a disservice to clients.

This book discusses how lawyers can obtain more business by specifically improving their service to clients. Besides providing numerous specific innovative legal service applications, this book will discuss the theories and actions for creating, implementing, and evaluating innovative legal service applications.

Improving customer service is not intended to just enhance marketing; there are other significant benefits for doing so, such as reducing negligence claims and lowering complaints against lawyers. Providing better service also has nonmonetary advantages such as reduced stress, more enjoyment, and a greater sense of satisfaction. This book discusses these and other benefits that improving client service brings. This book will provide a jump start for lawyers to enhance their service to clients by suggesting numerous innovative legal service applications. I have developed and used many of these applications during my 42 years in practice. This book will provide an overview of these many service applications, which will be useful for one or more areas of law. I will also discuss applications that I left on the drawing board but never implemented and applications I formulated while writing this book. Also, on occasion, I will discuss some service applications developed by other lawyers. This book does not just say to listen to your clients and give them what they want. Instead, it will provide applications that lawyers can immediately use to improve their quality of service to their clients. In addition, this book will offer theories that will allow lawyers to find as well as create new applications themselves.

I will also include a suggested process for implementing service applications. Next, this book will discuss strategies for the formidable challenge of ensuring that ideas turn into reality and then a chapter on measuring a service application's success (analytics). Throughout the book, I make some observations and practice tips that I am not claiming are innovative. But for some newer and perhaps even some experienced lawyers, they are not so well known. Finally, I will look briefly at the big picture. I will provide my theories on why lawyers have not evolved, what lawyers can do individually, and what the profession should do about growing.

Therefore, though I may be biased, I think there is a lot of practical information in this book which will help lawyers obtain more business, reduce client complaints and negligence claims, and result in lawyers finding more enjoyment in the practice of law.

1.2 What Is an Innovative Legal Service Application?

The word "application" most often connotes a computer software program. But I use it to mean any physical item or activity used in processing a client's file. For example, a client manual that provides clients with articles and a place to organize the file's documentation is a physical application. Obtaining client feedback at all stages of a file is an activity application. By the word "service," I mean that part of a lawyer's work for a client that does not involve legal functions such as drafting and advocating.

A purist might say that "innovative" means something has to be new and original that no one has done before. My definition is not so narrow. I would say that an innovative application can also be an existing application that has been redesigned to be improved.

An innovative legal service application does not have to involve the use of technology. Allowing a purchaser to buy something in installments was a great business innovation that had nothing to do with technology. Finally, a bank figured out it would be of great service to their customers to have one line to see a bank teller rather than separate lines for each teller. Now, even more so because of COVID-19, I have noticed some grocery stores are using the one-line concept. There is no question that technology can and should be used to create innovative legal services, but technology is not always needed. An innovative legal service application can be something simple. It does not need to be complicated. Having one line is not complicated. Providing a client manual is not a complicated service application. A major application of mine is a client manual for each of my areas of practice. I elaborate on client manuals in chapter 4.1. The father of modern management, Peter F. Drucker said that business managers often wrongfully believe that something innovative must be complex. It does not.

1.3 What Are the Topics Covered in This Book?

I have divided the book into five parts. There are 14 chapters plus an Appendix with examples. The parts are (1) Opening Remarks [chapter 1], (2) Benefits and Elements of Innovative Legal Service Applications [chapters 2 and 3], (3) Innovative Legal Service Applications [chapters 4 to 9], (4) Creating, Implementing, and Evaluating Legal Service Applications [chapters 10 to 13], and (5) Conclusion [chapter 14]. Below I discuss the basics found in each chapter.

1. **Opening Remarks:** I give my definition of what an innovative legal service application is. I explain what topics are in this book, why lawyers should read it, in what order they can read it, the book's writing style, and where my ideas originated. I also explain why lawyers have not evolved and have not improved either their services to clients or their management techniques, as compared to other businesses.

2. **Benefits of Using Innovative Legal Service Applications:** I explain some of the benefits lawyers derive from using innovative legal service applications in their practice. It is not just a matter of better marketing: some of the benefits may not be readily apparent.

3. **Some Fundamental Elements of Legal Service Applications:** I present 20 elements that lawyers could include in applications to improve their legal services. I divided elements into two categories; first, client needs, and second, recommended lawyer actions. I sometimes provide a specific application to illustrate the principles. The 20 elements will help lawyers invent applications and understand why my suggested applications are of service to clients.

4. **Innovative Legal Service Applications:** I present many service applications that I suggest lawyers can use for most areas of their practices. I give some examples and sometimes relate the applications to the elements.

5 to 9. **Innovative Legal Service Applications for Specific Practices of Law:** I propose numerous service applications particular to five major areas of general law practice.

10. **Finding and Creating Innovative Legal Service Applications:** I present some methods for finding legal service applications and discuss how to create applications.

11. Implementing Innovative Legal Service Applications: This chapter suggests a process that helps in deciding which practice area is the best place to start the innovation journey and which applications to begin with and develop.

12. Ensuring Innovative Legal Service Applications Are Implemented: This chapter provides some practical methods to ensure lawyers put the applications into their practice. At first glance, this chapter may seem out of place in this type of book. It would appear to be more appropriate for a motivational/goal-setting self-help book. It is a critical chapter because it is challenging for lawyers, probably more so than for other businesses, to have their ideas come to fruition.

13. Analytics and Applications: This chapter provides ideas on evaluating an application's value using some analytical techniques.

14. Closing Remarks: If you make it to the book's end, I provide some final thoughts, which I hope will be helpful and inspirational.

Appendix: In the Appendix, I have some statistics tables but mostly samples of various applications discussed in this book. Rather than use these samples directly as precedents, lawyers should modify them to fit their practices and jurisdictions. They are in the book to show the format, style, and type of content of a specific application. They will often discuss matters that most lawyers would never have thought of when talking with clients, let alone put in writing to them. They are numbered based on the section in the book where I discuss them.

1.4 In What Order Can This Book Be Read?

In many business books, authors discuss the order in which the chapters in their book may be read. That is probably because the authors know readers might not finish their book. They do not want their readers turned off early, so they suggest readers can jump to the practical chapters and skip over the earlier, more theoretical chapters.

I was going to suggest an alternative order of reading this book, but then I decided to arrange the chapters in the order in which they really should be read. That means starting with reading about the many benefits of using innovative legal service applications in order to be motivated to read the rest of the book. Then, I follow the benefits chapter with some theories of client needs and recommended lawyer actions. Hopefully, I will keep you interested by presenting some applications in those discussions before moving to general and specific applications.

I do not suggest skipping over areas where you do not practice. Those other practice areas may contain applications that you could adapt to your practice. However, though not suggested, because it is an interesting and important chapter, you do have permission to skip chapter 10, "Finding and Creating Innovative Legal Service Applications," on the first reading if you are so anxious to implement my or your own applications right away. I admit Chapter 4 is tedious to read so I am not offended if you skim through parts of it. Knowing many readers will still skip sections, I sometimes make references prior and forward if I provide more detail about an application somewhere else in the book.

The section numbering system in chapters 5 to 9 is not sequential; it is based on the specific section number in chapter 4 that describes an application in general. The reader can then easily find more information about an application by looking at the specific section in chapter 4 as well as being able to see how that application was used in other practice areas as the section number will always be the same.

1.5 Who Is Lawrence S. Pascoe, and What Is This Book Based On?

It is appropriate for readers to know who I am, as my background and experiences have influenced my thoughts and suggestions in this book. While writing this book, I talked to lawyers who had practice areas different from mine, and I discovered that my experiences influenced me more than I had realized.

I graduated with an undergraduate degree in business and a law degree from Dalhousie University in Halifax, Nova Scotia, Canada. I was admitted to the Law Society of Ontario in 1977. I then practiced law in Ottawa, Ontario, for 42 years. Ottawa, the capital of Canada, is a government, university, and high-tech city. With a population of one million people, it is not a huge city, so I often dealt with the same lawyers and judges.

For my first 10 years of practice, I was in a small firm, a true partnership with first one, then two other lawyers. For my last 32 years practicing law, I was a solo practitioner with other lawyers on a cost-sharing basis. I retired in April 2019 (thankfully not a year later, during the COVID-19 pandemic).

After a few years of doing any legal work that walked through our door, I practiced primarily family law (75 percent), but to keep my sanity, I also had a wills and the administration of estates practice. In addition, I practiced residential real estate (5 percent). I dropped that practice in the early 1990s.

A significant interest of mine was continuing legal education. In addition to organizing programs, I wrote several papers. I gave presentations on family law and law office management issues on local, provincial, and national levels. I taught a few semesters in the Legal Assistant program at a local community college. I was a seminar leader at the Ontario Bar Admission Course, and I joined the American Bar Association (ABA), attending several family law conferences, ABA meetings, and the ABA tech shows.

As a commerce graduate, I was interested in the management aspect of the practice of law. I especially enjoyed marketing with an emphasis on producing a better product. Over the years, I researched management issues. That involved reading many legal and even more nonlegal management books. As a result, I created and implemented many innovative legal service applications.

In 1979, when advertising was first allowed in Ontario, my partner and I were the first lawyers in the City of Ottawa to advertise. In 1994, I launched one of Ottawa's first websites, then called "home pages." I had written many articles for a community newspaper, which would print them when the paper ran out of ads to insert. I, therefore, had a lot of ready-made material to post to my new website. In 1995, because of all the informational articles, checklists, intake forms, and a schedule of fees, I won an honorable mention in a local computer magazine's "Best Home Page" contest. Yes, I admit there was not much competition back then, but it was a useful website. I obtained a fancier name, "KnowYourRights.com," which I sold a few years later to a Minnesota law firm for US $10,000 ($15,000 Canadian). I changed the name to www.thepascoedifference.com. Surprisingly, no one has ever offered to buy that name. Over the years, I significantly increased my website's size and format.

My philosophy regarding my family law clients was that as they were going through such a hard time in their lives, if not the hardest, I tried to make the legal process easier. I worked to provide excellent and innovative service applications. I applied some of those ideas to my other practice areas.

I based this book on my experience with applications I developed and used my research of other lawyers and businesses and some legal and nonlegal authors' writings. I have also included numerous applications that I never got to implement. For some of them, it's because I did not find the time during my years of practice to create and implement these applications. Many other proposed but untested applications came to my mind while writing this book, so, yes, I actually used my own book's suggestions on how to create a service application.

1.6 What Is the Writing Style of This Book?

I would describe my general style of writing to be like a conversation with my readers. I want this book to be effortless and enjoyable to read, hence the informal style. I am not a writer or academic, so I could not write much differently anyway.

There will be no complicated flow charts and diagrams of wheels with principles going in different directions. There will be some forms which will be helpful to make decisions. Occasionally, for some readers, I may write what may seem obvious. I am doing this because perhaps what I think is obvious might not be so to others. I apologize to those who believe that, at times, I have "dumbed it down" too much.

To illustrate suggestions, I often add an experience I had. I will try to ensure my "lawyer war stories" are at least somewhat relevant. Sometimes, however, I may not be able to control myself, and I feel compelled to tell a good story. And the odd time, again, I will not be able to help myself, and I will get on a soapbox to render an opinion that may not exactly be on the book's topic. I will also make some suggestions that are not innovative applications but just practical suggestions about which perhaps not all lawyers are aware.

My wife always reminds me that not everyone gets (I say appreciates) my sense of humor. But I will occasionally try to be humorous to break from this book's seriousness. So, this book will hopefully be enjoyable to read. Often, I will put my so-called humor in endnotes to a chapter where the comment was not really necessary in the main text.

I want this book to be very helpful for lawyers. I will present numerous theories and ready-to-use service applications rather than concentrating on making a few major points. Therefore, I will not go into great depth for some of my discussions. I will sometimes reference the source of the idea or application to facilitate further reading on the concept, but there will not be footnotes and exact references to where I may have discovered the idea. I might not be able to recall where the idea came from during the last 40-plus years. Most of the legal service applications were my own inventions.

I will sometimes find it necessary to discuss a specific application or theory in more than one place. If I do so, I will go into great detail in only one of those places. In the shorter discussion, I will try to note where in the book the reader can find more detail about that application. However, I found that I did repeat myself in detail on certain matters. There were a variety of reasons for this. First, I know my audience. Most lawyers will not read this book as they should, cover to cover, so they may miss a good point I am making. Second, repeating a major point reinforces its importance. Third, for different reasons, the application or story does belong in more than one place. Fourth, the book may be more readable if the important points are found in more than one place.

1.7 Who Should Read This Book?

Much of this book applies to lawyers in all different practice areas and firms of any size. Parts even apply to lawyers not in private practice. Legal assistants should also take part in developing innovative service applications as several applications will be performed by them. For some practice areas, they are closer to the clients and have more contact with them than the lawyers do. Therefore, they may be better suited to know the clients' needs and have solutions to satisfy those needs. Marketing personnel at large law firms would also benefit from this book. Producing a better product with better service is key to better marketing.

Larger firms can afford to hire more extensive support staff. They should be working on improving their product rather than being so concerned about their social media platforms. Larger firms may have many partners and practice groups that probably need to consult and agree on implementing a new application, so an advantage that solo and small firms may have is that they do not have the bureaucracy to approve an innovative application. They also probably might not have the resistance to change that lawyers in some of the larger firms would have. Therefore, they can move quickly to implement an application. Solo and small firms have to differentiate themselves from the large firms. Using innovative service applications is a way they can do so.

1.8 Why Have Lawyers Not Evolved?

Lawyers were in existence in ancient Greece and later in ancient Rome. Lawyering became more of a defined occupation in the early Middle Ages, when England in the 1200s enacted statutes governing lawyers. I suspect the ways lawyers serviced their clients during ancient times are not significantly different from how lawyers service clients today. I believe there are several systemic reasons why lawyers have not evolved very much in the ways they service their clients.

The legal profession's culture is still primarily that lawyering is a profession and not a business. Many lawyers believe they should not get their hands sullied by using standard business practices. As members of a "profession," they think they're above that. This attitude has changed only somewhat over these thousands of years, and then just relatively recently. This culture prevented lawyers from even being allowed to advertise in the United States until as late as 1977.[1] The legal profession has discovered how technology and some business practices can improve the production of legal services and create additional ways to market them. However, the profession has not used either technology or new business practices very much to improve the service aspect of their products. And it appears the legal profession was/is not the one

---

[1] In 1977, the Supreme Court of the United States, in a 5 to 4 decision, ruled in Bates et al. vs. the State Bar of Arizona 433 U.S. 359 (1977) that lawyers had the right to advertise. The court held that lawyers had that right because the Constitution's First Amendment gave everyone the right to free speech. However, my theory is that lawyers were allowed to advertise because television stations suffered a significant loss in revenue when tobacco advertising was banned on television a few years earlier by the Public Health Cigarette Smoking Act. Television stations needed lawyer advertising to replace the lost tobacco company revenue. The jury is still out on whether society would have been better off with the tobacco ads rather than the Personal Injury lawyer ads.

that invents and produces these new products to help lawyers manage their practices. Software companies that seem to be made up mostly of non-lawyers and young ex-lawyers with some legal experience are the ones who did and do so. I suspect there is not much input into these products from older, experienced, practicing lawyers. If this older group was involved, I think there would be more client service applications.

The legal culture encourages lawyers not to change. Law schools teach their students to rely on precedents and laws that are generations old. So why should the practice of law change with the times either?

For cultural reasons, the legal education system does not teach law office management in any significant way. Law practice management is almost nonexistent, let alone a core part of law school curricula. A survey in a 2008 article in the *Albany Law Review* found that only 61 of 195 law schools' websites in the United States listed any courses in law office management. That is 31 percent. I conducted my own survey of law schools in the United States for the 2020 school year. I wrote 161 law schools, asking if they had any courses in law practice management. Of the 72 that replied, 23 schools had law office management courses, producing the same 31 percent rate as in 2008.

In my research, five law schools did have such courses but discontinued them. These cancellations occurred because the students lacked interest or lecturers did not want to teach them anymore. I reviewed the descriptions of the courses presently being offered. I found most of them not to be comprehensive. Marks were generally based on attendance, and many were pass/fail courses. In my six-month Bar Admission course 44 years ago, there were only two days on law office management. Most of those two days focused on legal accounting. When my son took the Bar Admission Course in Ontario in 2013, nothing was taught or tested on law office management. It also seems that though state Bar exams may have some questions about legal ethics, there is no testing on law practice management issues. Managing a law office is finally taught to lawyers at continuing education courses once they are practicing lawyers. Those courses are probably there at the insistence of the companies insuring lawyers to help reduce negligence claims. Insurers and Bar societies know from their statistics that lawyers' lack of knowledge of the law does not cause the most significant number of complaints and negligence claims against lawyers. Rather, business management mistakes are the primary culprits of claims and complaints.

In Ontario, the number of continuing education hours required for these "professional" hours is very minuscule, in my opinion. What qualifies as professional hours is also broadly interpreted and not always a fundamental law office management topic.

Lawyers have also not evolved as law office managers because they lack the time to invent service applications. Lawyers' time is taken up accomplishing the many tasks they must do to run a law practice. This situation is especially true if the lawyer is practicing solo or is in a small firm. Besides having the primary job of being the line worker who produces the product, the solo lawyer has many other responsibilities. These lawyers are the chief executive officers, comptrollers, marketing directors, heads of human resources, and purchasing agents. Add to this the time devoted to keeping up with the law, and when is there time for lawyers to also be in charge of the research and development department? Unlike those other business functions, research and development are not necessary to operate a law firm. Accordingly, law firms have left that department out of their organizational structure.

Unfortunately, another reason for the lack of evolution is that some lawyers think too highly of themselves: they believe they can operate a law practice without learning the many skills needed in running a business. It is analogous to the university professors I am sure we all had who were brilliant in their field of expertise but were poor teachers because they were not taught how to teach. Universities just expected that PhDs could teach even though real teachers go to teachers' colleges. Not all people in business have a business school degree. Still, it certainly helps to have some training to run a business.

In the final chapter of this book, I will discuss how individual lawyers and the legal profession as a whole can evolve faster.

1.9 Conclusion to This Chapter

This book contains my observations based on my experiences and what I have read. Some readers may disagree with my opinions and have other ideas on the subject. That is great! This book is just a small start on the vital matter of improving legal services. I could do only so much to create and implement applications and research the subject matter. There are many great ideas out there that could be developed and used by lawyers. I hope that what I am presenting is a good beginning for lawyers interested in improving their legal services. I am hopeful that lawyers think about what I have provided and use my applications and create some themselves.

I also realize that the vast majority of lawyers will "just not get it." They will say that lawyers will survive without worrying about producing better service because they have lasted this long without changes, so why should they change now? Their lawyer culture, lack of management education, and lack of time to think, let alone time to work on service applications, have made them that way. I hope this book changes their minds so that they change their ways, adopt some of my suggested applications, and create some of their own.

I hope that the legal profession will follow the lead of another long-time conservative business, the banking industry. That enterprise has evolved to serve its clients much differently and better than it formerly did. When I was younger, banking hours were from 10:00 a.m. to 3:00 p.m. every weekday except Fridays when they stayed open until 6:00 pm. Banks in the 1970s changed their hours: they opened earlier, stayed open later every day, and were accessible even on some evenings and Saturdays. Then banking services became available 24 hours every day with the introduction of ATMs. Then more 24-hour services became conveniently available at a customer's home with phone and online banking. Customers can now take pictures of checks and deposit them without even visiting their bank. Bank websites contain their customers' banking, investment status, and history, and have practical information on investing and specific reports on their customers' investments. In addition, these sites have several mathematical calculators to help their clients make financial decisions. If banking, an age-old and conservative institution could evolve its customer service, the legal profession surely can as well.

PART 2

Benefits and Elements of Innovative Legal Service Applications

2

Benefits of Using Innovative Legal Service Applications

This chapter discusses some good reasons why lawyers should pursue an active program to develop and implement innovative legal service applications. Besides being good for marketing, having more service applications will also benefit lawyers in several other ways. I hope these reasons will encourage lawyers to introduce more service applications into their practices.

2.1 Reduced Malpractice Claims

Appendix 2.1 and Appendix 2.2 are two statistics tables that I assembled from Lawyer's Professional Indemnity Company (Law Pro) publications. Law Pro provides malpractice insurance for lawyers in the province of Ontario. I would assume other jurisdictions would have the same experience as Ontario. The first table (A 2.1) shows four specific years, their four-year average, and a 10-year average percentage of each type of malpractice claim to the total number of claims. The second table (A 2.2) shows the percentages for types of claims over 10 years for different practice areas. These statistics reveal a lot of thought-provoking information. Except in the practice area of criminal law, lawyers' lack of knowledge accounts for a low number (18 percent) of claims. The remaining 82 percent of claims are primarily because of practice management issues. Almost one-third of those claims are related directly to poor communications between lawyers and their clients; therefore, I suggest all can be categorized as service issues. Eighteen percent of claims are because of inadequate investigation, which would also partially be a service issue. Providing legal service applications that improve communications between lawyers and clients and those who gather the facts would reduce negligence claims against lawyers. Malpractice claims cost lawyers money and time. The experience of being sued is very stressful. The worry about being sued is also a constant stress for lawyers.

Fortunately, Law Pro produces a great deal of information on how lawyers can organize their practices to reduce the number of negligence claims. I assume other insurance companies that provide malpractice insurance to lawyers would also offer the same type of information. This knowledge would also be a valuable resource for creating innovative legal service applications to reduce malpractice claims.

2.2 Reduced Client Complaints

Clients can complain about their lawyers in many other ways without going to the extent of commencing a negligence claim, and unfortunately, all these methods will cost lawyers time and money as well as creating enormous stress.

First, clients can complain by communicating with the lawyer directly. Second, clients can give lawyers bad reviews on Google or a variety of lawyer rating websites. Third, clients can make a formal complaint to their lawyers' governing bodies. Fourth, clients can go to court to complain about their lawyers' accounts if the governing body does not deal with billing issues. Unfortunately, at the very least, and perhaps most harmful and problematic to determine, is the client who badmouths the lawyer to all their friends and maybe to others who had been good referral sources.

Looking again at Ontario statistics as published by the Law Society of Ontario in its 2019 Annual Report, the number one complaint clients had against their lawyers was their lawyers' failure to serve them properly. That type of complaint included a failure to communicate. In 2019, 48 percent of clients' complaints claimed the lawyer failed to serve the client properly.

As with malpractice claims, when lawyers know what causes complaints, they can create service applications to mitigate these complaints and be motivated to implement more service applications.

2.3 Improved Marketing

Improved marketing is probably the leading benefit lawyers derive from innovative service applications. I admit that improving my marketing was the original reason I became interested in producing my applications. I did not join an established law firm; instead, a law school classmate and I started out on our own, so we needed to find clients. Fortunately, I had an undergraduate degree in business and very much enjoyed my marketing course at university. I found that when the floodgates opened and lawyers were allowed to advertise in the United States in 1977 and Ontario in 1979, lawyers started to market their services heavily. The increasing competition made it a necessity for lawyers to be interested in marketing. That competition has only increased: lawyers now compete with more lawyers and with others doing work once done only by lawyers. In some types of practice, like family law, there are also many more people representing themselves.

I learned two fundamental principles in my marketing course that have stayed with me my whole legal career. First, there are four P's to marketing: Product, Promotion, Price, and Place. Second, a successful marketing program has to have the proper mix of all the P's. However, in my opinion, most lawyer marketing is based mainly on just the promotion "P," with little, if any, consideration for the other P's.. And even the Promotion activities are done mainly by advertising. A person can build the world's best mousetrap (Product), but if no one knows about it (Promotion), if its cost is too much (Price), and if its location (Place) is inconvenient for buyers, no one will buy that world's best mousetrap. The mousetrap was the example used in my university days, but I assume professors have changed that example to an item like "drones." I found many comments about Ps and marketing (I do not know why the fixation on the letter "P" by marketing professionals) when I was researching the up-to-date relevancy of the four P's to marketing. By my last count, commentators were now at 15 different P's in the marketing mix. These commentaries did not agree on which Ps belonged, except the original four P's were always part of their lists.

On the Place "P," I made the simple decision to always practice in the suburbs where office space cost less, free parking was available, and people resided nearby. Concerning the Price "P," I probably should have done more analysis because there are some theories on the pricing of legal services, but I did have a strategy. (section 4.13).

I concentrated on the Product "P," creating innovative legal service applications, because I thought that was the most important "P" in the marketing mix. Besides, for the good reasons set out in this chapter, a better product was the most beneficial to clients. Promotion is about benefiting lawyers. Place is a slight convenience issue, and I found it was not significant for most clients. Though clients want to keep their costs down, most clients accept that legal services are expensive and cost what they cost. Lawyers should not target very price-sensitive people as clients, so I did not concentrate on the Price "P." But it is of significance to all clients that they have a better product.

Even with the introduction of lawyer advertising and more aggressive marketing, the top methods of obtaining work are return clients and client referrals. Lawyers with innovative legal service applications will have more satisfied clients, resulting in return clients and referrals.

Implementing innovative legal services will also differentiate that firm from other law firms in the eyes of prospective clients. According to well-known author Jack Trout, differentiation is an essential marketing tool, so much so that a book he wrote was titled *Differentiate or Die.*

2.4 Clients Can Judge Service Better than They Can Judge Legal Skills

A lawyer's end goal, like that of every business owner, is to have a satisfied client. Measuring satisfaction is very subjective and differs from client to client. It is irrelevant whether a lawyer believes that their unhappy client should have been happy with the lawyer's service. It only matters how the client perceives the quality of the overall legal services. Satisfaction may be largely, but not entirely, measured by results. Many legal services do not have winners and losers, because not all legal services are about two-party conflicts. But even in a legal matter of resolving a dispute between two parties, it is often difficult for clients to judge how well their lawyers performed their job. A lawyer may have done a fabulous job. It may have been impossible to obtain the client's desired result, but the result was much better than it could have been. Or a lawyer may not have done such a good job but was lucky that the judge deciding the case was predisposed to their position. Unless clients are lawyers, they cannot fully judge how well their lawyers performed or how other lawyers would have done.

A client once fired me on a file where I believed I performed exceptionally well and took extraordinary measures to find information about a husband's substantial foreign property, which he would never have revealed. Though the husband retained an aggressive senior lawyer, I had the husband removed from the house right away, and my client received good child and spousal support immediately. I was sorting through all this husband's complicated foreign property when my client fired me. She said it was taking too long to complete the file. The client even asked the court to reduce my account. My client was unsuccessful in lowering my account, and I obtained more than my hourly rate because the court realized what a good job I had done. However, the client did not appreciate my good performance and was unhappy with what I thought was excellent work.

Fortunately, though rarely, a client's wrong perception can work in the lawyer's favor. I had a motion with a seasoned litigator on the other side. In court, I spilled water on some of my papers. I could not find what paragraph in my client's affidavit I was relying on during my argument. I could not answer, even to my satisfaction, a question the judge put to me. The opposing lawyer, much more experienced, out-argued me. The judge's decision was all right because of who the judge was, and sometimes the facts and the law do matter, but it was not as good a result as I had hoped. Before I could apologize to my client, as we were leaving the courtroom, she said, "You really showed him." I wanted to ask her if we were in the same courtroom or perhaps in a parallel universe but was happy to find she did not think, as I felt, that I looked like a complete idiot.

Clients may not be able to judge how good a legal job a lawyer does, but clients can judge the speed with which a lawyer returns a phone call or an email. They can evaluate the service aspects of the whole legal product.

In his ABA book *Think Again: Innovative Approaches to the Business of Law*, Jeffrey Nischwitz writes that as lawyers cannot control the results, they need to focus on improving the quality of service to be great, because clients can judge service.

2.5 Creativity, Satisfaction, and Fun

Though producing innovative applications is more of a management science process than an art form, there is an inherent creative aspect. Even if lawyers, as I suggest, copy my or other lawyers' applications, they will still have to modify the applications to reflect their own practice. Being creative is fun and has been found to also improve one's ability to solve problems. The health benefits of being creative are that it increases happiness, reduces dementia, improves mental health, boosts immune systems, makes one smarter, and reduces stress. It also has been found that a person lowers their stress level even if they are not good at that creative activity.

I got great satisfaction and a sense of accomplishment when I created and implemented an innovative service application. In addition, I had fun and felt good about adding value to my legal services.

2.6 A Matter of Survival

The titles of two marketing books, Jack Trout's *Differentiate or Die* and Mathew Kiernan's *Get Innovative or Get Dead* may be a little overdramatic about the need to differentiate and innovate. I do not know of any cases where a lawyer died from not differentiating or not being innovative. However, we should go back to the even more fundamental theory of evolution of Charles Darwin. As I understand it, the theory is that individuals who do not adapt to a new environment are less likely to survive and less likely to reproduce. That theory will apply to lawyers who do not evolve with the changing legal business environment. Times have changed. Like many businesses, the law has seen a lot of changes to its environment. There is now major competition with other lawyers, other related businesses, and self-represented clients. The loyalty factor, which lawyers have heavily relied upon, is no longer so strong as it once was, as discussed in the book *Loyalty Myths* by Keiningham, Vavra, Aksoy, and Wallard. Lawyer websites allow prospective clients to shop around and compare law firms, something they could not easily do in pre-internet times.

For some law firms, it may be a matter of surviving, not a matter of thriving.

2.7 Being a Happy Lawyer

Several studies have shown that many lawyers are not very happy. I am sure readers have heard the following information or variations thereof: Numerous lawyers leave the profession at all stages of their careers. As many as 66 percent of lawyers want to quit the profession. In addition, lawyers rank fourth in suicides among all occupations and are 3.6 times more likely to be depressed than non-lawyers. The number of unhappy lawyers is so high that there is an industry specializing in helping lawyers find new occupations.

There are many reasons for a lawyer's unhappiness, one of which is that the work is boring. I would assume that also includes the fact that many files are quite similar, and therefore their work is somewhat repetitive. I would suggest that lawyers spend part of their day working on applications that improve their service to their clients. Then they will be doing something that is not boring but is mentally challenging, creative, and rewarding.

I include rewarding because Clio's *Legal Trends Survey* in 2020 measured what defines law firm success. By far, the number one item that lawyers define as success is making clients happy and satisfied, which, obviously, good client service does.

The issue of how lawyers can be happy is much more complex than having satisfied, well-served clients, but this is a component. I would recommend lawyers read the excellent classic book *Stress Management for Lawyers* (third edition) by Amiram Elwork for ideas on reducing stress.

2.8 The Untapped Legal Services Market

Lawyers who use innovative legal service applications obtain more of the existing legal services market. But there is another large and growing legal services market that lawyers should address.

There are many people whom Jack Newton, co-founder and president of Clio calls the "latent legal market." It consists of people who represent themselves, who use non-lawyers, or who do not deal with the legal issue at all. In his excellent book *The Client-Centered Law Firm,* Mr. Newton states from his own company's research that the main reasons for not using a lawyer were that doing so was too costly, the benefits did not justify the cost, and people disliked not knowing the final costs of the service.

Technology may have sped up the time it takes to deliver legal services, but it has not decreased legal fees, which are now often so high they are out of reach for many clients. Instead, legal costs have gone up because life and legal disputes are more complex. For example, when I started my law practice, family law did not even have to deal with the division of assets because the spouse in whose name the asset was registered kept that asset, and it was just a matter of arguing support. In addition, the parties generally assumed that the mother would obtain custody, so few cases were arguing over custody.

Lawyers have been creative with legal fees by offering contingency fees and unbundled services for specific practice areas. But I am still amazed at how few law firms post their prices or do a better job estimating or even trying to predict their costs, even as they expect clients to discuss retaining them without knowing what their fees might be. It is no wonder this latent market is so large.

I believe using more innovative service applications will convince potential clients in this latent market of the value of hiring a lawyer rather than trying to represent themselves or doing nothing at all.

3

Some Fundamental Elements of Legal Service Applications

This chapter presents two fundamental types of elements, one or more of which would be present in a successful legal service application. The first element type contains several client needs that service applications must address. The second element contains many actions lawyers need to use to produce better legal service applications.

Some elements are more significant than others; depending on the area of law, some client needs and lawyer actions are more critical than others. Some elements may not even be relevant for specific areas of practice. Some elements' significance will also vary depending on individual clients' different personalities and their diverse backgrounds. Lawyers must recognize the diversity of their clients and safeguard the dignity of all their clients.

Knowing these elements—client needs and lawyer actions—will help explain the reasoning behind the applications I suggest in this book. Lawyers can also look to these elements to customize my suggested applications and to develop their own. To better explain a client's need or a lawyer's action, I will often provide a specific application as a demonstration. Discussion of an application might appear more fully later in the book when I am discussing an application generally or for a particular practice area. I provide many specific applications in detail in the Appendix section so that lawyers can better understand the application and implement it immediately.

There is no direct relevance to the order in which I have listed the elements. These lists are not exhaustive but are a start. In addition, lawyers will have their own elements that they can use to create better and more innovative legal service applications.

3.1 Client Needs

Lawyers should have applications that satisfy their clients' needs. Sometimes clients will not even know they have a specific need until an application meets it. Studies have shown that what clients say and do are different, which shows their lack of self-awareness of their real needs. Because clients' needs vary in degree from practice area to practice area and from client to client, lawyers should offer their clients all the available applications and not try and figure out which needs are for which clients. There will be elements that will be more significant to some clients than to others. I am presenting the most important client needs based on my experience and research. Other lawyers may find other needs are significant, and these could be satisfied with a new application. I provide a list of all the elements in Appendix 11.2. I discuss using this list in chapter 11 when talking about processes to implement legal service applications.

3.1.1 Clients Want to Be Confident That Their Lawyers Are Very Competent

The reason for retaining a lawyer can be one of 'the most significant events in a person's lifetime. Next to death, and sometimes worse than dying, divorce can be the most traumatic event a person may experience; therefore, clients want to have confidence that their lawyers really know what they are doing. They want to see that their lawyers know the law, are comprehensive, organized, and do not make mistakes. Clients can lose confidence over what the lawyer may see as minor matters, such as typographical errors. Sometimes clients will compare their lawyer's actions to the lawyer's actions on the opposing side.

To build that confidence, clients want to know as much as they can about the lawyer. They would like to see the credentials and experience of their lawyer. At medical appointments, I always look at the doctor's office walls to read their diplomas. I look for when and where they went to medical school. Before retaining a lawyer, clients check them out through friends, websites, and rating services (though this is sometimes dangerous, the way rating services operate). Therefore, it is essential, as it will be discussed in section 4.2.3, for lawyers to provide clients with as much information about themselves as possible.

3.1.2 Clients Want Their Lawyers to Be Empathetic

In my family law experience, a significant criterion for clients hiring a lawyer was whether the lawyer believed in their positions in the case. Clients would seek out lawyers who would agree with their demands, even if the demands were not realistic. Clients want their lawyers to be empathetic to their cases.

When I taught the family law practical course at Ontario's Bar Admission Course, the course materials suggested lawyers be sympathetic, not empathetic. The dictionary difference is that empathetic means putting oneself totally in a person's position and feeling the way they feel. Sympathetic, however, means showing sincere concern when something terrible happens to someone. When lawyers are too empathetic, their advice and action may be based on too much emotion and what the clients want rather than on rational reasoning. Early in my career, during a hotly contested settlement conference, a judge gave me good advice. The other lawyer and I had been arguing quite strenuously and with much emotion. We were not getting anywhere when the judge put up his hands, smiled (which this judge rarely did), and said, "Hold it guys, it is the clients who are supposed to be emotional, not the lawyers." We had lost our objectivity being too empathetic. Another local judge, who, as a lawyer, was quite emotional himself, remarked that as judge, he found that lawyers lose their credibility when they get too emotional. He also said the same was true when lawyers were not civil with each other (which can result from being too empathetic).

I believe lawyers should be empathetic *and* sympathetic because the clients want and need both from their lawyers. The lawyers will do a better job if they appreciate better what their clients are going through. From my experience of numerous matrimonial files, I tried to have the right mix of empathy and sympathy for my clients' situations. However, I am sure many lawyers would disagree with this self-assessment.

Unfortunately, simply being empathetic in many family cases resulted in over-demanding clients hiring over-aggressive lawyers who would follow their clients' overreaching instructions. This pairing often results in unnecessary arguing and going to court in cases where the parties could have settled. I blame this situation much more on over-aggressive lawyers, because it is their job, in my opinion, to advise their clients to be reasonable.

How is this need for empathy applied to creating a service application? I suggest lawyers must regularly communicate at every opportunity that they are empathetic as well as sympathetic. Also, lawyers should provide resource material for nonlegal aspects of the case. For example, I asked a local counselor to write an article about the psychological aspects of divorce. Lawyers should also provide a list of other professionals or businesses that may help clients with nonlegal issues. By doing this, lawyers show that they recognize clients may have these psychological issues and that they want to help even though this help is outside their job description. Sometimes, lawyers should just listen to their clients vent their frustrations, even though what the clients are espousing is not relevant to their legal case. And yes, lawyers should allow venting even when they are charging on a set fee basis.

3.1.3 Clients Want Good, Timely, and Understandable Communications with Their Lawyers

Lack of good communication between the client and the lawyer is the number one cause of clients' malpractice claims and complaints to lawyers' governing bodies. Clients want their lawyers to regularly communicate with them throughout the file and on a timely basis.

Clients want their lawyers to return their telephone calls within a reasonable time. Incredibly, lawyers have to be continually reminded to return telephone calls promptly. And of course, now that applies to replying to most client emails. If I was able (and I tried) to return calls right away, clients often remarked they were surprised and impressed that I got back to them quickly.

As I will discuss in more detail in section 4.27.6, a stated policy of returning calls and emails should be established and followed.

3.1.4 Clients Want to Know What Their Costs Will Be

Like any other product or service consumer, clients want to know what the product or service will cost. There are a variety of reasons why they want or need to know. First, they may want to see if they can even afford the service at that time. For instance, for a young couple without children, wills and powers of attorney can sometimes wait. Second, if it is a service they must have, such as representation in a criminal matter, they have to know so that they can plan where they will obtain the money if they do not have it, or if they have it, but it is not accessible immediately. Third, they may want to know the costs because they are shopping around and looking for the best price. This search for the lowest price is especially true for what clients consider are commodity legal services, like representation on a residential real estate file or the drafting of wills and powers of attorney. For other matters, the price is not their primary criterion for choosing a lawyer, but they still want to know what it will be.

Many legal services have fixed prices, so there is no reason for lawyers not to post their fees on their websites, yet few do. It is as if lawyers are embarrassed to tell the client what the service will cost until they have their first consultation. It is often the last issue discussed at the first consultation. In other businesses, you would not see an advertisement or website selling a product without listing the price, so I do not understand why lawyers do not post their service prices, especially those with fixed fees. Section 4.13 discusses many aspects of legal fees.

3.1.5 Clients Want to Know the Timing of Their Matter and Want It Completed Quickly

Some clients can be like children on a long car trip. They want to know when they will get to their destination, and they want to be there as soon as possible.

For many types of files, the lawyers and clients alone cannot control the timing and speed. In those cases, timing and speed will also be dependent on many other people, such as the opposite parties, the other side's lawyers, the courts, experts, and other participants.

In matters like a wills practice, where lawyers and clients have complete or almost complete control of the timing, lawyers should write out the process time frame for the clients. I did this without difficulty for my will files and uncontested divorce files and was usually correct. For uncontested divorces, I gave a spread of dates because the court timing could vary slightly on a few of the steps that involved the court.

Concerning speeding things up in those controllable matters, I employed process maps with a realistic schedule based on everyone doing their tasks as soon as possible (A 5.13.2 and A 6.12). Having client information forms sent out by email or filled out on the firms' websites before the first consultation will speed things up. Doing so lets clients know what information and documentation are needed to bring to their appointment. Then the processing time is not prolonged, waiting for information to arrive after the consultation. At the end of clients' first consultations I made a date for the will-signing appointment to speed things up and be on track with the schedule. This set appointment date pressured the clients to provide further instructions, if necessary and forced me to draft the wills quickly, often right after the clients left the first appointment. It also reduced follow-up phone calls to make the appointment to sign the wills.

3.1.6 Clients Want Their Tasks to Be Easy to Do

Though it was about 35 years ago, I still remember completing two complicated projects in my personal life. We had a nanny for our older son (now a 40-year-old entertainment lawyer). Though the premium was small, the government required that I complete a workman's compensation application. It was the most challenging form I ever had to fill out in my life. I recall that I even had to take out the carbon sheet and insert it in two places. I was very frustrated and wrote to the Worker's Compensation Board, complaining that even with two university degrees, I had trouble with their form and instructions. Around the same time, I bought a new gas barbecue. It came in hundreds of pieces that I had to assemble. It took a few hours, but I enjoyed putting it together. I had no trouble doing so because it came with the most detailed instructions; a monkey could have probably put the barbecue together. That I remember these experiences more than 35 years later shows the importance of making clients' tasks as easy and uncomplicated as possible.

Lawyers should analyze every task that clients must do and make it easier for them to do. One of the first applications I developed was to write a very detailed article for my clients on how to fill out the mandatory Family Law Financial Statement, a form necessary for all family matters where the client is claiming support or a division of property. I also eventually produced videos on the same subject. I posted those videos to my website and YouTube (where they still are today).

3.1.7 Clients Want to Understand the Substantive Law and Legal Process

When a person does not fully understand how a vacuum cleaner works, it does not affect how well the vacuum picks up dirt. However, sometimes a client who does not understand the law can affect the outcome of their case. The client's lack of this knowledge may result in their not providing facts relevant to the case and not fully comprehending what they agreed to.

Lawyers will serve clients better if they communicate easily and understandably with them on all aspects of their legal matters. Lawyers should explain any legalese and speak in plain language to their clients. I suggest providing clients a list of definitions of legal terms lawyers use in the file's particular law area, as I did for family law (A 5.12.2). Lawyers should provide memorandums that annotate standard document clauses.

The use of short articles written by lawyers on substantive law and the legal process will substantially meet this need. However, just orally explaining these subject matters may not be good enough because there is already too much information for clients to absorb all at once.

Lawyers should routinely ask at the end of any interaction with the client, whether in a consultation, phone call, or even a letter: "Do you have any questions?" Clients may not think of or want to ask questions even when they do not understand if lawyers do not encourage them to ask. Asking clients if they have any questions may remind them of something they wanted to ask. It also shows the client the importance lawyers place on making sure clients understand everything. I even added that question to my interview checklists.

Depending on the matter, lawyers should also encourage clients to bring a family member or good friend to their consultations. Then there is another set of ears to take in the sometimes voluminous legal information given. Sometimes these third parties also provide clients assurances that the advice lawyers are offering makes sense. For example, in matrimonial matters, I often found clients would have a friend or relative accompany them to the office but would ask permission for these people to sit in on the interview. They thought these third parties were not wanted when the opposite was true.

3.1.8 Clients Want Their Service Personalized Based on Their Preferences

Clients do not want to feel that they are buying a commodity when they retain lawyers. Legal matters are customized depending on the facts of the particular file and, if possible, so should aspects of the service components. For matrimonial matters, I had a Client Preference Questionnaire that asked the client among other questions, for their preferred type of communication, the best times to telephone, and the time of day to have appointments. It also asked the clients to rate the priority of the issues that could become contested in their type of case.

3.1.9 Clients Want to Participate in the Process

The dynamics between the lawyer and the client may determine the outcome of the file. It will undoubtedly affect the satisfaction rate of the client. Many clients are sophisticated about the law, more so than in past years. From various sources, they may know a lot about the law for their legal issue. Yes, their television, internet, and friends' sources are often wrong, but not always. Clients certainly know more about the facts of their case than do their lawyers.

Lawyers must inform their clients that they are part of a team and that their participation is needed and wanted. No question of fact is irrelevant until the lawyer tells them it is not relevant.

Most clients want to be part of the process and not be just bystanders. They can help if the lawyer's office keeps them up to date with all the case developments. Therefore, they should be given a duplicate of the file documentation not just on a timely basis but immediately. If there is a client portal to their file, their lawyer's office should notify them when the lawyer puts something in their file. If there is no portal, the law office should immediately copy the client with all outgoing and incoming material. The client's immediate comments on that material may be helpful. Clients are not truly part of the team if lawyers do not share information with them without delay.

For my family law clients, I always had an article setting out what each of our roles was and what we should and, importantly, should not expect from each other (A 5.12.5.1).

At times, clients were reluctant to get very involved and apologized for not knowing the law, to which I would always tell them to stop apologizing because if they knew the law, I would not be in business. I said they were not on the team for their legal knowledge but with my help their role was to make decisions.

As clients are now more sophisticated, many want to do some work on the file themselves. That may be entirely appropriate. For my administration of estates files, I broke down the many tasks required to administer an estate. I classified them as ones the client can do, what generally only lawyers do, and what either the client or the lawyer can do. If they chose to do any of the tasks, their fee was lower. The odd time they wanted me to do some of the tasks they usually would do, so they paid more (A 7.10).

3.2 Recommended Lawyer Actions

Recommended lawyer actions are activities lawyers should do to better serve clients.

3.2.1 Lawyers Should Recognize That What Is Important to Lawyers May Not Be Important to Clients and What Is Important to Clients May Not Be Important to Lawyers

I had a rude awakening early in my practice when I called a client about her recently drafted separation agreement. My small firm in the early 1980s bought one of the first word processors. It was expensive, took up a whole room, and required a secretary to take a four-day course to learn how to operate it. Besides a fancier font, this machine's advantages were that agreements would be right-hand margined and had proportional spacing, so an "h" took up more room than an "i." These features resulted in the agreement looking very professional. I excitedly phoned the client to tell her I had the agreement back from our word processor and that it looked great. It had a professional-looking font, was right-hand-margined, and had proportional spacing. I heard only dead silence on the other end of the phone until the client said, "I don't care what it looks like, what does it say?" Lawyers want to look professional; however, substance over style is what clients want.

Substance over style is fundamental in lawyers' websites, though it is not a principle, in my opinion, generally followed by lawyers. Another one of my war stories illustrates this. My first website in 1995 was all print, no images, and no color. As I mentioned in chapter 1 (and as I remind people often), my website won an honorable mention in a local technology magazine's "Best Home Page in Ottawa" contest. I talked to the editor of the magazine at a trade show sometime after the contest. I told him I was thinking of adding some graphics and colors to my site. He looked at me as though I had lost my mind and said, "You are a law firm. People want information. If they want graphics and color, they'll go to the Louvre's website."

An example of where clients find something important but lawyers do not, is websites. When advertising was first allowed, and lawyers could put ads in the Yellow Pages, many lawyers were slow to advertise there. Lawyers could not imagine anyone would use the Yellow Pages to choose a lawyer; as it happens, maybe lawyers do not choose lawyers that way, but many regular people do. The same has happened with websites: not everyone, but now numerous people use websites to select their lawyers. I have much to say about law firm websites in this book (section 4.2).

3.2.2 Lawyers Should Use All Three Time Periods (Before, During, and After Being Retained) to Provide Service to Their Clients

Many products and services have three time periods when vendors provide service to their clients. The first is the period before the sale, when the product's attributes and costs are explained. The second is the period when the product or service is delivered. The third period occurs after the sale, when warranties covering problems with the product or work or routine maintenance of the product or work are provided. Legal services are no different and have three periods when lawyers can offer their clients service. The first period occurs when clients are looking to retain lawyers. The second occurs when the clients have retained their lawyers and the lawyers have completed their work. Last, there is the period after the lawyers have ended the matter, and their files are closed.

I believe that lawyers are not providing the service applications they could in the first and third periods, because they believe the second period is the only one in which they need to serve their clients. Lawyers miss the chance to provide significant value to their products if they do not have service applications in the first and third periods.

In the first period, prospective clients know they need to hire a lawyer but do not know which lawyer is the right one for them. Even if they get a recommendation from a friend or have used a lawyer before, they would like to have information before choosing a lawyer for their new matter. They also want to know something about the law for their particular case. They would like to see the lawyer's expertise, office location, and approximate costs. Many will want to know about the process and timeline of a typical file like theirs. They may wonder, even at this searching stage, what information and documentation they are expected to provide to process their matter. Many lawyer websites do not provide significant amounts of this information when these websites could easily do so.

After the file is closed in the third period, probably because there are no foreseeable billings, most lawyers do not offer any further service. However, lawyers can provide many easy and inexpensive applications to add extra value to their products. Doing so may result in future business, but even if not, they enhance the service provided. Using this period to provide service also differentiates a lawyer's service from other lawyers' services because lawyers do little of it. When I finalized a will file, I, with the client's permission, wrote the client's executors a letter informing them where the client has stored the original wills and provided them with some articles I had written about the duties of an executor. I also gave my clients a list of free follow-up legal services, unrelated to their file that I would provide to former clients, like swearing (not drafting) simple affidavits for something like insurance loss claims.

As explained by Dan and Chip Heath in their book *The Power of Moments,* clients do not average out their total service experience but remember, besides the highs and the lows, the beginning, and the end of their experience. Therefore, it is essential to have helpful service applications in the first and third periods of servicing clients. Lawyers should not forget the age-old principles of the importance of making good first impressions and that one never gets a second chance to make a good first impression.

3.2.3 *Lawyers Should Use Available Legal Software*

Because law firms do not have research and development departments and individual lawyers do not spend the time to work on service applications, technology companies that deal with legal products have built some service applications into their products. Though these programs primarily appeal to lawyers for document production and financial matters, they have some client service applications. For instance, some do have the ability to allow clients to book consultations online. Also, through the cloud, they have the beneficial ability to create client portals to allow clients to access documents on their files. Lawyers should try to be up to date regarding what these products can do to improve their service and, when appropriate, should purchase them. They are worth the money, though they may cost more than generic software made for all business types.

A significant reason to use these legal software programs is that they must know changes in the law that might affect that particular practice. For example, without the legal software, the lawyer might miss some small updates, such as a court form change.

3.2.4 *Lawyers Should Use General Software*

The primary software programs, such as Microsoft Word and Excel, have many service applications that lawyers can use in their practice. For instance, all word processing software like Microsoft Word can produce a table of contents and indexes. At times, I have used them for separation agreements so clients can find a particular subject matter in a lengthy contract rather than searching through the document, frustrated they cannot find what they are looking for. For draft wills, I used the line numbering feature to show the document is a draft and make it easier for clients to ask whatever questions they have. Lawyers can use features of Excel or any spreadsheet program to produce service applications. Word and Excel are mainstream software programs that all lawyers and most clients would have. People are developing many apps every day, some of which lawyers could adapt to their practice to improve their service.

3.2.5 *Lawyers Should Indulge Clients but Give Realistic Expectations*

A marital breakup can be one of the worst experiences clients will go through in their lifetime. The clients are often not themselves. They will stress about small things they would not generally worry about and will not register in their brains everything told to them. A lawyer told me her theory that matrimonial clients are temporarily insane while going through their divorce. I would not go that far, but I recall seeing matrimonial clients months after their file was closed and often found them different people from when they were going through their matrimonial case.

Therefore, to reduce stress, lawyers should have many additional helpful features, even minor ones, like providing a map showing where the parking lots are surrounding the courthouse they will attend.

Lawyers must be careful that they do not feed into their clients' unrealistic expectations. Lawyers must carefully manage clients' expectations; they should explain that what clients may want as an outcome may not be possible to obtain. Some lawyers promise their clients more than can be delivered to make their clients feel better. On the other hand, some lawyers will forecast a poor case outcome, so the lawyer looks good if there is a better result than predicted. Lawyers should give a realistic assessment to clients. That is what clients deserve. Clients must also be in the best position to make decisions if required to do so. They cannot be in that position if the predicted result has been overstated or understated.

3.2.6 Lawyers Should Provide Information about Nonlegal-Related Resources

Lawyers are most often just one component of their clients' total project. When clients buy a house, they also need to retain a real estate agent, a mortgage broker, a mover, and other businesses to complete the project. A matrimonial client might need a psychologist, financial advisor, and all the people involved in a real estate transaction. A will client might need a financial planner and insurance agent. Lawyers are often asked for recommendations for those other fields but should not wait for the client to ask; instead, they should have a list of their own suggestions ready to provide in written form. I went one step further by getting these other service providers' business cards to give to my clients. I placed a plastic insert holding these business cards in the client manual.

I would not go so far as many other businesses do and have referrals or arrangements with unrelated businesses, as my mobile phone carrier does with restaurants. A lawyer who does that would lose some credibility about their professionalism, in my opinion.

I did have a list of lawyers who practiced other areas of law, because lawyers are often asked for a recommendation for a lawyer in another field of practice. Lawyers should be ready to provide recommendations that are of service to their clients. I had prepared for clients and even nonclients information about other lawyers that I could recommend for files in which I had a conflict, files that were not in an area of law I practiced or for files in areas of law that I practiced but that I did not want to take on. At one point, I also had these other lawyers provide short biographies, including details about their fees and location.

3.2.7 Lawyers Should Create Moments of Exceptional Service

As I discussed at the end of section 3.2.2, the service that clients remember the most takes place at the beginning, the end, and at the highs and lows of the file. But according to Chip and Dan Heath, authors of *The Power of Moments,* clients also remember small special extras of the service. These extras significantly increase their overall rating of the service given to them.

I created a small moment by providing clients with a free good-quality three-hole punch they could use when inserting the copies of documents I had sent them to put into their client manuals. Also, walking into my office and seeing a monitor for them was a moment for most clients.

3.2.8 Lawyers Should Have Some Physical Aspects in Their Applications

In his excellent marketing book, *Selling the Invisible,* Harry Beckwith states that service providers like lawyers have an invisible product, in contrast to a company that produces a physical product. That and other differences make it more challenging to market a service business. Beckwith's books, therefore, discuss how to market service businesses better. He suggests that a service provider should "make the invisible visible." He argues that potential clients do not like things they cannot see. Perhaps this is more of a marketing principle than a service principle. But I would say that a useful physical object like a client manual is a good service application for a client and makes the invisible feel visible. Physical applications must have practical functions: I provide my clients with my magnetic business card, which, besides reminding them of me when they look at their refrigerator, has the beneficial role of holding up grocery lists and family photographs.

3.2.9 *Lawyers Should Use Humor to Put Clients at Ease*

Many clients are understandably nervous about using a lawyer, especially at their first consultation. I have found that using some humor sets them at ease and makes me look somewhat human, which reduces their anxiety.

The nature of my practice was that I had primarily one-off clients. I, therefore, got away with not changing my jokes much in over 40 years. I just had to put up with my assistants if they were in the room, rolling their eyes because they had heard the joke so often it was no longer funny to them. I still thought I was funny. I tried to find something humorous in every type of file, even in serious cases.

When clients were signing their wills, I always told them that they should read them over carefully as from the draft to the final copy, I had inserted a clause in two-point type giving me their entire estate.

I am sure many readers may not find my humor amusing or appropriate but in over 40 years, not one client complained, and they did occasionally laugh.

3.2.10 *Lawyers Should Recognize That Most Clients Are First-Time Users of Legal Services*

For most general practice areas, the clients will have only one similar file with the lawyer and will use lawyers very few times in their entire lives. I had only two clients who divorced three times and only a handful who had divorced twice. A client going to a lawyer is not the same as a patient going to their doctor or dentist. Those patients have been to the doctor's or dentist's office many times before. In those cases, patients know what to expect.

Not having been to a lawyer before, and probably not for a contentious or emotional matter, the first-time clients are likely to be apprehensive and stressed about this new experience. There are so many things they may want to know.

The solution is quite simple: lawyers should let these first-time clients know in writing beforehand everything possible about what their experience will be like, what is expected of them, and how the law firm operates. Lawyers should also anticipate common questions about the process and the fundamental law for that area of law. They should put that information in writing to the client beforehand.

Lawyers can disseminate this information in a variety of ways. They can put it on the website. The website would also include their client contact and factual questionnaire, which would let the client know what information and documentation are needed. Lawyers can also have this information in an appointment confirmation letter. Some information that can wait can be in a New Client Memorandum, which is found in the client manual. Lawyers must be careful not to overwhelm clients with too much information at once.

As will be discussed later, for the first interviews, I had a slideshow (like a PowerPoint presentation) showing what I would discuss with the client during the consultation. I posted the slideshows to my website so my clients would know all the subject matters intended to be discussed at their first interview.

3.2.11 Lawyers Should Show Appreciation to Clients and Others Who Refer Clients to Them

If a client is nice enough to recommend you to friends or relatives, which might amount to thousands of dollars for just one file, then they deserve more than a standard two-line thank-you note the assistant typed and the lawyer simply signed (and maybe a holiday greetings card). Almost all, if not all lawyers, will say their business mainly comes from repeat clients and client referrals, yet most lawyers do not adequately thank the client or person who referred clients. I will be discussing my practice of sending maple syrup at the end of the year to anyone who referred clients to me.

3.2.12 Lawyers Should Always Remember What Business They Are In

When designing an application and serving clients, lawyers should never forget what business they are in. What business is that? They are, for most, practice areas in the business of helping people through the most significant and sometimes the most challenging events in their lives. A wills and powers of attorney practice is not just about producing documents that say where one's assets go on death or who is in charge when one becomes incapacitated. It is about planning what happens so as to ensure the client has the peace of mind that their worldly possessions go to the right people, that loved ones are financially taken care of, and that it will be made easy for the survivors to manage the estate. It is about ensuring the client is looked after if they become incapacitated. Family law is about helping people obtain a fair settlement or good court order for themselves and their children if their marriage fails. As well, family law lawyers must make sure their clients get through the legal separation process as painlessly as possible because separation from a spouse can be one of the worst events that can happen to a person in their lifetime. Estate lawyers are usually helping people deal with the final affairs of a loved one. A real estate lawyer is helping people complete what is more than likely the biggest financial transaction of their lifetime. And corporate lawyers are helping set up and resolve problems about their clients' livelihood. Criminal lawyers are like family lawyers who guide their clients through a difficult and traumatic incident in their lifetime and advocate on their behalf. Personal injury lawyers fight for proper payments for their clients to compensate them for their injuries and loss of income, determining their finances for the rest of their lives.

All of this means, first, that it is important to provide not just excellent but extraordinary service to help clients get through these major events in their lives. Second, the legal aspect is just one part of the client's events. Often, lawyers need to collaborate with nonlegal service providers to assist their clients and, in some cases, complete nonlegal functions on behalf of their clients.

There is also a self-interest reason for lawyers, like other businesses, to remember what business they are in. It can be a matter of survival. Kodak forgot they were in the photography business, not just in camera film production; therefore, they did not adapt when the digital camera came along, even though a Kodak engineer invented digital photography. This principle does not apply only to individual companies: there is the age-old example that horse-drawn carriage companies went bankrupt because they forgot they were in the transportation business, not just in the business of producing carriages. Lawyers must change with the times as new technologies as well as non-lawyers provide services to clients that were previously the domain of lawyers.

3.2.13 Lawyers Should Ensure Clients Use the Service Applications

Clients should be reading the articles and letters and filling out the questionnaires; many clients do not read as much as they should, which diminishes the lawyers' service to their clients. Getting clients to read the many articles and long reporting letters is no easy task. This subject is discussed more fully in sections 4.5.9 and 4.12.12.

PART 3
Innovative Legal Service Applications

4

Innovative Legal Service Applications

This chapter will present legal service applications that lawyers can use for most practice areas of law. In chapters 5 to 9, I will set out specific detailed applications for individual practice areas. I have based the order in which I present the service applications in this chapter on a combination of when they occur in processing a file and what I consider are the essential applications for providing better client service. I sometimes note the elements discussed in chapter 3 that the application achieves (listed in Appendix 11.2), though it should be apparent which element the application satisfies. Some of these applications in themselves are not new and are therefore not technically innovative; sometimes, however, when certain content and other features are added, these applications become innovative. Like the elements I outlined in chapter 3, not all applications are relevant to every practice area or every client in the same practice area. Like the elements, some applications' significance will also vary depending on clients' different personalities and diverse backgrounds. I may use examples to explain the service application and refer to where the reader may find a fuller explanation and sample.

4.1 Client Manuals

For the last 30 years of my legal career, I gave each of my clients a customized client manual for each area of the law I practiced. The standard matrimonial file clients received a large high-quality three-ringed binder entitled "The Family Law Client Manual." If the matter went to court, clients received volume 2 of this manual. If the file was an uncontested divorce or a marriage contract /cohabitation agreement, they received different manuals with less material. I also had a Wills and Powers of Attorney Manual and an Administration of Estates Manual. Before I stopped doing residential real estate, I had a Real Estate Manual.

4.1.1 The Manuals' Purposes

Manuals have different content for different practice areas but have several common purposes. First, they are a place to provide written information for the client on various subjects as set out in this book. The second objective is to hold material sent or given to the client throughout the file's life so that the client has an organized file for the legal services provided. Third, manuals may contain information for the client to keep up to date after closing the file. Fourth, manuals may include nonlegal information related to the subject matter that the client chooses to store in the manual.

4.1.2 Organization and Contents of the Manuals

Each manual has sections separated by numbered tabs. The organization and content would vary significantly from practice area to practice area but generally would have the following sections: an index of what was in the manual, an introduction section, an article section, a section to hold letters, a section to keep documents, a section relating to the retainer and accounts, a section for notes and to-do lists, a section related to information after the file is closed, and a section for related but nonlegal written material. Because there was more correspondence, the Family Law Client Manual would subdivide the letters and document section based on the source.

4.1.3 Keeping the Manuals up to Date

When I gave clients copies of documents at their appointments, I would three-hole punch them and have the client insert them in the appropriate section. If I sent clients copies by email, clients were to put them in their manuals themselves. Clients could keep their index up to date themselves if they so wished.

4.1.4 Why the Client Manuals Are So Important

The manuals provided clients with an organized, up-to-date, client-friendly copy of their file.

The manuals made it easier for clients to participate and to understand what was going on. Since lawyers keep their files organized, why should clients not have organized files? Otherwise, clients would have to devise their own system for managing their files. More likely, they will have all their letters and documents in many different-sized envelopes, which can be easily misplaced, whereas clients cannot easily lose a three-ringed binder. In addition, it was a convenient record for clients when the file was closed.

Having a lot of written information, including matters that the lawyers and clients may not have fully discussed, ensures that clients understand the law, the process, and the lawyer better. Some of the articles can be about minor matters which might not be that important to lawyers but may be essential to clients. Providing a memorandum on the firm's practice policies helps first-time clients. The client manual and the three-hole punch are both a physical element and a moment. Lawyers can make some client tasks easier with good explanations found in articles in the client manuals. The memorandum "How to Complete a Financial Statement" in the Family Law Client Manual is a good example of that (5.12.6). The manuals can provide information on other related and nonrelated resources. I have already mentioned the plastic business card holder page for my and my assistant's business cards as well as cards for other services: accountants, financial planners, psychologists, or whoever might be helpful to the client. I put in some recommended advisors' cards, and clients added their own cards if they already had advisors or as they hired them.

Lawyers can show clients empathy by helping them with nonlegal issues by providing resource articles from other professionals in the manuals. I will explain the client manuals in much greater detail when discussing the individual practice area manuals and presenting many examples of their content in the Appendix section.

Besides being a major second-period (active file work) service application, manuals can be a useful third-period (after the file is closed) service application. The Wills and Powers of Attorney Manual's instructions and information sections are an excellent example of this (sections 6.1.2 and A 6.1.2.2)

I received positive feedback from clients about my manuals. Along with detailed reporting letters and to-do lists, they liked having something in writing that they had discussed orally but had not fully understood or had forgotten. For example, one client told me she liked all my written material and read it all because she, like others, digests information better when it is written down instead of being given orally. Another client liked my process articles because that information is not easily found elsewhere for clients. He found those articles got him more engaged in the process.

4.1.5 Electronic Version of the Manual

When I started using manuals, there was no internet, and lawyers did not have paperless practices. Even in the later years of my practice, I did not go completely paperless, preferring to work mostly with paper for active files, but I did store closed files electronically. The big advantage of an electronic file in the cloud is that clients may access their complete files, including financial matters, from anywhere at any time. There is no reason why the client manual cannot be in paper and on the cloud. The many articles that are in a manual can be posted to a client's cloud file in the same format as the physical manual. Additions such as letters, documents, and checklists inserted and updated on the cloud file can be also in the same format as the physical file. Because technology changes and the cloud file may not be in existence in the future, the physical manual is the best way for clients to store their closed files.

4.2 Law Firm Websites

Along with the client manuals, law firm websites are, in my opinion, the most beneficial service applications lawyers can use. However, my observation is that most lawyers have squandered the website's great potential. Instead of using the website to provide an abundance of client service benefits, lawyers use it primarily as an advertising device. The law firm website is often just a glorified brochure about the firm. Worse, I find many lawyer websites a little offensive because they use marketing slogans that mean nothing and that can apply to any law firm. What law firm is not "understanding," "dedicated," "high quality," "innovative," "the most trusted law firm," "the creative at its best law firm," "the different law firm," or "the firm who are there when you need them." Yet, these are the types of assertions seen when visiting almost all law firm websites. Lawyers must have watched too much *Mad Men* when they agreed to have those slogans on their websites. Or, more than likely, firms hired marketing companies to create their websites, and for those marketing company's other businesses, catchy slogans are common. If your firm is the most trusted law firm in the city, something I have seen a law firm proclaim, then prove it. Lawyers should delegate the technical aspects to these marketing companies but control their website's slogans and content.

Though I could comment much more about law firm websites, I will limit my discussion to some key issues.

4.2.1 Why the Law Firm Website Is So Important

The website, unlike other applications, can be used to service clients in all three time periods of the file. It is crucial in the underutilized first period of service (before the firm is retained) when that all-important first impression happens, and the decision of who the prospective client chooses as a lawyer occurs. The number of new clients a good website can obtain is significant. Consistently for over 20 years, 15 percent to 20 percent of my new clients chose me as their lawyer because of my website. These new website clients came from a new circle of people other than my current and past clients. They, therefore, generated new communities of referrals and were also a source of repeat business. As about 70 percent of my new files came from repeat business or were referrals, there was a multiplier effect. That made the value of new clients from the internet much higher than just the direct 15–20 percent of new clients it produced. Because the website can also hold an unlimited amount of information, providing a lot of beneficial information for clients, many of the elements of legal service applications set out in the previous chapter can be satisfied using the website.

Many lawyers say they do not need much more than a limited website because most of their clients are referrals or previous clients. Therefore, they do not spend time and money on a website full of information. They reluctantly have a website because other law firms have them, and they do not want to look like they are not keeping up with the times. To these lawyers, not having a website would be like not having a business card. But when a prospective client receives a referral, the person will probably still check out the referred lawyer's website to find out more about that lawyer. The prospective client will also seek out the information they would like to know right away about their legal matter. Prospective clients will not be impressed with a limited website that has little information about the lawyer or the law. They will seek legal representation elsewhere. So, lawyers with limited websites are missing out on a significant direct business source and some referral business.

4.2.2 Why Lawyers Should Provide Free Information on Their Websites

Another reason lawyers have limited websites is that they do not like the idea of giving away free information because they believe knowledge is what they are selling. However, content is everything, according to experts, to be a good website. A lawyer's job is much more than providing general legal information. It also involves applying legal knowledge to a particular case, negotiating, advocating, and drafting documents. Imparting general information will not lose lawyers' business. Giving out free general information will obtain business. When I asked clients what they liked about my website, they said it was because of how much free information was on it; they specifically pointed out that other lawyers' websites did not have so much information. Lawyers will not be losing much billable time by providing clients with a background of general knowledge. Lawyers cannot assume that clients have read all the material on their websites. Lawyers will still have to discuss the content of the articles with their clients. The articles will reinforce what the lawyer and client discussed, add some detail, and be a written record for the client.

Clients will find general legal information on the internet on other lawyers' websites, government publications, nonlegal websites, or a book with general legal information. But they would rather obtain that information conveniently, for free, and in a condensed form from someone they may be choosing to be their lawyer.

4.2.3 What Information about the Lawyer Should Be Posted on the Website?

For the first period of service, prospective clients visit websites for numerous purposes, but generally, the prime reason would be to choose a lawyer. Prospective clients want to know all about the lawyer who may be handling their legal case.

However, most of the websites I studied had little more than a paragraph about their lawyers. The profiles state what areas each lawyer practices, and sometimes something personal such as that they enjoy skiing and walking their dog, or their cat's name. Prospective clients are looking for a lawyer, not a date! Some lawyers' profiles on their dating sites are probably not much different from their law firm website profiles. It is good to have some personal information in the lawyer's profile, but it must be accompanied by an extensive curriculum vitae (CV), as I now find on more websites. My CV has always included when and where I received my education as well as my legal associations. It listed all the articles I had written and legal conferences and public speaking engagements where I had spoken.

I decided on my last website revision to be more assertive with the information about me. On the first page, I had a link to a section called "Why Choose Me?" I openly said that as the prospective client was probably on my site looking for a lawyer, I would give specific reasons why they should choose me. I went with what I thought were my strengths and what I thought would be relevant to a prospective client selecting a lawyer:

1. I had experience, as I had been in practice for over 40 years.
2. I was different and innovative. To prove that claim, I explained some applications I am discussing in this paper.
3. My peers had recognized my abilities.

I verified that latter point by mentioning that I had taught family law at the bar admission course and had spoken at many conferences locally in Ottawa, provincially in Toronto, and nationally. I suggested that the reader who was choosing a lawyer ask essential questions, such as what experience does the lawyer have? Does the lawyer have value-added service? Have other lawyers recognized the lawyer for their legal skills?

Many law firms have testimonials from a few clients, a concept partially akin to "Why Choose Me?" but not as assertively worded. I think many people realize that some testimonials are somewhat suspect. I resisted putting testimonials on my website for a long time because I did not believe prospective clients liked or trusted them; however, the marketing experts say they work, so I reluctantly put a few on my website. No, they were not written by a cousin or by me. I asked some satisfied clients if they would write something, because clients are not forthcoming with their spontaneous praise.

My favorite "Why choose me?" story, which occurred pre-internet, demonstrates the effort some clients put into their process of choosing a lawyer. A prospective client brought to a consultation a piece of paper about three times the standard letter size, attached to a large board for note-taking. During the consultation, he would make notes on this paper. At the end of the appointment, he retained me. I asked him what that piece of paper was. He explained that he was a psychologist working for a large technology company. His job dealt with product development. His form was a chart of the many attributes he was looking for in choosing a lawyer. He had visited or called 10 lawyers, and they were all rated on this chart in his different categories. I said I was honored to come in first. He then told me I came in second, but the lawyer who came first was too busy to take his case. A point of this story is that clients choose lawyers for many different reasons and in many different ways, so lawyers should provide a lot of information about themselves and their practice.

4.2.4 How Should a Website Be Organized?

There are numerous ways lawyers organize their websites. The simpler, the better, as I find it very difficult to find my way around many lawyer websites. I think the way I laid out my website was pretty user-friendly. After an introductory opening page, I organized my website by my practice areas: Separation and Divorce, Marriage and Cohabitation Agreements, Wills and Powers of Attorney, and Estate Administration. I also added a heading, "About Lawrence," which had detailed information about myself as discussed in section 4.2.2 and articles about my office procedures and service principles. For each practice area, I generally had five sections: (1) First-Time Client, (2) The Law, (3) The Process, (4) Fees and Forms, and (5) Resources. For each of those sections, I had articles or forms. There were just three tiers below the initial page. I believe three levels are the optimum number a website should have. For one or two of my four website incarnations during my 25 years of having a website, I had an Index page and search feature, both useful but not necessary if lawyers design their websites well. When searching the internet, many people will not necessarily land on the home page first, so the need is to have each page on the website include contact information and to return to the home page effortlessly.

So as not to overwhelm clients in my last website makeover, my webmaster convinced me to have a small "First-Time Client" drop-down for each practice area. It contained basic information. There I also posted slideshows (section 4.4) of the first consultation for that practice area.

On reflection, I would suggest adding a section that describes what type of work the firm does for each of its practice areas. Most lawyer websites do that already, especially those that do corporate law, because it has so many different areas of practice. I did not find that necessary because in my case, it was so obvious what wills and powers of attorney law and administration of estates law covered. I thought family law was obvious also, but the odd time people would ask if being a family law lawyer, which I liked to say I was, meant I did wills. I did do wills, but not because I was a family law lawyer. And if I had described on my website what I did in my family law practice, I would have said I did not do child welfare matters or adoptions.

4.2.5 What Content Should Be On the Website?

The website should not just be a dumping ground for previously written papers given at legal conferences. Those papers that are of interest to clients may be posted to the website but should take a back seat to the bulk of the material found on lawyer websites. Lawyers should write specifically for a website reader.

Law Drop-Down Menu

I suggest that under the "The Law" drop-down menu, the website have short general information articles on that practice area's central common issues. For instance, for family law, that would be parenting, division of assets, and child and spousal support. Those articles should be the first ones in the "The Law" drop-down and not lost among articles addressing issues of little interest to most separating couples, such as an article on fertility and reproductive rights. Those introductory law articles should have necessary information without getting into too much detail. The article should not overwhelm the prospective client, especially with topics not generally relevant to all cases.

Many of my articles and some forms that were in my client manuals were on my website. But there were articles and a questionnaire on my website that I did not insert in my manuals. For instance, I had articles about psychological assessments and a questionnaire about contested custody matters that I did not want to clutter the original client manual with because they might not have been relevant. If a subject became relevant, I could refer to an article the clients could download from my website.

If they are not strong writers, I would recommend that lawyers contract someone to edit their articles. I also recommend computer software such as Grammarly (professional version) to fix spelling, punctuation, grammar, and sentence structure. I am not the best editor, so my wife and her parents edited many of my website articles.

Process Drop-Down Menu

Another drop-down menu for some practice areas is "The Process." It has information about the legal process and lawyers' processes. I have not found many process-type articles on websites I have looked at, yet that information is of interest to clients.

Fees and Questionnaires Drop-Down Menu

Each practice area should have a drop-down for "Fees and Forms." I will discuss questionnaires and forms in the next section. I do not understand why law firms generally do not post their fees on their websites. One of the first answers clients want to know is what it will cost. It is hard to predict costs for some practice areas, such as some Family Law or Litigation matters, but many legal services can have fixed fees that lawyers can post to their websites. There is nothing wrong with stating that specific fixed prices are subject to change if something arises, resulting in the lawyer spending much more time than anticipated processing that type of file.

Resource Drop-Down Menu

For each area of practice, websites I suggest have a "Resource" drop-down with links to various legal and nonlegal websites that could help clients. A little bit of internet history: in the early days of the internet, the Resource section was widespread, voluminous, and the website's most extensive section for many websites. That occurred because it was easier to find and list other useful websites than to do original writing. Also, having a link to another website was a significant criterion to help a website's search engine optimization. Besides other law firms located far from

Ottawa, I often got invitations to exchange links to nonlegal websites. I always vowed to build better Resource sections but never did. I think it is an excellent way to serve clients in the first and third periods of service. I did, however, link to good lawyer family law sites that had large Resource sections. Lawyers can at least list those links with little effort.

First-Time Client Drop-Down Menu

For each practice area, I had a drop-down menu called "First-Time Clients," which contained a one-page summary of the essential articles and questionnaires that first-timers would want to know quickly. There were links to those articles. And then, I would have in a different format the first consultation slideshow. Prospective clients would then not be overwhelmed with my large website and be shown where to start.

4.2.6 Forms and Questionnaires

First-time clients want to know what information and documentation are needed to process their case. They do not want to wait until their appointment date to fill out a client information form themselves or be asked questions by a paralegal or a lawyer. When surveying lawyers, I was surprised to learn that many lawyers have no standard questionnaires to gather clients' basic information.

These lawyers say they like to get that information at the first interview as a way to warm up clients. I think that is a waste of time and costs the client unnecessary billable hours. Lawyers can warm them up by quickly reviewing the completed forms and questionnaires. More importantly, clients may not know all the information and documentation needed. If lawyers send out questionnaires beforehand, clients have time to collect all the information and not be rushed to fill them out. Clients' anxiety will be reduced if they know what information and documentation lawyers expect from them before the appointment.

Some clients may not even want to wait until they receive forms and questionnaires, which often accompany their appointment confirmation letter. Lawyers should put the forms and questionnaire on their website. Then clients can, without pressure, fill them out electronically at their own pace on their own computer. Clients have time to think more about their answers and make sure information is correct. There will also be no mistakes because of hard-to-read handwriting.

I would suspect a reason that questionnaires are not on more websites is that lawyers are afraid other lawyers will copy their questionnaires. When speaking at a lawyers' conference, I mentioned that I had found that a law firm had copied my client matrimonial questionnaire onto their website. A lawyer in the audience implied that should have bothered me. I said no; I was flattered. It would have been nice if the firm had at least thanked me for it. What does it matter if another firm copies it? The original firm can brag that other firms think highly of their firm that they are being emulated.

I also had on my website a client preference questionnaire. It asked clients about their expectations, priorities, and how best to communicate with them. I should have done more with this questionnaire than I did.

4.2.7 Videos

Though it is probably the most labor-intensive legal service application to produce, I believe lawyers should be using videos much more on their websites than they currently do. They are useful for the client; however, what I have mostly seen is that lawyer website videos are just television commercials. They state how tremendous and caring the law firm is.

I use YouTube frequently to learn how to perform various computer procedures and household maintenance. I need YouTube to review how to clean my Dyson vacuum cleaner, so why should there not be videos about legal tasks?

It took me many years of contemplation, but I finally produced six videos totaling just over an hour on the vital topic of "How to Complete the 13.1 Financial Statement." This task of completing a financial statement needs the client's input but is very daunting for clients. To help clients fill out the statement in my videos (which I broke down into the separate sections of the financial statement), I virtually went through the statement explaining it line by line, sometimes adding my editorial comments and explaining the law. In my video, I stated that my goal was to go into so much detail that a monkey could fill out the financial statement. I also tried to make it a little amusing, however as my wife remarked when I made her watch the videos, "The subject is so boring, it is a reason not to get divorced."

I purchased a relatively inexpensive computer program, my legal assistant figured out how to add music and slides, and I recorded the video just using my DSLR camera. I did not need to hire anyone outside the office. The other significant advantage of using videos is that lawyers can, as I did, post them on YouTube as well as on their own websites. Posting on YouTube also gives added exposure as prospective clients search YouTube for legal information. Also, at one time and perhaps still today, having videos helped increase a lawyer's search engine optimization ratings. Though my website is no longer in existence now that I have retired, my videos on YouTube live forever. Search on YouTube.com "Lawrence Pascoe Financial Statement" to find them.

For one of my website incarnations, I wanted to do a video explaining what I posted on my website and how to navigate the website. However, as it would have been so much work, I settled for a much easier voice-over. Because lawyer websites have a lot of information on them and can be difficult to navigate, I recommend lawyers make an audio file introducing themselves and explaining what is on their websites and how to navigate them.

Clients can read the legal information articles on the site, so it is unnecessary to have a video duplicating that type of information. Usually, the videos or audios I see on websites are recycled television or radio appearances. They give the lawyers credibility but may not be of great interest to clients.

4.2.8 Resource Pages

Lawyers can add value to clients' service if they advise them about other resources found on the internet or elsewhere (like using old technology—the book). They can be legal resources or related to the legal matter. A link to a psychologist's website with articles dealing with emotional aspects of separation would be on the family law resource page. I do not think there is a need to list and link to government statutes. I think it best to keep it to what information clients will want and, if possible, to hyperlink to local sites so that if clients are looking for a local mortgage broker, psychologist, or financial planner, they will get the contact. Having useful resource pages for each practice area (and I suggest lawyers group them by practice area) can take a lot of work. At the very least, I suggest that lawyers should find and link to other lawyers' sites that have helpful resource pages.

4.2.9 Third-Period Uses of Websites

Lawyers should use websites to provide the often neglected third period of service, which takes place after the file is closed.

Lawyers could provide contact information about several nonlegal resource professionals and companies that clients could use after the file is closed. For real estate files, the website could give information on local snow removal companies and gardeners. Financial planners are relevant for matrimonial clients as well as for wills and estates clients.

Months and even years after files were closed, former clients often asked me to recommend lawyers for matters not in my practice areas or located in another city. I had a list handy with names of lawyers for each practice area and contact information. I collected some general information about these lawyers to provide to clients. I had considered getting more information from those lawyers and putting it on my website but never got around to doing it. I could have put this list in all my manuals, but it would be better on a website, which would be updated and changed. Lawyers could ask for reciprocal referrals from these resources, but that is not the main objective for lawyers to have this service.

As will be discussed later in the book (section 6.1.2 and A 6.1.2.2) in my Wills and Powers of Attorney Manual, I had many forms where clients kept up-to-date information, like their financial assets and burial instructions. As this information was always changing, and it was better to have these forms filled out digitally so there would be no illegible handwriting issues, an extra set of these forms was on my website. I also thought about providing a digital copy of the forms for clients, so that when I took down my website, they would have the forms in a digital format and create and fill in the forms themselves.

4.2.10 Making Appointments

Many law firm websites have the application of allowing clients to make appointments directly from the lawyer's websites. Though I understand the frustration of playing telephone tag, I never did use that application for various reasons. For my family law practice, I wanted to ensure I would take on the file, so I had several screening questions before my assistant, or I would book an appointment. I liked having the first contact communication between the office and the client to be real and not digital. In retrospect, I probably could have had them book an online appointment application for non-family law files.

4.2.11 Promoting Clients

Using a website to promote clients who would appreciate the promotion of their business would be a rare event, but it is possible and appropriate for an entertainment law practice and perhaps other commercial types of practice. The website promotions would be more of a profile for these companies, whereas their special upcoming events would be on the firm's Facebook page to be delivered on time as clients do not check their lawyer's websites regularly. It would not be appropriate for family law lawyers like me to have a "Recently Divorced and Now Available for Dating" list for my divorcing clients. But at one time, I thought of having a miscellaneous resource page of links to any of my clients' websites who asked to be on the resource page. They could have done a small write-up about their business and then provided the link to their website. It would be sort of like a free community advertising bulletin board you see at grocery stores or restaurants that allow patrons to leave cards at the cash register. In the early days of search engines, a significant criterion that helped one's search engine optimization was to have many links from other sites. I do not know if that criterion is still relevant, as in later years of my practice, people no longer inundated me with requests for reciprocal links for sites with no geographical or content relevancy.

4.2.12 A Legal Quiz and Other Uses for Lawyers' Websites

In one of my website's incarnations, I had a separate section, "For Lawyers Only." It contained several papers I had written over the years for legal conferences. A few of them would be of interest to some clients, in which case those would also appear in one of the areas of a practice section. My webmaster decided I should drop that section for lawyers, though it could probably be of interest to, or even impress, some clients. Also, the extra volume would help my ranking with search engine optimization.

To show my personality and creativity, for years I had a legal quiz on my website. There were 10 questions that were not easy. The average score was about five. I do not think anyone received a 10. As the response to this quiz was so good, I spent too much time marking the test and replying. I changed the process so that the answer would be revealed on the website after the user answered the question. I also explained the reason for the answer.

Over the years, I had collected a series of lawyer cartoons I considered posting on my website or putting in my manuals but never did. Again, I wanted to add some humor and show my personality.

I am sure there are many more applications for websites if lawyers put their minds to it. I hope this book will motivate them to create more website applications.

4.2.13 Conclusion about Websites

Lawyers' websites are extremely valuable because they can achieve for all practice areas of law several elements of legal service applications that I outlined in chapter 3.

It takes a lot of work to get good websites up and running, but they are not high maintenance for the solo or small firm, which will probably not have a constant turnover of personnel like the big firms often have. Lawyers' websites must look professional, but they do not have to be fancy and artsy. Prospective clients are looking for information, not a flashy website. A good website should be a law firm's priority.

Websites can start small with just some necessary information and slowly grow with the addition of new articles and applications. For most practice areas, an article's shelf life can be many years, because the law does not change that much. It is a fallacy to believe that lawyers must continually change their websites, because most visitors to lawyer websites are there for the first time looking to find a lawyer. They are not repeat visitors looking for what's new on the website. They do not know that lawyers may not have changed their websites in a long time. However, it is good to try to keep the website relatively current, especially if there has been a significant change in the law. It also helps for better search engine optimization to change and add significantly to a website.

As will be discussed (section 13.2), a website is an application from which lawyers can easily obtain analytical data, which is not the case for other applications. Lawyers, without much work, can collect data themselves and can also receive some from their hosting provider. That allows lawyers to determine the websites' effectiveness and see what aspects of the websites work best.

Some websites give out legal information only in a PDF booklet if prospective clients send in their email addresses. I believe that is a mistake; many people searching on the web are there because they want to be anonymous. If they give out their email address, they lose that anonymity and worry that they will be harassed with numerous emails in the future as to why they have not made further contact with the law firm. Email harassment happened to me when I requested a booklet from a matrimonial lawyer. The constant emails may bring in some new clients but could lose other prospective clients. Therefore, it is best to have the contents of that booklet on the website. Furthermore, it will reduce staff workload, because they will not have to send out e-booklets.

Lawyer websites have endless possibilities for improving the quality of service lawyers provide their clients. After I retired, I took down my website, but with the magic of www.archive.org, which archives websites periodically, my last version of www.the pascoedifference.com can be found at http://web.archive.org/web/20181229082606/http://the pascoedifference.com/.

4.3 The Client Monitor

One of my favorite innovative service applications, about which I received a lot of positive client feedback, was a second computer monitor on my desk which faced my clients. I introduced that application many years ago before the technology for it was not as easy as today. Its purpose was to mirror for the client what I was doing on my computer during the consultation. The monitor started as a relatively small one, but a client complained of its size. I replaced it a few times, and my clients' monitor at the end of my career was larger than mine.

I made use of the client monitor in many ways. For each practice area, I showed a slideshow on the monitor, like a PowerPoint presentation. It outlined the issues discussed at this essential first consultation.

Because I have trouble reading my handwriting, I used my computer to make my consultation notes. Many clients followed my note-taking on their monitor, and some clients asked for a copy of my notes. The notes reminded them of what we had discussed and what advice I had given them.

Most law areas will necessitate some number crunching, even calculating the matter's estimated cost. I found clients could better understand these calculations if they saw me doing the math before their eyes on their monitor rather than just being told the numbers or even being handed the printed result.

The client monitor's most useful function in my practice was reviewing and changing documents that I drafted for court. That was especially true for the financial statement in matrimonial matters. My clients and I checked the documents using our monitors and made appropriate changes based on the clients' inputs. During this application, most clients voiced their appreciation for being provided with a monitor but jokingly requested I also give them a keyboard. They found my typing skills lacking, and they often corrected my typos.

As will be discussed (section 4.9), using Excel, I produced to-do lists for clients, myself, and the other parties, which my clients and I reviewed together on the monitor before printing out and giving to the client. Again, it is better if lawyers and clients do this together, which the client monitor allows.

When lawyers use the second monitor application, they must remember when moving around in programs to turn off the client monitor so clients do not see other clients' names. During those brief times, my clients got to see my screen saver, which had pictures of my adorable grandchildren.

The client monitor application satisfies several of my elements that should be in service applications. I believe my clients understood me much better when they could see with their own eyes what I was saying, especially when I was talking numbers. It made the drafting of documents and to-do lists easier and faster. I found that having a monitor was a moment: many clients were impressed and showed appreciation when they walked into my office and saw they had a monitor just for them. Finally, but most importantly, the monitor implements the element that the client is an integral part of a team—a teammate, not a bystander.

4.4 The First Consultation Slideshow

The first consultation for most practice areas is generally the longest and most important meeting. For all my law practice areas, I produced a slideshow setting out the issues we would discuss at the first consultation.

Lawyers have only one chance to make a good first impression; hence the reasons for having good websites, intake processes, and appointment confirmation letters. However, the lawyer-client relationship really starts with the first consultation. Lawyers want to impress clients at their first face-to-face meeting. Lawyers want to look like they know the law, are organized, knowledgeable, and empathetic to their client's situation. Having this slideshow and having it made available beforehand helps create that good impression.

There is a lot to cover in the first consultation. It is easy for either the client or the lawyer to get off track and spend too much time on one topic or skip an issue. Having a slideshow (or PowerPoint presentation) on both monitors with a detailed agenda of all the topics helps the lawyer get back on topic and not forget to cover everything.

I also used my own printed, prepared checklist to ensure I had covered everything I wanted to discuss, marking off each topic as we finished discussing it. If we did not cover an issue, it was a reminder to mention it in my reporting letter after the consultation.

For clients, the slideshows were like lecture notes providing a list of all the main subjects, but not all the particulars, of most issues. I had posted copies of these slideshows on my website. It was surprising how many clients would print them out and bring them to their appointment. However, they would then watch the monitor, which was more comfortable than flipping their printed-out version pages. But I think the fact that they printed them out, which I never asked them to do, showed they felt they were of value.

Clients are provided with the first consultation agenda beforehand to ease their anxiety about what will happen at that meeting. Knowing the schedule also allows them to be better prepared to ask questions. The slideshow informed them of topics they might not have even known applied to their legal matter. And if they printed it out, they had something physical to put in their manual.

I have set out three of my first consultation slideshows in a table format in Appendix 5.4 (Family Law), Appendix 6.4 (Wills and Powers of Attorney), and Appendix 7.4 (Administration of Estates). I detail the topics, starting with preliminary matters for new clients, then the areas of discussion and closing matters, explaining the manual, and even reminding myself to ask whether the client has any more questions.

4.5 Client Questionnaires and Forms

The concept of having client questionnaires is not innovative. Most lawyers, though, surprisingly, not all, use them to collect client contact and factual information to process a file. What can be innovative is the types of questionnaires possible, the information requested, and the process for filling them out.

There are several different types of questionnaires and forms, which I set out in this section. Generally, the difference for me between a form and a questionnaire is that lawyers or their assistants fill out the form, whereas the clients complete the questionnaires.

Concerning the process for completing these questionnaires, as I stated in section 4.2.5 when discussing websites, I believe that all the questionnaires should be available on lawyer websites. Clients could fill them out electronically from the websites and then have them forwarded by the website directly to an email address at the law office. Clients need time to collect the information and not be under pressure to fill out these questionnaires. There may be many questions that the client did not even consider and may need a lot of time to think about and even want to discuss with other people. If lawyers do not like to put their questionnaires on their websites, they should email them with the client appointment confirmation letter, again providing them time to fill them out. Some questionnaires, such as the performance questionnaires and surveys, can also be inserted in the client manuals, and clients can fill them out by hand. Having these types of questionnaires in the client manuals is a reminder to complete them. Lawyers should not ask clients to fill out the questionnaires in their office waiting rooms just before their appointments. For some questionnaires, lawyers should ask clients to send the questionnaires back in enough time for the lawyers to review them before the clients' meetings. They may have to prepare for some issues raised in the questionnaire. Lawyers will then also have a better idea of what the case is about from the outset, that is, from the first consultation.

4.5.1 Client Intake Forms

I had an extensive client intake form that the person (my assistant or myself) booking the first appointment would complete when making the first appointment. The form had different sections for different types of files, even within a practice area. Besides the necessary contact information, the form had questions to ensure I could and wanted to take on the client. The form had jurisdictional questions as sometimes the client required a lawyer in another province or another city. The form, especially for family law matters, asked questions discussed in section 5.5 to help decide whether I wanted to take on the matter. For a conflict of interest search, the form requested the full name of the spouse. The form did not have just questions but also reminders of information to tell the client, such as to advise the client of my hourly rate and the retainer amount. I was far from being the most expensive lawyer, but still, being a senior lawyer, my hourly rate was not at the low end of rates lawyers charge, and some prospective clients balked at the cost and declined an appointment.

There were various ways a client chose me as their lawyer. The method was something we noted on their intake form. We requested further information, if appropriate, such as if a friend recommended the client, we would ask who the friend was and whether we could send the friend a thank-you letter. Knowing where a client came from was very useful for marketing purposes and for showing appreciation to those who referred clients to me.

At first glance, this client intake form does not seem to be a service to clients but instead a benefit to lawyers. But it is of service to both. It weeds out clients who the lawyers cannot have or does not want to have as clients. Both parties save time and money by not having a useless first consultation that will lead no further. Prospective clients, therefore, should be thoroughly screened.

4.5.2 Client Information Questionnaires

Each practice area should have a substantial client questionnaire that clients complete before their initial consultation. It may contain several different sections, depending on the practice area. One section would be the necessary information such as contact information, personal information of the client and their family, and previous court proceedings history. But these questionnaires should also request facts related to the practice area. The questionnaire could ask the clients what issues they believe are in dispute and which are not, and if not, what the parties tentatively have already agreed upon. For some practice areas, like wills, the questionnaires can ask for tentative instructions like whom the clients want as executors. For litigation areas of practice, the questionnaires could ask clients their issues in a multifaceted matter, their priorities, and expected outcomes. There can be a detailed questionnaire asking questions the client probably never thought relevant for some issues with many relevant facts. If the case was a contested custody matter, I had a four-page questionnaire with questions ranging from which parent took the children to the doctor to what would be the daycare arrangements. My initial client questionnaires again asked why the client chose me, and if referred, I requested that I be allowed to send that person a thank-you note. I also asked for that referral source's email address if I did not know that person, because sometimes it was a friend of a friend.

4.5.3 Client Preferences Questionnaires

Client preference questionnaires, which the client completes before the first consultation, can collect some useful information. I developed a client preference questionnaire only for my family law practice, but it could be used for all practice areas. The preference questionnaires could cover several subjects. They would include ones that were not actually preferences but rather priorities and expectations, both of which are important to know.

Priorities: There can be several major issues and issues subsidiary to the main issues. Lawyers need to know which subjects the client believes the parties have agreed upon, and those not yet decided upon, and which issues are most important to the client.

Expectation of Results: Lawyers must know what are the clients' expected outcomes of their legal matter to make sure they have reasonable expectations.

Expectation of Timing: Lawyers must also know what clients expect the time frame will be to complete their legal matter, to ensure clients have reasonable expectations.

Communications: The questionnaire can ask clients what the best forms of communication are in their case. Do they prefer only telephone calls, or do they want emails? Can they be called at work? Do they mind being called on their cell phone? Can they be called at home, and if so, at night or on the weekend? In some cases, lawyers should not telephone them at home. In the post-COVID-19 world, perhaps for certain types of consultations, clients would prefer a teleconference and select one platform over another.

Delegation: The questionnaire could ask clients if they minded (which almost all do not) having a legal assistant communicate some issues with them, rather than the lawyer.

Approval of Correspondence: The questionnaire would ask if the client needed to approve the final version of all correspondence sent out to the spouse or the other lawyer. Their approval was important to a few clients who wanted to ensure my letter had the right tone for their spouse.

Timing of Billing: The questionnaire could ask if the lawyer should bill at the end of every month, when the work in progress reached a certain level, when a significant task had been completed, when the retainer was exhausted, or when I believed it was appropriate.

Detail of Legal Information: The questionnaire could ask how much detail the client requested concerning the law involved in their case. In some family law matters, the rare client would want copies of the case law presented to the court.

4.5.4 Lawyer and Staff Performance Questionnaires

Inserted in my manuals and on my website was a very short Lawyer and Staff Performance Questionnaire. The questionnaire asked a few very general questions about how my staff treated them. It also asked if clients thought my fees were reasonable and whether they were happy with the results. Finally, I had clients grade me from Excellent to Poor. This questionnaire could have used a lot of improvement, though it did accomplish two things: it allowed clients to thank me easily and notified me after the fact if I had done something wrong. I did not keep statistics as I should have, but I would estimate that 90 percent said Excellent and 10 percent marked Very Good. I cannot recall any negative replies, which to me shows not that I was perfect, but that people have trouble or cannot be bothered to give negative feedback. I regret I had only two performance questionnaires about myself and my staff. Most of these completed questionnaires came from my wills clients and not my matrimonial clients. I know I had some unhappy family law clients over the years; it would be impossible not to. Sometimes it may have been my doing, but as discussed in section 2.4, a problem lawyers have is that clients cannot easily judge how well or badly a lawyer performed their matter's legal aspects.

I would recommend that each practice area have a section of questions specific for that practice area, such as whether the lawyer and staff met the higher priority needs.

I would also suggest that clients complete performance questionnaires at the various stages of the file's life. I had only a questionnaire about my website articles and one at the end about my and my staff's performance. I regret that I had only two performance questionnaires. More questionnaires would provide lawyers with more information. In addition, it would allow lawyers to rectify some problems with clients when there was still time to do so. However, I do not think it is a good idea to have too many performance questionnaires, which some other businesses seem to have, as it is asking too much from clients, and they get tired of being continually asked to fill out surveys.

4.5.5 Marketing Questionnaires

Over the years, I had questionnaires that I asked clients to complete even before their file formally started. These questionnaires were more for my benefit. I had a questionnaire about my website—its ease of use and content. I asked them about their thoughts on my articles: were they too long, too detailed? I asked what other subjects I could write about. I asked about fees. I gave them several factors that I thought went into choosing a lawyer and asked them to rank them in importance. Being a specialist in the law area they required seemed to be the most critical criterion, though I did not take a good accounting of the answers because I did not get a lot of replies. I did not press clients as much as I should have to fill out these questionnaires, though, as discussed in the next subsection, I did give clients an incentive to do so.

4.5.6 Survey Contest

I had a contest whereby on January 31st of each year, I awarded a prize of a pair of Ottawa Senator hockey tickets, plus a voucher for free parking and $20, which could have bought a beer and part of a hot dog. To win the contest, the person had to suggest a way to improve my service to clients. I had only a few good suggestions over the years, but it was a very worthwhile application.

In 1994, I was doing a will for an engineer from Nortel. I told him about the contest I had just launched. He asked, "Have you ever heard of the internet?" I said, "No, tell me about it." So, he told me about this new technology and the World Wide Web and "home pages," which were what websites were called then. My initial response to him was that I did not think this "internet" would ever amount to anything. However, the next week I saw an ad in Ontario's *Lawyer's Weekly* inviting Ottawa lawyers to come to hear a lecture about the internet. I had thought about this internet thing since talking to my client and decided it was worth checking out, which I would never have done if the client had not mentioned it, and he did that only because of the contest. Only about 20 lawyers were at this lecture listening to a legal technology lawyer/writer, Lewis Eisen, talk about what the internet could do. I was hooked when he showed us that the internet could tell when the next subway train left the Dundas Street station in Toronto and arrived at the Queen Street station. He also brought two very young people to the lecture whose small business set up an internet home page for $200. As I had all these articles to put on a home page which I had already written for a local community newspaper that published my articles when it ran out of ads to print, I hired the two kids, and I had one of the first lawyer websites in Ottawa. My interest and a significant head start using a website for marketing and service purposes all started because of my survey contest.

Besides pushing more for clients to complete these questionnaires, I should have drawn one entry at random to win a good prize, or perhaps had one more detailed questionnaire which gave clients a small reduction in their fee if they submitted all their questionnaires.

4.5.7 Change of Information Form

On my website, I had a Change of Information Form. This form effortlessly allowed clients to advise me during the file or after it was closed, if there was a change in their contact information in case I had to get hold of them. I did have to find old clients when I retired, because I had an obligation to contact clients whose original wills or powers of attorney I had in safekeeping. Again, in retrospect, I should have had this form in all my manuals. I should have impressed upon the clients the importance of telling me of a change in contact information. I should have also had a list of circumstances they should advise me about, which might have resulted in a need for updated legal help such as marriages, separations, deaths, and changes in financial circumstances.

4.5.8 Getting Clients to Fill Out Questionnaires

I rarely found it a problem getting clients to complete the questionnaires related to the facts of their case. However, if they did not complete them fully, which did happen occasionally, I would put them in a boardroom and ask them to finish filling them out. I explained that it would save them money it would cost to fill them out with me as I would have to charge for my time.

The more difficult task was getting clients to fill out the other questionnaires related to my service and what they thought of my articles. As mentioned, what helped a little was that I had a survey contest with a prize for clients who handed in these surveys about articles and other matters. I have discussed the survey contest more fully in section 4.5.6.

4.5.9 Conclusion about Questionnaires and Forms

Completed questionnaires provide information necessary for processing the matter, which might not be uncovered by just orally questioning the client. A significant cause of malpractice claims in all areas of law is "inadequate investigation." Detailed questionnaires will help reduce that problem. Questionnaires help the communications between lawyers and clients and personalize the service. These questions on communication show that lawyers have empathy. They help the client participate more in the process. They let lawyers know the priorities and preferences of their clients. They can gather valuable information that lawyers can use to improve their marketing. Therefore, lawyers should use them more and have them available on their websites.

4.6 First Appointment Confirmation Letter

Lawyers emailing clients to remind them of their first consultation date is not innovative, but a substantive letter can be. For each of my practice areas, I had a lengthy standard confirmation email sent out within a day of making the appointment with at least the following information:

a. confirmation of the date and time of the appointment;
b. my policy regarding changing or canceling appointments;
c. the list of forms, with hyperlinks, to complete and send in before the consultation and a suggestion to also print them out;
d. guidance as to which articles (again with hyperlinks) on my website they might want to read;
e. a suggestion they review my first consultation slide show to see the agenda of the meeting;
f. a discussion of fees and my process for being paid and what I expect from them at the first consultation, which included signing my retainer;
g. a reminder to bring to their appointment photo ID because it was a requirement of the Law Society of Ontario for new clients;
h. a suggestion they write out questions they may have;
i. a note advising them that it was okay and even a good idea in some cases to bring in a family member or friend to sit in on the consultation.

Finally, since I asked them to do so many tasks, I ended with a checklist to mark off each one.

At one time, I had an assistant who was particularly sensitive to strong scents, so my letters requested that clients not use scented perfume or aftershave.

Having such clear instructions and easy access to the forms with the hyperlinks reduces clients' stress and makes their tasks more comfortable. I included my family law first appointment letters in Appendix 5.6.

4.7 Appointment Letters for Subsequent Appointments and Reminders

I did not do it for all my practice areas as I did for the first consultations, but I suggest it is a good idea to always do confirmation letters for subsequent consultations. Besides confirming when the appointment is, lawyers can draft agendas to insert in the letter. Included could be a checklist of the client's tasks before the meeting and what the client is to bring to the meeting. By having the agenda, clients could better prepare for the consultation and have time to think and formulate questions they had.

To remind clients of their appointment, my staff generally called them two days before the date. Often, they were also reminded that we had not received their questionnaires, other requested information, or documents needed for the appointment. Some software programs have an automatic feature to email clients to remind them of their appointments.

4.8 Consultation and Telephone Notes and Agendas

When I had a phone call or consultation with a client, lawyer, or anyone on a file, I recorded my notes on the computer file about the communication. I did this by using a template I created in my practice management software, Time Matters, using their "Outline" feature. All practice management software would have a similar function. Lawyers who do not use such legal software could purchase cheap outline programs to accomplish the same result. Calling up and saving the note to a particular file would be much easier within a full practice management program. My template was different depending on the type of file and the person with whom I was communicating. The notes did have similar headings, such as what each party said and the next step each party had to do. Besides being a good record for my files, my clients often asked for a copy for their records.

If it was a consultation or a phone call I was initiating, I also had a "purposes" section. Before the appointment or telephone call, I noted what information I would give or what questions I wanted to ask.

This service application made it easier for me to recall what we discussed and what the next step was. It also made the process easier for the clients, especially if they had the written notes and an agenda, which had the element of obtaining something physical (A 5.8).

4.9 To-Do and Document Lists

There are so many tasks to be completed, even in the most straightforward legal file. Lawyers should have a system to keep track of those tasks. They have their own to-do's and have to control their clients, their staff, and the other sides' lawyer and opposing clients' to-dos. In some practice areas, especially those where there is no other side, the to-do lists are shorter, but lawyers should still have a written record of their status.

For every client, I set up an Excel file for all my practice areas. I used Excel, but any spreadsheet program will do. Each client file had at least separate tabs for the lawyer, the client, and the legal assistant. For family law files, I also created tabs for the opposing lawyers and their clients to keep track of what I had asked them to do. The type of file dictated the number of columns under each tab. For a wills and powers of attorney file, there were simply three columns: the task column, the column to note whether the client was required to do that task or had already done it, and in the final column, the client's confirmation that they had completed the task (A 5.9; A 6.9; A 7.9).

Though there was room to add more tasks, for wills and powers of attorney there was a standard list of tasks that the clients and I would review on their monitor at the end of their appointment, and then I would print it out. Clients would then insert the to-do list in their Will Manual. On that to-do list, we also inserted the date and time of their signing appointment, which I generally scheduled two weeks after the initial meeting.

Matrimonial to-do lists were more complicated. There were more parties involved: the opposing lawyer and their client. At one time, I also added columns for the date and how the party was asked the request (email, call, consultation), so I would know when to follow up. Each Excel file would also list tasks that might be required in the future; this list acted as a checklist to ensure that I requested all appropriate tasks from the opposing side or from my clients.

This application makes it easier for clients to keep track of their tasks. It is an excellent use of nonlegal software. I gave clients printed copies of their to-do list, but if they had access to a client portal, they could also follow the status of the to-dos of everyone involved in the file. The printout is also another physical item the client receives.

Lawyers can use Excel to keep track of documents in the same manner: having separate tabs for each party and columns for their status. This method could effortlessly track what documents were still outstanding and I needed to receive. Each Excel file could also list documents that might be required acting, again, as a checklist to ensure lawyers ask for all required documentation.

4.10 Calculation of Estimated Costs Forms

Another way I used Excel in my practice was to estimate the total fees and disbursements for my administration of estates clients. Using an Excel form I devised, listing the specific tasks, the fees for those tasks, and confirming whether the client or I was responsible for the task; the form then calculated the fee. See section 7.10 and Appendix 7.10, which makes it much easier to understand what I did.

I did not need the fees form for my wills and powers of attorney, uncontested divorces, or marriage contracts files, because I based them on a fixed amount.

I never got to do my project of estimating a contested matrimonial file's costs based on the stages reached in such a file before settlement or a trial. I think that lawyers could do that, and they would use a spreadsheet program like Excel. I would suggest most practice areas could use Excel to estimate the legal costs to a client by having all the possible disbursements in the calculation as well as estimates of legal fees.

For various reasons, as previously discussed, most clients want to know the cost of the legal services they are buying. Therefore, having an application that calculates that estimate quickly and easily and produces a printed form that displays it is a significant benefit to clients.

4.11 Client-Helpful Word Processing Software Features

Several word processing software features make legal documents easier for clients to navigate in and easier for clients to communicate with their lawyers.

Word processing programs can number the lines in draft documents. I did this for wills, which clients seemed to appreciate, but lawyers can do it for any long document with many subparagraphs.

These programs can generate a table of contents. Lawyers should use them for extended agreements. They make finding specific topics much more manageable. I know from experience that when I am reviewing another lawyer's separation agreement, if there is no table of contents, I sometimes have difficulty finding what I am looking for.

Such programs can also produce indices for agreements, though the process for doing so is more difficult, again, it is helpful to find a subject that may not be easily found in the table of contents.

These are small applications, but besides being more straightforward ways to find something, they demonstrate that lawyers are looking to make life easier for the client and are using simple technology to do so.

The occasional client used the Microsoft Word feature to make suggested changes in documents. It allows lawyers to accept changes automatically. I was not too fond of that feature; however, I do like the ability to let the client insert comments and questions on the document. I also think the "compare documents" function is useful; lawyers and clients use it to see how a document has been changed.

Lawyers should keep abreast of the new features continually added to their everyday software programs, such as their word processing, spreadsheet, and even email programs. Most of the new features make the production of documents easier for the user, but when a feature that makes it beneficial for the clients comes along, lawyers can add it as an application. As these new features may not be simple to use or easy to remember, I suggest lawyers write a brief article for their client manuals about using the feature. If there is a YouTube video explaining the function, lawyers should include its URL in the article. I never ended up tweeting, but when I opened a Twitter account, I put in my manual an explanation of how Twitter worked and how clients could open a Twitter account and could follow me.

4.12 Articles for Clients

Many useful articles written by lawyers for their clients should be made available to them. Lawyers can put the articles on their websites, in their manuals, or both places. Articles are one of the few applications that lawyers can use for all three time periods of service, including the underused third period (after the file is closed). The following are the categories of these articles, with some examples. These articles provide practical information that is often not found elsewhere and that show the lawyers' personal opinions and procedures. The articles can go into greater detail than just an oral presentation, and being in writing, can be reviewed and retained better by clients. Clients will be able to reduce their note taking and concentrate on listening to their lawyers if they recall that the subject was discussed in an article that they read beforehand.

4.12.1 *Substantive Law Articles*

Lawyers should write one or two-page articles on substantive law issues of interest to clients. Without getting into great detail, it is not hard to outline the essential factors upon which the law is based for specific topics. For instance, I had an article on the formula in Ontario's Family Law Act that determines how the law divides assets on marriage breakdown. Most clients believe assets are split 50/50, whereas the values of assets brought into the marriage and assets inherited are part of the formula. For this division of assets issue, lawyers can discuss the legalities of tracing and proving values later with the client, but the clients would like to have, and should have, some knowledge about the law at the initial stage. These articles can dispel clients' misconceptions about even some fundamental law.

4.12.2 *Definitions and Annotations*

Lawyers and the law often operate in a different language, often known as "legalese." Legalese has changed somewhat over the years as many legal terms in Latin have been replaced. In Ontario, "Ex parte" was finally changed to "without notice." However, lawyers should still explain some words and phrases for clients, which can easily be done in a list of definitions.

More importantly, lawyers should write articles explaining the plain meaning and purposes of standard clauses found in such documents as wills, leases, purchase and sale agreements, and shareholder agreements. The client would better understand these standard documents, and lawyers could spend less time explaining them. Those oral explanations are not usually as thorough as a good article about each clause. I have to admit I often refer to my article "The Plain Meaning and Purposes of Will Clauses" to remember the purpose and how to best explain some archaic clauses we still use in wills.

4.12.3 *Legal Process Articles*

I suggest lawyers provide short articles about each practice area's legal processes. There are many steps in a litigation file, whether family, civil, or criminal, that lawyers could explain in articles. Flowcharts could even accompany those articles. For family law, I also wrote an article outlining the different processes available to resolve a marital dispute. They range from client–client negotiations to having a case decided by the Court of Appeal's judges. There are also five alternative methods in between that clients can use to resolve the terms of their separation. I spelled out the advantages and disadvantages of each process in the article. See the article in Appendix 5.12.3.3.

As these are once-in-a-lifetime events for most clients, lawyers should write out in fine detail practical questions that clients have about the processes. Concerning court appearances, I included information such as what time they should arrive at the courthouse, where they should meet me at the courthouse, and how they should dress.

I discovered it was necessary to tell clients how to dress and specifically instructed them to dress as if they are going for a job interview—no jeans. I once made the mistake of telling a not-too-bright client to "dress up" for his uncontested divorce hearing. The client came wearing a white dinner jacket and red bow tie. I looked at him and said, "You are getting divorced, not married." The judge looked at him, asked one question, looked at me, and said, "Divorce granted, get him out of here."

4.12.4 Law Firm Procedures Article and New Client Memorandum

All law firms have different ways of processing files and serving their clients. Lawyers should write out that information for clients in the form of an article in what I called the "New Client Memorandum." I had information on topics such as how best to communicate with my assistant and me, and how we stored files when the matter was closed. I also advised about some minor free services that I provided all my clients no matter what type of file they had, such as swearing affidavits even unrelated to the file (A 4.12.4).

How clients could retrieve their files and original wills could be in this memorandum or in a separate article. These are important issues that I believe should not just be part of a long reporting letter at the end, because they deserve special attention right from the beginning of a file.

4.12.5 Client-Lawyer Relationship and Client Expectation Articles

The relationship clients have with their lawyers differs significantly depending on the practice area, the personality and expectations of the client, and the lawyer's management of the relationship. In a matrimonial matter, the association will last for months at least and may last for years with numerous consultations, phone calls, and court appearances.

Because of their emotional state, the client may rely heavily on the lawyer for even nonlegal matters and see the lawyer as a psychologist. In many areas like wills, real estate, and the administration of estates, the client may meet with their lawyer only one or two times and even then briefly the second time. Therefore, the lawyer needs to discuss orally and write out each of their roles so clients understand their and their lawyer's role and what each should expect and not expect from the other. Lawyers can set out their roles in an article, in the retainer agreement, or in initial letters; but this should be in writing somewhere (A 5.12.5.1).

For areas of practice where there is a conflict, like family law, litigation, and criminal law, the client's expectations of the result must be managed by the lawyer. In all areas of law, the lawyer must manage expectations as to the timing and cost (A 5.12.5.3).

4.12.6 How-to Articles

If there are tasks that the client needs help doing, then lawyers could write articles to help them. One of my first, longest, and still favorite articles was about filling out the clients' financial statements in matrimonial matters. This is a very long, complicated form. I also made an hour-long video for my website and YouTube about completing the form. In my opinion, I found some lawyers did not do a proper job of completing their clients' financial statements before presenting them to the opposing side and the court. When writing about questioning (cross-examinations), I wrote an article advising clients on how to act when being cross-examined. For executors, I had an article on what their primary duties were. I am sure I could have done more of these articles to benefit clients.

4.12.7 Legal Fees and Billing

Hiring a lawyer is a very significant, complex, and costly purchase for clients. Unlike physical products and even most other types of services, there is often not a fixed fee. Fixed fees are not possible for several kinds of legal matters, because lawyers cannot estimate the amount of work needed to complete the file. A straightforward case, which the parties could have settled, may become hotly contested. There may be some unexpectedly high disbursement costs if experts are needed. I took the time to explain to clients why I could not set a fee in a standard matrimonial file. But I also put the reasoning behind the hourly rate and how

I based my fees on the time I spent on the file in an article I placed in their client manual.

Legal services are also very different from physical purchases and other services in that the client is actually a factor in how much the fees will be. A client who is unreasonable in their demands, overly needy, or not as helpful as could be in gathering evidence can increase the final costs. The other party or their lawyer or both can be challenging and run up the costs. I had a section in my fees article about how my clients could keep their costs down in matrimonial matters. I said the best way to keep costs down was for them to be reasonable in their positions on issues in dispute.

Though I used a prominent company in the legal accounting software field, I found my invoices in certain respects challenging to understand; so I wrote a short memorandum on how clients could better understand them.

Though technically not an article, lawyers' retainers can contain information about legal fees helpful to clients. I did explain in my matrimonial retainer the procedure for clients to contest my accounts. I also pointed out the consequences if clients did not pay their invoices and were not reasonable in their claims. As Canada has the concept of a losing party in litigation possibly paying all or part of the winning party's legal fees, I made this clear in my retainer. Such advice should be in writing, and I thought the retainer was the best place to do it.

4.12.8 Articles Written by Other Local Related Service Providers

Lawyers could request local services that were not legal but related to the area of law, to write articles that would help clients. I had a local family counselor write a relatively short article about the psychological aspects of going through a divorce. This article benefited my clients and introduced them to a nearby person they might want to retain. I suspect that obtaining articles for other practice areas would be a little difficult but worth the effort.

4.12.9 After the Fact, Third-Period Articles

I had a two-page article in my wills manual entitled "Changing Your Will." The article discussed times when people should change their will and pointed out when their actions like divorce or marriage automatically affected the will. I also had an article called "Preparing for an Easier Administration of An Estate." It outlined the many things a client could do to make life easier for their executor.

Instead of giving more detailed advice in long reporting letters that clients probably never read, lawyers could place it in articles that they would put on their websites and in their manuals. Separate articles, rather than many parts of a reporting letter, have more impact and are more likely to be read. They are also suitable promotional materials.

4.12.10 Promotional but Informational Articles: Why Use a Lawyer?

Each practice area could have an article about why clients need the legal services. The articles would be beneficial to clients and would perhaps advocate for retaining a lawyer and not handling the matter themselves. I believe the first article I ever wrote, over 30 years ago, was "The Reasons for Having A Will." It discussed the reasons for having a will and what would happen, including the problems, if one died without one. It was promotional as well as informative.

Though it is not technically an article, all lawyers should have a comprehensive CV about themselves on their website so prospective clients can read about the lawyers' expertise.

4.12.11 Format and Writing Style of Articles

A widely used format for lawyers' articles is the question and answer. I used it a few times but preferred good old-fashioned regular prose. In prose, lawyers can include minor points that they might leave out in a question-and-answer format. What matters more is the length of these articles; clients will not read articles if they are too long. What matters the most is that lawyers write these articles for clients, not for other lawyers. If a subject matter necessitates a lengthy discussion, lawyers should break the articles into many small sections and use section headings. Lawyers should also not get into the minute detail that some legal issues and processes may have; otherwise, the articles will be too long, even if divided into pieces, and clients will not read them. If it is a complicated, detailed subject, the fine details can be in a separate article.

There is nothing wrong with lawyers putting on their website articles that they wrote for a legal conference. Those articles will increase the lawyer's credibility as having expertise in that area of law. But the lawyer should advise clients that the lawyer wrote those articles for lawyers and not necessarily for clients to read. These articles should only be on the website and not in the client manuals.

4.12.12 Making Sure Clients Read the Articles and Reporting Letters

Many lawyers, especially corporate lawyers I have talked to, were adamant that their clients read next to nothing they sent them, including reporting letters. Real estate lawyers said the same. By way of proof, they pointed out that a very high percentage of clients never cashed refund cheques sent with the final reporting letter (because often lawyers overestimate the final costs). These clients probably never even opened the envelope containing the last reporting letter, or if they did so, never made it to the end of the letter and the attached check.

In retrospect, I do not know how much my clients read. I did not ask my clients what they read and did not read. However, I know that many wills and powers of attorney clients read the articles because many completed the survey about the initial articles that I asked them to read. I had the same type of survey for my other practice areas, but clients rarely completed them. There is so much value to the client when they read these articles and letters; it will also reduce communication problems (thus lowering complaints and malpractice claims). Therefore, I have thought of some ways lawyers can get clients to read these materials more. I admit some of them are a little radical and not for everyone. They are as follows: (a) explain in the first consultation the importance of reading the articles and letters; (b) in any articles, like my matrimonial lawyer-client relationship article, write that reading the articles and letters is as much of a client obligation as paying the lawyer; (c) put in the written retainers that the client must read the articles and letters; (d) have clients fill out surveys about each article and provide a prize or a reduction in their fees for completing the survey; and (e) have clients sign and send back reporting letters confirming they have read them, and follow up until the client has confirmed reading the final reporting letter.

4.13 Legal Fees

Legal fees are a significant issue for both lawyers and clients. I believe a significant client need is to know how much their legal costs will be. A very high percentage of formal (and likely nonreported) client complaints about lawyers concerns legal fees. I believe fees are an issue that lawyers should realize (but most do not) is more important to clients than to lawyers. Therefore, lawyers should be taking this subject very seriously. There are many ways to set fees and numerous aspects relating to legal fees. I will start with the standard methods of setting fees, then I will comment on important lawyer fee issues not always discussed with clients, followed by how I set my fees. I will also briefly discuss unbundled services or limited scope retainers because it is somewhat of a fee issue. Much of my discussion is not so much about innovation but rather my opinion on some aspects of legal fees.

4.13.1 The Different Methods of Determining Lawyers' Fees

Lawyers use various methods to determine the legal fees they charge. Those methods include the hourly rate, the fixed fee, the contingency fee, and combinations and variations of these methods. The pricing method will depend on the lawyer, practice area, and file type. Determining legal fees that are fair to both lawyers and clients is not an easy subject. The following are some of my thoughts.

The Hourly Rate (Billable Hour) Method

The hourly rate (or billable hour) method has historically been the most commonly used method for lawyers to determine their legal fees. This method is based on the principle that a fair cost is determined by multiplying the hourly rate by the time spent on the file. Because value is subjective and can vary significantly between lawyers and clients, the billable hour method is not always a fair judge of value for lawyers or clients; but lawyers tell clients the billable hour method is the most appropriate way for lawyers to charge because what lawyers are selling is their time. However, clients see several problems with this method. They find there are generally no limits on the number of hours lawyers might take, and clients want certainty about what their matter will cost. Clients may think the lawyer is spending more time on the file than is necessary. Clients see the billable hour method as one that does not reward efficiency, but the opposite is true. Lawyers argue they do not know how long it will take to complete a file, because every adversarial type of file may settle at any point along the way to the courtroom or to the arbitrator's door. Lawyers point out that the number of hours spent depends not only on their and their clients' actions but also on how the opposing sides and their lawyers proceed. New issues and problems might arise that were not known at the first appointment when the lawyer and client discussed costs. Experts who were not anticipated might have to be retained. Issues the parties thought they settled may become contested. Lawyers sometimes find that the value to the client was far greater in cases where lawyers accomplish a lot for the client with very few hours taken. Though there are good reasons for many practice areas to charge by the hourly rate method, I doubt many lawyers in their professional or personal life would like to buy any service using the billable hour method. Lawyers must be more sensitive to clients' legitimate concerns. Saying, as I often did, "Trust me, I'll be reasonable and try to keep the costs down," may not cut it for clients who have just met their lawyers for the first time. Though clients do not like the unpredictability and the possibility of abuse by lawyers, they are at the mercy of their lawyers because they will generally need legal services. As most lawyers in practice areas charge the same way, clients will often shop around for lawyers with lower hourly rates. Choosing the lawyer with the lowest hourly rate may or may not be beneficial for the client, because the higher hourly rate lawyer should be more efficient and, with more expertise and experience, get a better result and so may be worth the higher hourly rate—though, of course, this is not always true.

Though I disliked it and did not do it myself, many law firms bill the time spent for secretarial and legal assistant services. I believe lawyers should take those costs into account when setting an hourly rate or a fixed fee. If lawyers charge for that time, it should also be estimated, which may be hard to do and should be told to the client. Some lawyers would argue, though, that charging for secretaries' and assistants' work reflects the actual legal costs of the file.

Lawyers must therefore be very mindful of clients' legitimate concerns with the hourly rate method. Lawyers should try, if possible, to move away from a strict hourly rate basis. When lawyers use the hourly rate, they should try to provide realistic estimates of how much time will be needed and explain why the hourly rate is the fairest method for their type of case.

The Fixed Fee Method

The fixed fee method is where, as the name says, the lawyer and client agree on a fixed fee to complete a legal service, no matter how much time the lawyer spends on the file. However, as it should, the agreement will probably provide an increased cost if something completely extraordinary happens on that type of file that results in the lawyer having to spend much more time on the file than expected. Clients like this method, because they may need to budget for it, there will be no surprises, and they can compare costs among lawyers. It should also be acceptable to them that they can appreciate a higher price if something extraordinary occurs. Lawyers like it because they will probably base the fee on the amount of time it takes, on average, to complete that task, plus a little extra time as insurance. Lawyers can also increase that set fee if they believe there is more value to the service than just their hourly rate dictates, and they can take into account perhaps the legal work assistants would do on the file. I also considered it a fixed fee method when I charged a tiny percentage on higher valued estates when clients retained me to do the legal work to administer an estate. The amount I charged extra in those cases was minuscule compared to billing estate work by the tariff, as was once recommended by my county law association, which made estate work quite lucrative for lawyers but overpriced for clients, in my opinion. As the estate's value is generally known at the first consultation, I do not consider this is a type of contingency fee but part of a fixed fee.

Using the fixed-fee method allows lawyers who have produced more efficient ways to work those types of files to make more than just their hourly rate. Lawyers who use technology, good precedents, and excellent processes should be rewarded. Using a fixed fee method, like for any product's sticker price, allows both clients and lawyers to decide what they consider to be a fair value for a legal service. Lawyers set a price they think is reasonable for the value the client will receive. If clients believe the value is less than the price, they will shop elsewhere.

The Contingency Fee Method

The contingency method occurs when lawyers agree to charge an agreed-upon percentage of their client's settlement or judgment. If the client is entirely unsuccessful, the lawyer gets nothing. My practice areas did not lend themselves to using a contingency fee. Each jurisdiction has different rules about when and how lawyers can use contingency fees. The rationale for the contingency fee seems to be twofold: it allows clients who could not afford a lawyer an opportunity to have legal representation, and it rewards lawyers for taking the risk they may get nothing or very little for their efforts if their clients lose.

Call me cynical, but it seems to me that lawyers who work on a contingency fee basis will not take on losing cases, so there is no real fear their clients will not pay them from their settlement or court-ordered judgment. I also believe that often, the percentage lawyers charge is much too high in relation to the legal work done and the risks taken. In deciding whether to settle a case, as lawyers are, in effect, parties to the case when charging a contingency fee, they must be influenced in the advice they give. I do not know if anyone has conducted a study on the advice lawyers give when on a contingency fee, but I read about a study that showed that real estate agents, when selling their own homes, gave different recommendations of what to agree to on the final purchase price compared to when selling clients' houses. I would think the same is true for lawyers.

The Combination and Variations Methods

Lawyers can be more creative and use a combination of methods and a variation of fees. Instead of charging an excessive amount for a contingency fee, they can charge a multiple of their hourly rate if a claim is settled before trial, and a contingency fee after that if the matter goes to trial. Lawyers can charge some aspect of the file on a fixed-fee and part on an hourly basis.

4.13.2 Estimating Fees When Using the Hourly Rate Method

As a family law lawyer, I found it extremely difficult to give, at the start of a file, anything but an extensive range of estimates for the final legal costs. I believe other family law lawyers do the same. A major project

I left on the table would have somewhat rectified that impreciseness. Going forward from the start of the project, I would have recorded my time for each major step in the process for each contested matrimonial file. I could have tried doing this for closed files, though it would not be as easy as for the files yet to be done. I would take the numbers to show the client the range of what costs could be, based on how far the case had gone before being settled or adjudicated. When I first started as a lawyer, I did legal aid matrimonial work. The Legal Aid Tariff had, and still has, time limits on how much time a lawyer can spend on a family law matter. Though, as I recall, a little stingy on the amount of time, it showed what Legal Aid thought lawyers would need to do their work. That and similar guides might also help in this project. Lawyers could do this for any practice area that uses the hourly rate method to determine their fee.

4.13.3 Discussing Fees with Clients

There are several topics about fees that lawyers should discuss with their clients. Lawyers can do this in an article inserted in the manual and discuss it at a consultation. The range of topics is wide: it goes from why the lawyer's method of calculating their fee is being used to how a client can keep their costs down. It also ranges from the components of the account to how to read and understand an account. In Appendix 5.12.7.1, I have a list of topics I suggest lawyers could discuss.

I never bargained about my fees with prospective clients. I felt that I would be betraying my other clients, who never tried to negotiate a lower fee. That is not to say I would not reduce my fees if a client had a valid complaint about the fees or if I believed the final cost was much too high under all the circumstances.

4.13.4 Ensure Getting Paid, and How Clients Can Pay Accounts

The best advice about fees that I could give young lawyers starting in practice is that they must remember they are not a bank. Lawyers should obtain good money retainers and not finance their clients' cases unless, of course, it is a contingency fee type of file. Lawyers should not work on files unless they have the money in trust to cover their work or, because of the nature of the case, they know that clients will definitely pay them. In my family law practice, I probably could have bought a house with all the bad debts I had in the first half of my legal career. Some bad debts will be inevitable and almost beyond the lawyer's control, so lawyers should accept some bad debts as part of doing business but most bad debts are avoidable.

One method I used early on in my family law practice that considerably reduced my bad debts and benefited my clients was allowing clients to use credit cards. Their use had to be combined with timely and frequent billing. Like a hotel, I had the client sign a credit card authorization at the end of the first consultation to allow me to charge their credit card upon rendering an account. I did not need my client's permission to charge their account upon issuing a statement of account with this authorization. Therefore, the client was generally billed smaller amounts but more frequently and did not have to come up with a hefty retainer before I did any work. Clients also like getting loyalty points from their credit cards, which can generally work out to be a 2 percent discount on their fees. Lawyers pay a cost to the credit card companies, but I believe it is worth it because of reduced bad debts, and it is a service they are offering to clients. Also, I think lawyers who do not take credit cards are looked upon by prospective clients as antiquated and not keeping up with the times. As seems to be the case for everything lawyers do, there are rules for using credit cards, set forth by the lawyer's governing bodies. Lawyers should check them out.

Not every client wants to use credit cards; some prefer to pay upfront retainers. Financial institutions have come up with different electronic ways for clients to pay their lawyers other than the old-fashioned check. Lawyers should offer these payment methods to clients.

4.13.5 Tax Deductibility of Certain Legal Fees

I found that many of my clients thought that their legal fees were tax-deductible when for most types of work I did, they were not. And when the fees were a deduction, the rules of their deductibility often changed. Lawyers must be clear and in writing from the beginning about what, if any, part of the legal fees may be tax-deductible. Although some fees in matrimonial matters are tax-deductible in Canada, I found that some lawyers did not even discuss this subject with their clients unless asked.

Considering that the benefit could be substantial to the client, I think lawyers should take a proactive approach to this issue. I never finalized my process completely on this issue, but I would always advise about it at the first consultation, in the first consultation reporting letter, and in the final reporting letter. I would provide my clients with a letter to provide to the tax authorities. I would include a final ledger of the account and calculate what part of the fee was tax-deductible and why. I would even, at one point, in my letter to my client state where on their tax return they should insert the deduction (which changed over time). I planned to produce something similar to a tax statement given by employers and financial institutions, which would have the information to insert on a tax return.

I believe that lawyers could use this process for any practice area where the legal fees are tax-deductible.

4.13.6 Retainers

Every type of file needs a written retainer signed by the client. It is not good enough to set out the financial arrangement and perhaps other essential matters a lawyer would put in a written retainer, in a first (sometimes called the engagement letter) or last reporting letter. A written retainer is primarily an acknowledgment that the client agrees to the legal service's cost, but it can do much more. It can confirm what are, and what are not, the lawyer's and client's respective responsibilities. It can reiterate and emphasize critical advice given to clients. Clients may forget that advice, especially if they do not read the reporting letters, which is the case for many clients. I had a wills and powers of attorney retainer that dealt with several issues besides the cost. It stated the clients were responsible for providing the correct information about their finances. It discussed what would happen to their wills that I had in safekeeping when I retired. It discussed what would happen if there was a conflict when I did wills for a couple and it reminded clients again that a future marriage automatically revoked their wills (A 6.13.6).

4.13.7 Unbundled Legal Services

In the past several years, to deal with the problem that many people cannot afford lawyers and therefore do not have access to justice, the practice of unbundling legal services has developed. It occurs when the lawyer does some legal work and the client does the rest. This service is also known under other names, including "Limited Scope Representation,"

"Limited Scope Retainer," and "A La Carte Services." It probably is, as in Ontario, subject to the Rules of Professional Conduct. It is specifically discussed in detail in Ontario's Rule 3.2-1A. There is more written about the subject in Law Pro, which provides errors and omission insurance to Ontario lawyers because there are major risks involved. Law Pro provides sample retainers, checklists, and helpful practices. It is beyond this book's scope to go into all the details of this service. I would point out that lawyers should consider offering it, because it can be beneficial to both clients and lawyers. But lawyers must follow the process and the rules.

4.14 Follow-up Legal Services: Free or Reduced Fees

Some clients might feel hesitant about calling their lawyers on minor matters after the file is over, because they might worry about receiving another account. As I did for matrimonial matters, I suggest lawyers set out their pricing policies on providing follow-up legal services.

I would suggest doing several minor legal services for free or at a reduced cost. In my New Client Memorandum article, I set out some minor free legal services to all my clients, past or present. Those services did not always relate to their file, such as swearing affidavits for other matters. Often people would require an affidavit sworn for a minor insurance claim, a lost check, or a requirement to receive a bequest under a will from outside of Ottawa. I did not charge for swearing these affidavits, provided the clients had the forms all filled out and made an appointment and did not just drop into the office (which they did anyway). Often my legal assistant, as a Commissioner of Oaths, was able to swear such affidavits. I was generally needed only if the document was from out of province, and therefore my Notary Seal was required. As stated earlier in this book, I did not charge for consent to travel forms.

Though it was not a chargeable legal service, I did state that I would help my clients find a lawyer if they needed one in a law practice area that I did not do.

4.15 Letters to Affected Nonclients

Sometimes people, though they may not be clients, will be affected by the legal services provided. Lawyers should contact them after obtaining permission from their clients. In wills and powers of attorney matters,

I wrote to the named executors and attorneys to advise them where the clients were storing the original will and provided them with articles or links to articles that I wrote about what their duties would be (section 6.15.1 and A 6.15.1). I also wrote lawyers holding on to previous wills of my clients (section 6.15.2).

4.16 Following Up with Clients after the File Is Closed

There are many reasons to follow up with clients after a file has been closed. I suggest the follow-ups fall into the following categories:

1. *Reminders:* Clients had to do or had the option to do specific acts according to an agreement or to-do list.
2. *To help clients do actions they had to or should do:* For family law, examples would be lawyers helping clients calculate annual changes in the support amounts or lawyers helping clients at tax times with tax issues related to the separation.
3. *To possibly obtain new business:* After a certain number of years, lawyers could inquire of wills and powers of attorney clients whether circumstances changed to warrant a change in the wills or powers of attorney.
4. *Just to check in to see how clients are doing:* If a client was having a hard time emotionally dealing with a divorce or the death of a spouse, lawyers could call months after the file was closed to inquire how they were doing.

4.17 Providing Clients Resource Information

Lawyers should provide clients with information about legal and nonlegal resources related to their type of file. Such information would come from all levels of governments, other lawyers, and even from other disciplines that clients would benefit from knowing.

Besides adding value to their services, lawyers would show they are empathetic, because they acknowledge that the legal aspect is just one component of their clients' needs. A home purchase may also need a mortgage broker, mover, and house inspector and not only a lawyer.

Reading lists of books and other material could be made available to clients. But the best places to find this type of information are other websites. Lawyers can use hyperlinks on their own websites for clients to access the resource websites.

Providing resource pages with links to other sites is not that innovative; most law firms do have them. As more fully discussed previously (section 4.2.5, sub-section Resource Drop-Down Menu) when websites first appeared in the early-mid 1990s, the resource page was the major component of websites. It was easier to find another site that provided relevant information for the client than to have lawyers or someone else write it. Because some law firms put so much work on their resource pages, lawyers can refer and link to another law firm, especially in another city, and therefore not in competition for the same clients.

Another way to provide resource information is to have local experts write articles about nonlegal related topics to help clients. Besides providing information, this approach would also introduce clients to experts who could help them with their nonlegal but associated issues. I have not seen lawyers do this. It may be because getting local experts to write such articles is not easy. It took me many years to finally get a local family counselor to write an article about aspects of a marriage breakdown, but I persisted until I received the article.

Resources could be posted on the firm website or be placed in the client manual or in both places. Producing a resource page is neither time-consuming nor costly. There could even be possible referrals from those local experts the lawyers asked to write something for the resource page.

The resource application is relevant to all three periods of service. Perhaps one of the resources might be crucial to the client though not so important to a lawyer.

4.18 Reporting Letters

Lawyers producing reporting letters is, of course, not a new idea. All lawyers use them to some degree at the beginning of the file, during the file, and on completion. What can be innovative and vital is how much lawyers include in those reporting letters and how many they write throughout the lifetime of a file.

There are several purposes for reporting letters. Lawyers should use them to confirm important information that they provided orally to their clients. The reporting letters would set out the substantive law and the procedure that applies to that specific case. I suggest, subject to obtaining final information, lawyers in some practice areas should set out what they believe the likely outcome, or the range of outcomes, will be for the issues in dispute. It is critical for reporting letters to confirm the facts and instructions their clients gave to their lawyer orally or in writing in a questionnaire or letter. For letters confirming settlement instructions, lawyers sometimes even have clients sign that letter confirming they agree and send it back to their lawyers. Reporting letters should also advise on matters that the lawyer and client did not discuss in consultation because of time constraints. Reporting letters should set out the steps each party and their lawyers are to do next. When sending documents to clients, the accompanying reporting letters can summarize in plain language, and not legalese, what the documents say and mean. If, as suggested, lawyers have produced articles annotating standard agreement clauses and articles with definitions for legal words, they will have an easier time writing these letters. With these objectives in mind, lawyers should write reporting letters at the beginning and throughout the file after any significant action and not only at the end of a file. Final reporting letters are often done to protect the lawyer from the client but should be much more. Besides recapping what went on during the file, the last reporting letter should set out tasks the client might have to perform going forward, and what future events might necessitate action. The final letter should also point out that it is not the lawyer's obligation to advise former clients of changes to the law that could affect them. Therefore, if they hear of any changes through the traditional media or social media platforms that they believe affect them, they should contact their lawyer, or any lawyer if theirs is no longer in practice.

Comprehensive ongoing reporting letters satisfy clients' needs for good communications and personalization.

4.19 Social Media

There are numerous social media platforms where lawyers can build digital communities. It seems the most popular for lawyers are Facebook, Twitter, Instagram, YouTube, blogs, and podcasts. I used social media very little in my practice. I had only a Twitter account that was hardly ever used, a personal Facebook page not for my law practice, and a YouTube channel just for my six videos on how to complete a Family Law Financial Statement. I believed that social media platforms were more of promotional advertising devices than services to clients. As a one-lawyer established firm, I did not want to spend much time and financial resources on social media.

Having researched social media for lawyers for this book, I see some service applications that I would like to list that are used by lawyers. I believe I did have one important innovative application for Twitter which I would recommend doing for all social media platforms. In my client manuals, I had a one-page article about my Twitter account. I stated my Twitter account name, why I was using Twitter, why clients should use Twitter, and how clients could set up their Twitter accounts and follow me. I believe lawyers should discuss those four aspects in articles for every social media platform they use. That would get clients not already on those platforms to use them and follow or subscribe to the lawyer. Clients who do not become addicted to social media would also reap the benefits these platforms provide. I would suggest that lawyers also offer a complimentary lesson given by their legal assistants for technically challenged clients. Their assistant would help set up the client's social media account, and then the client would become a follower or subscriber of the lawyer.

The services these social media platforms can provide are numerous:

- **a.** they can provide information very quickly and directly;
- **b.** clients do not have to check the lawyer's website daily for new information;
- **c.** they can announce a new article, video, or podcast recently posted on the firm website;
- **d.** they can announce a free seminar the firm is giving to the public;
- **e.** they can announce a change in the law, one that would not necessitate a major article but would still be of interest;
- **f.** they can easily, in the case of Twitter, provide other people's articles by simply retweeting;
- **g.** using a blog, they can discuss some minor substantive law issue that may not necessitate a longer article;
- **h.** they can promote a client's services or public appearance;

i. they can announce changes to the firm;
j. they can announce honors (like a Nobel prize) members of the firm may have received; and
k. they can provide more of a personal connection than a website does.

A benefit to lawyers of having a social media presence, besides the marketing aspects, is that they project an image that the lawyer keeps up with and embraces the latest technology. As Facebook may be around for eternity, it provides a way to connect to previous clients for a long time. Clients may move, change phone numbers, and sometimes email addresses, but they will always update their Facebook account. Another advantage to lawyers is that many people now search for services on Facebook the same way they do a Google search. A Facebook presence helps in the marketing, as does Facebook's feature allowing paid posts to designated demographics to be sent to non-Facebook followers of a particular lawyer.

Social media platforms change their features and technology and require time and money to keep up to date. The advantage of the website is that it can remain more static and does not need to be changed or updated so often. Because there is so much technology to know and keep up to date, small firms should hire consultants to do the technology side of the social media platforms, leaving the lawyers to write the content, which should be primarily informational and not promotional. However, lawyers must ensure coordination among the social media platforms, the website, and the law firm brand.

4.20 Client Newsletters

Client newsletters are an excellent way for lawyers to keep in touch with former clients and impress prospective clients with their expertise. It also shows both groups that the lawyers care about their clients and are willing to provide free information to former and prospective ones. Of course, the hope is for lawyers to obtain new or further business from these groups, but still, it is an added valued service provided by lawyers.

The key to these newsletters is to have brief helpful information written in terms the readers will understand. They are not to be promotional; the readers already know who the lawyers are and what they do.

Unless a new area of practice is now being offered, a firm member was honored for something, whether in the legal field or not, promotional items should not be in these newsletters. The newsletters can keep the readers up to date about new developments in the law, and they can remind clients of ongoing obligations they may have to fulfill. Newsletters are generally for one specific practice area. They are not general firm newsletters covering many different areas of law. Readers have no interest in other areas of the law. If they did, they would sign up for those specific emails.

Newsletters are suitable for many clients who are not on social media platforms. Otherwise, would lawyers not be notifying them by a tweet or Facebook post of a development that the lawyer may have posted to their website. They can be printed and mailed out to clients, but that can be expensive. As about 90 percent of adults in the United States use email (and I suspect many of the remaining 10 percent cannot afford lawyers), I think it is better to have an electronic newsletter (e-newsletter). An email would be so much cheaper to produce and send. But just because they are electronic does not mean the newsletter should look like a long email. They should have color, a banner head, columns, and headlines, and should be visually appealing.

The chances of the followers receiving and reading the e-newsletter are probably higher than their chances of seeing a Facebook post because not everyone checks their Facebook page as much as they check their email. The Facebook post can be easily lost among the many other posts on the receiver's page if the receiver is not continually checking for new posts. The disadvantage of an e-newsletter compared to Facebook is marketing, because prospective clients search Facebook for clients; however, there is nothing wrong with having both.

Short of doing a complete newsletter, lawyers can do something like a weekly (or any period or even random) email to clients containing one recent development in the law. I know of a solo lawyer who subscribes to many free newsletters related to his area of practice. Almost every week, he attaches an interesting article from one of those newsletters to his brief commentary on the issue. He then sends it out to clients interested in that practice area and to people who have subscribed to his weekly commentary. This simple process requires very little work on his behalf, keeps his name out there, and provides his clients a valuable free service. There is the issue of an email sent en masse being filtered as junk email by the recipients. Lawyers should investigate prevention techniques to avoid this problem.

4.21 Radio and Television Advertising

In the pre-internet days, for a short period, I had radio ads for each of my three law practice areas. The 60-second ads were informational. In the first ads, I was interviewed, and I told prospective clients that they should know their rights and obligations. To do so, they could call my office (or visit), and my office would send them a free packet of information about the substantive law, the process, me, and my fees. The packet was about 20 to 30 pages long. It was really a short version of a website. After each airing, we would receive 20 to 30 telephone requests. Radio ads were not that expensive then, but the number of clients I received made it just slightly worthwhile, even though they were good-paying files.[1]

However, I did learn a very important and recurring lesson from the radio ads. Another similar-sized radio station called me to advertise on their station when they heard my ads on their competitor's station. Their salesman convinced me to do a very artsy dramatic ad. It started with the loud sound of a door slamming, then dramatic music, and then an actor saying something like, "If your spouse suddenly leaves you and wants a divorce, call Lawrence Pascoe." There was not enough time to explain the packets in detail as in the other radio station's ad. The response to this ad probably averaged only four calls per airing and resulted in no new clients. Lawyer marketing should be strictly informational. Clients do not need the dramatic and the overly promotional.

[1] Ironically, one of the good files I obtained from those radio ads was because of someone I never met. On a Sunday morning, I was in my office when I received a call from a man who said his brother had just died. He was looking for his brother's will, which he could not locate. He found in his brother's papers my wills and powers of attorney packet. He, therefore, phoned me thinking his brother might have retained me to draft his Will. I checked my files and said no, he had not retained me, but he must have just ordered the packet and not acted on it. The caller then said he had made an appointment for the next week with a lawyer recommended to him, but could he ask a few questions that he needed quick advice on. I obliged him, and by the end of the conversation, he decided to cancel the other lawyer and made an appointment with me. The estate was not large, but it was complicated because there was no will, and we had to deal with two ex-wives and a common-law spouse.

Television stations approached me to do TV ads, to which I had an easy response: "My wife hates the radio ads; she'll divorce me if I do television ads." My observation is that primarily Personal Injury lawyers use television ads because of the costs and returns.

4.22 Radio, Television, and Public Speaking Appearances

Being interviewed for radio or television is done mainly for marketing purposes. For prospective clients, being on radio or TV gets a lawyer's name out in public. The lawyer looks like an expert in their field for both prospective clients and ongoing clients. Why else would the radio or television station want to interview them? However, the interviewed lawyer often just happens to know someone who knows someone who knows the reporter, or their name appeared somewhere prominent so that the reporter just chose that lawyer for a timely interview.

To be a public speaker to small groups like faith groups, financial advisor meetings, and companies with a speaker's lunchtime program, a lawyer also does not have to be an expert but should look like one to the audience. Again, speaking to these types of groups is mainly done for marketing purposes and is a service in the first time period to prospective clients but not generally of service to the ongoing clients. However, it can also be a service to ongoing and former clients if the public speaking appearance is recorded and then posted to the website for clients in all three periods to view. I liked to speak to these small groups more as public service, though I did obtain some clients from them. I realize now that if I had recorded some of those appearances with my hosts' permission, I could have put them on my website and YouTube. Former clients may have learned of developments in the law since they were clients. Lawyers who are interviewed on radio and television will generally post the interview to their websites. Time permitting, they will announce by Facebook and/or Twitter when they will be on radio and television so their clients can see or hear them live and, if not then, later on on the website.

Some lawyers believe that being on television will surely bring in clients. The two times I was on a cable TV phone-in show and my one television interview on a local television station did not result in any new clients. On one phone-in show, only one person called just as the show was ending, and there was no time to answer their second question.

These shows and interviews were also of no service to my clients. My favorite television story happened to a good friend of mine. He was interviewed by a local cable show live about matrimonial matters one night for one hour in his office. He sat in his office the next day, expecting his phone to ring off the hook with calls from new people wanting to hire him. No calls came until about one minute to 5:00 p.m. when his receptionist excitedly told him a lady was on the phone who had seen him on television. He was thrilled to pick up the phone. The caller said she had seen him on television and had a question for him. The question: "How do you get that plant you had behind your desk to grow inside? I have a similar plant, and mine will not grow inside, only outdoors."

4.23 Physical Applications

There are not too many opportunities for lawyers to provide a physical aspect of their practices. But here are some, in addition to the client manual, which is the primary physical application.

4.23.1 Three-Hole Punch

When I provided clients copies of correspondence or documents at appointments or by email, they placed them in their manual's appropriate tab. Because they received a lot of material, mostly by email, they needed a hole punch; so I gave all my clients a good-quality three-hole punch for free. I bought them in bulk, so they were not that expensive. I stuck on a label that said, "Compliments of Lawrence S. Pascoe."

I would assume many readers think this application is corny, but it is a functional and innovative application. Besides being physical, handing clients the hole punch is, though small, a memorable moment of the service. Because it was near the beginning of my services, clients remembered it more. Once, many years later, when a returning client called me to make an appointment for something new, she mentioned that she always remembered receiving the three-hole punch.

4.23.2 Business Cards

With the advent of smartphones, lawyers giving clients business cards is not as beneficial as it once was. Clients will add the lawyers' contact information to their smartphones rather than carry business cards in their wallets. However, I suggest that lawyers still use business cards, as I do, but be more creative by using the back of their business cards to promote themselves. On the back of my business card, I set out my service principles by stating, "As well as providing competent and economical legal services, I am committed to delivering a product that is innovative, client oriented and value added." I went on to say that these features are found in my services and ended with my original marketing slogan, "Know Your Rights and Obligations." As I did, I suggest having a business card for legal assistants, to impart to your clients and the assistants their importance. I also went through five incarnations of a magnetic legal business card, which were more functional when there were not as many stainless-steel refrigerators to which they could not stick.

Besides being useful to hold up grocery lists and family photos, the magnetic business card was like a mini-billboard on display 24/7. Though very minor, these cards were a physical reminder of my legal services.

4.24 Proper Thank-Yous to Referral Sources

As I experienced, most lawyers find that referrals from former clients, other lawyers, and related business associates are their most significant source of new clients. At times in my practice, referrals accounted for as much as 50 percent of my billings. Most of those referrals were generally from former clients. My observations were that lawyers did not adequately thank clients who referred clients. Lawyers are good at entertaining related business associates who can steer business their way; but for their former clients who may refer only one client, lawyers generally just write a brief thank-you note, send a season's greeting card, or donate to a charity in honor of the referring clients, if they do anything at all. I do not think any of those actions are enough. These former clients are probably responsible for a third of a lawyer's revenue, yet all they probably get is a thank-you note.

For almost my entire practice, I kept track of the people who referred clients to me. I could not open a file without knowing why the client chose me. I wrote a thank-you note to the person who referred the client. For the last 25 years of my practice, I also thanked these people by sending them a big bottle of maple syrup at the end of the year with an attached "Compliments of Lawrence S. Pascoe" sticker, and another thank-you letter. It was not an inexpensive gesture with the cost of the maple syrup, the boxes, the postage or courier costs, and the time it took, but it was an appreciated surprise for the recipients and the right thing to do. It was a moment with a physical element.

My office was in Ottawa's west end, not far from Lanark County, Ontario's Maple Syrup Capital (so says the sign at the county line), so it was very high-quality maple syrup—like the best brand of Scotch whiskey to some people. I was also lucky because a former legal assistant owned a sugarbush that produced and packaged maple syrup, so I always had a good supply. I suggest lawyers surprise their clients who refer clients with a nice gift at holiday times to thank them for the referral. Though the intent was not to receive more referrals, my assistant was convinced that one bank financial officer referred clients just to get the maple syrup.

I also sent the big bottles of maple syrup annually to my actuary, accountant, tech support person, court office estate clerks, night cleaner, and anyone else who had been good to me during that year. That even included some lawyers who had given me some good advice. My wife and her family taught me the art of appreciation. In December, my wife bakes for anyone who has been good to her that year. I believe this application applies to all practice areas; all clients appreciate that their lawyer thought of them enough to send a nice present.

4.25 Legal Software Programs

Software programs that lawyers can apply to their practices represent a sizeable subject about which I will only make limited comments. A significant observation I have made before is that lawyers are using technology more to improve the production of their legal products than to improve client service, other than to speed up the process. Those same software programs that make the production easier have features to enhance client service. They probably could do more for client service by producing more specialized client reports.

I am sure some lawyers will disagree, but I believe in the following principles about software programs.

Lawyers should:

a. avoid trying to save money by purchasing generic software not specifically designed for lawyers, when software designed for lawyers is available.

b. buy from companies with robust customer support. The cost of waiting to be adequately served outweighs the cost of a strongly supported product.

c. use the legal practice management software for accounting, client, and file management.

d. purchase software programs designed for their practice area of law. These products will ensure lawyers have all the required and latest updated court forms.

e. use features in the general software like word processing and spreadsheet programs that improve client services.

f. not waste their time being lab rats in testing new programs to save money.

g. be careful not to overwhelm their clients and judges with technology, and use it only if it serves a valuable function and is not used just to impress.[2]

4.26 Decision Making and Formula for Determining Whether to Settle

The application discussed in this section may more aptly belong in a book about legal skills like negotiating and advocating, but it is also, in ways, a service application.

As there is significant uncertainty about the outcome, and there are high costs when taking a disputed legal matter to court, the vast majority

---

[2] I am dating myself when I say that I once used one of the original spreadsheet programs, Lotus 1-2-3, for a court motion to determine child and spousal support. The other side was asking for what I believed was an atrociously high amount of support. I thought their position produced such disparity and unfairness in take-home money after paying support and taxes. I thought the best way to show this disparity was to create pie charts in Lotus 1-2-3 showing how much of the pie each party received under different scenarios. The pie chart with the opposing side's numbers showed my client with a little sliver of the pie. I did not do well on the motion, and though he did not say anything, I do not think the judge was impressed with my pie charts and perhaps felt I was showing off using new technology when it was not really necessary for me to use.

of contested cases are settled somewhere along the road to court. With its built-in pretrial conferences, the legal system encourages settlement. These conferences help clients decide whether to settle by having judges give opinions on the outcome if the matter proceeds to court; but those opinions, for a variety of reasons, may not be helpful in convincing the parties to settle. In family law, the judges have so much discretion, and each has their different way of viewing the world, that who is appointed the trial judge significantly affects the outcome of a trial. A settlement conference may not have all the facts available, or the credibility of witnesses is not known; or, as happens on occasion, the pretrial judge is not prepared or not knowledgeable in that area of the law, so the judge's recommendation will not be a deciding factor. Fortunately, on the other end of the spectrum, I have seen judges do simply brilliant jobs of getting cases settled that I thought would never settle at the pretrial conference. In many matters, parties make serious offers to settle before any settlement conferences take place; therefore, clients can make decisions without a judicial opinion.

Regardless of the settlement conference's recommendations, it still comes down to both parties having to come to an agreement or let a court decide. Many factors go into the decision to propose or accept a settlement offer. An opinion by the lawyer or a judge that the client would win if the matter went to trial is but one of several factors when deciding to settle or proceed to trial. I reviewed my suggested criteria (for family law found in section 5.26) with clients and then helped them decide. I believe clients could have made their decisions more easily if I had finalized my project of creating a process to rate the different criteria on whether to settle for an individual case, which by its score would answer whether to accept the settlement offer. Decision making is much more sophisticated than the old-fashioned pros and cons method. In the meantime, the criteria, like those set out later in section 5.26, should be presented, and then the gut feeling method used to decide. As I understand it (and I may be wrong), according to Malcolm Gladwell in his book *Blink*, the client should consider their gut feeling as much as an over-analyzed decision-making process. But I would still suggest lawyers think about my proposed application for creating a mathematical calculation to make decisions.

4.27 Communications

4.27.1 Checking in with Clients

Many legal matters can take months to complete and often have long periods between an action happening on the file. Many clients think lawyers are like taxis, where it is not just how far they drive, but that they also make more money the longer a file takes to complete. I often had to point out to my clients that if nothing was happening on the file, I was not making money, and I had the same interest as my clients in having the file completed quickly.

I did not do it, but I think I should have noted the date in my calendar when I thought I should have received something like an answer, material from the opposing party, an expert's report, or a court decision. If I did not receive anything by that date, my assistant could call the client to confirm we were still waiting, just to be in contact.

Though not on a consistent basis, I often emailed the opposing lawyer, copied to my client, asking when I would receive a response as the other lawyer should have responded by then. With this approach, the lawyer then keeps clients up to date and is also trying to move the file along. Perhaps all files should be assigned deadlines for when the opposing lawyers should respond, and then some action is taken, either with the client, the other lawyer, or both. A lawyer I dealt with on several matrimonial matters, when asking me to do something would always request me to commit to a delivery date. I never would, because I would not let him dictate my schedule, but I bet it worked on some people.

4.27.2 Automatically Sending Copies of Received and Sent Correspondence to Clients

When any correspondence or documentation on a file came by fax or email to me, my policy was to send copies to clients immediately, even if I had not reviewed the correspondence or documentation yet; unless it was something that my assistant or I thought should be reviewed by me before the client saw it. Sometimes, though, clients saw correspondence or documentation from the other side before I did. If I had not reviewed the material, my assistant or I advised the client of this and that I would contact them once I had a chance to review the material. Also, when my assistant sent a letter to anyone else on the file, she automatically emailed a copy to my clients. If I was emailing any correspondence myself, I always copied it to my client.

4.27.3 Providing Clients with Copies of Court Arguments

When I went to court for a conference, motion, or trial, I would type up my oral presentation to the judge. I typed the arguments to make sure I covered everything I wanted to say, and so I would not have to worry if I could not read my handwriting. But I also gave a copy to my client to comment on before I made the arguments. Doing so would ensure the accuracy of what my client told me and wanted. As well, it allowed the client to participate in the process. The client would then have a copy of the arguments for their records. As I began my presentation I would give a copy to the judge (and the other lawyer) so the judge would not have to take as many notes and could listen more attentively. Judges appreciated this application.

4.27.4 Detailed Voicemail Messages

I changed my voicemail greeting at the beginning of each day, stating the day and advising clients whether I would be in the office that day and when I might return calls. I do not suggest going into detail, as some lawyers do, about how busy they are and all the things they were doing that day. It sounds like the lawyer bragging about how busy they are. If the lawyer will not be in the office the following day, I suggest leaving that on their voicemail greeting the night before; otherwise, clients will hear a day-old message and not know what to think. Clients do not appreciate waiting for a return call, only to receive a call back a few days after leaving their message because the lawyer was in court and could not return calls for a few days or even for a day. They would not be sitting and stewing, expecting a call back if their lawyer stated on the voicemail message when the lawyer would probably be able to return the call and why. In this world of instant gratification, clients expect a return call at least the same day, especially if it is something urgent. Even if the lawyer provides a good explanation why the return phone call took a few days, some damage has been done while the client waited longer than expected for the return call. The lawyer's voice message could say to call the lawyer's assistant if it is a pressing matter that needs immediate attention. I also tried to remember to put on my "Do Not Disturb" when leaving the office. Then clients calling would go immediately to voicemail and not have to listen to many rings before finally getting voicemail.

These are minor matters, but if used as suggested, they show a pattern of caring for the client in every way that lawyers can.

4.27.5 Virtual Consultations and Phone Calls

With COVID-19, everyone has become accustomed to, and many generally prefer having, virtual consultations and court appearances. I believe lawyers should offer clients the choice to have virtual phone calls instead of strictly audio calls. It will be more personal for the lawyer and client to see each other, even for a short conversation. It would not be proper if either one called from their home and dressed inappropriately, but it is easy to turn the video off or just have a regular phone call. Lawyers should also offer consultations virtually.

4.27.6 Telephone Calling Policies

I think it is a good idea for lawyers to advise clients of their telephone calling practice. I advised clients to call me any time during my office hours of 8:30 a.m. to 5:00 p.m., but I told them that I generally focused on files without interruption or had long appointments in the morning, so I might not get back to them until the afternoon. As crucial as returning calls is, lawyers should have focused time to work on a file or even a management matter. Some experts and I agree that multitasking is not as productive as focusing on one matter at a time. I did promise and did return calls always by at least the next day. If that was not possible, perhaps because of a court appearance, my assistant notified clients why I could not get back to them within the day and when I might return their call. I did try to return calls the same day, if possible.

As a marketing application, a friend of mine told his clients that he had a 60-minute guarantee that he or someone in his office would return a client's call. I never went that far and do not think his application lasted too long, but I could see it being more feasible setting up a "by the next day" guarantee.

4.27.7 Dictating Letters to Spouses or Their Lawyers in Front of Clients

When writing the opposing side, especially for the first time, I dictated those letters in front of my clients. I also sometimes did so while on the phone with the clients. This application moved things along and ensured the correct tone to the other side. This process sped up the file, more so in the odd case when clients wanted to approve letters sent out from our office.

4.27.8 Client Portal on the Cloud

When it became feasible to have my law practice management program stored in the cloud, it was too late in my practice for me to move there. But I definitely would have if I had been further away from retirement. There are many advantages for lawyers to being in the cloud, as clearly spelled out in the short booklet "Why Lawyers are Moving to the Cloud," written by Clio. Lawyers can find the booklet on Clio's website. I will discuss just the communications aspect.

Being in the cloud improves client-lawyer communications for both the client and the lawyer. If the client's file is in the cloud, all the client's documents, financial matters, and to-do checklists are available to the client as they are produced. Some of these statements are probably not routinely given to clients but may be of interest to them. The client can access the file at any time and from anywhere. Clients who want to call their lawyer from work have access to their files on their own office computer.

Lawyers who get an emergency email at home or just out of the office, perhaps in court, can deal with an emergency email or phone call because they will have access to the file from their smartphone or laptop.

Some clients still like working more with paper than having their files completely digital, so I would still suggest having the paper manual.

4.28 Flowcharts

Since all legal services involve processes that often have many tasks, besides explaining those tasks to clients orally and through long articles, I always thought it would be good to show an overview of the many steps in the order in which they occurred. For example, for a family law matter involving a separation, I counted 21 potential tasks if a case never got settled and finally was decided by the Court of Appeal. However, the whole process was not simple, because it was not linear: after certain events, the negotiation step would be repeated and then go on different paths depending on whether the negotiations settled the case. I also found the process was complicated because, after specific steps, the clients might agree to go to mediation, appoint the government's children's lawyer or obtain a psychological assessment.

I, therefore, looked, though not too hard, for a computer program that would produce this brilliant flowchart. I never did finish that project but settled on a simple listing of the steps and explained in words when there could be a repeat of the negotiating step and when some steps were optional (A 5.12.3.2). I also accompanied that oral explanation with the article explaining each step (A 5.12.3.3). When writing this book, I looked for that flowchart software program and found a flowchart feature in Microsoft Word and Excel that would produce boxes of different shapes (to designate the task) and arrows to connect the tasks. Next, I googled "legal processes flowcharts." I found some samples, information, and an article specifically about legal processes. However, I found that most of the flowcharts were so complicated that they were too hard to understand. I also realized they would be harder for me to produce, though they would look nice, especially in color. But then a complicated flowchart may be a case of overusing technology, and the looks would be something clients do not care about, as I learned from my client who did not care about the beautiful-looking separation agreement (section 3.2.1).

Some processes, like a wills and power of attorney file, are linear, so it is possible, as I have done in Appendix 6.12, to list the actions in a table format in the order in which they occur and a simple explanation of what is involved in that action. I think that is easier to understand and has more value than a flowchart. I am not ruling out the use of flowcharts to explain all legal processes, but I do ask lawyers to decide if they are appropriate for their clients or if a simpler, less sophisticated approach (like the table) would not serve their clients better.

4.29 Inventing New Processes

In the early 1990s, Minnesota lawyer Stuart Webb believed there was a better and less expensive way for clients to resolve their differences on a marital breakdown. He, accordingly, invented the new process of collaborative family law. He and others made up the process and basic rules and developed training courses for lawyers who wanted to use this it for their family law clients, when appropriate. It gave clients another option to resolve the terms of their separation.

In section 5.29 "Other Applications," I will discuss how a Toronto lawyer invented a process to deal with prenuptial agreements. In the wills and powers of attorney sections 6.35 and 6.29, another Toronto lawyer created a new method to deal with the practice of drafting wills. He used technology to generate a visual display of wills and a process that he turned into a software program to sell to other lawyers. It is possible to change a long-standing legal process partially or entirely.

4.30 Other Applications

4.30.1 Safekeeping of Client Documents and Assets

Lawyers sometimes hold on to client documents or assets. A widespread practice is for lawyers to keep their clients' original wills and powers of attorney, which I discuss in greater detail in section 6.29.1, and corporate clients' minute books and corporate seals (section 9.30.1). There are advantages and disadvantages for both clients and lawyers in having lawyers safekeep clients' documents and assets. The significant advantage for clients is that they will not lose these items. I was surprised to learn from experience when contacting clients about my impending retirement how many clients did not know where they kept their original will. The advantage of lawyers holding on to a client's assets or documents would probably be that it could result in future work. But the disadvantage would be that lawyers would have to ensure that they keep track of their clients and know where they lived throughout their practice.

4.30.2 Storing Clients' Completed Files

When lawyers finish their files, questions arise: Who will store the files, for how long, and how they will be held? How they will be held is a client service matter. Since the digital age, it is much easier to store completed files. It is also much easier to provide clients with a digital copy. Once, for an estate file, I needed the deceased client's tax lawyer's file. It was given to me on a compact disc (CD). That got me thinking that perhaps every client should get a CD of their file when finished. But then, like my 2018 car and new computers, I found CD players were becoming obsolete. That did not stop me from trying to put a CD into my new car's radio for five minutes until I realized there was no CD player. I guess now lawyers can put files on a USB. Maybe USBs will be around longer than CDs, but probably not forever. Then, there is the issue of whether the software programs used in the future will be functional with old technology storage methods. That brings me back to the client manual. Paper lasts a lot longer than the latest technology. If the lawyers and clients use the client manual correctly and the client uses it to store the letters and documents of a file, the client manual is the best way for them to keep their files forever, in my opinion. In the months leading up to my retirement, when many clients came to their appointments to update their wills and powers of attorney, I was pleasantly surprised to see clients come into my office with 30-year-old Will Client Manuals.

4.30.3 Discounts with Non-related Businesses and Free Parking

My cell phone provider and the Canadian Automobile Association (CAA), my automobile roadside assistance company, offer numerous discounts to many stores and restaurants.

I once saved more money on a pair of prescription glasses than I paid for my annual fee to the CAA. These member perks are not just confined to nonprofessional businesses. My new dentist gave me a coupon for free ice cream at a nearby ice cream parlor. On arrival at the new office, I was greeted with a menu board asking what show I wanted to watch on Netflix while in the dentist's chair, which the hygienist could put on a low vibration mode if I desired. I also thought I stumbled into a yoga studio rather than a dentist's office, with the waterfalls and the atmosphere in the waiting room. But then I thought of what a lawyer's office could offer regarding "members'" benefits. I do not think it is tacky to give out coupons for discounts at local (not chain) restaurants and certainly pay for parking if clients have to pay for parking to attend the law office. Many wills and powers of attorney clients would comment that a factor in choosing me was that they greatly resented going downtown to a lawyer where they would have to pay for parking.

I am sure lawyers who work in offices where clients must pay for parking think that clients should not complain about paying for parking when they are probably spending thousands for legal fees, so what is the big deal of the little extra cost? But for some people, it is a big deal that they have to pay for parking.

4.30.4 Hours of Service

I do not believe I have ever seen law firms compete based on being open on weekends. I think it is even rare to see a law firm available at night for appointments. I sometimes saw ongoing clients on the weekend, as I assumed other lawyers did because they had to complete something on time, but that is different. The banking industry finally extended its customer hours to service its clients better. I think it is time for lawyers to do the same.

4.30.5 Sales

I am sure almost all lawyers will say I am going too far to suggest that lawyers, like all other businesses, should have some type of sale when appropriate. The Ontario Bar Association has for many years made November "Make a Will Month." The Association produces brochures and buttons and provides seminars to the public. One year I offered to reduce my fees for wills and powers of attorney for that month. I did not do a thorough job analyzing whether it was worthwhile at that time, but I believe I broke even, because the number of new clients (they did not flock in) made up for the reduced revenue caused by the lower prices. But even if I lost a little money, I gained some new clients who could be return clients and referral sources. No clients said that it was unusual or wrong for a lawyer to have a sale. I believe it was appropriate timing for a sale. It was not as though I was reducing the price of uncontested divorces because I had an oversupply of divorce forms I needed to unload. (I stole that joke from an old George Carlin routine about having a reality TV show called *Divorce Game*).

4.31 Legal Service Applications for Specific Practice Areas

In the following five chapters, I discuss legal service applications that apply specifically to the following practice areas of law: family law, wills and powers of attorney law, administration of estates law, residential real estate law, and corporate law. A general practitioner would probably practice civil litigation and might practice criminal law, but I have no specific chapters devoted specifically to those two practice areas.

Family law is a form of civil litigation. I assume other jurisdictions like Ontario have their own set of procedural rules for family law apart from or in conjuncture with their Civil Procedure Rules; therefore, there is no need to have a whole chapter on civil litigation. I would just be repeating myself with minor modifications to what I wrote about in chapter 5 "Family Law Service Applications" (and I already repeat myself enough). The same is true about landlord and tenant law and employment law. There may be procedural differences but servicing the clients is similar to servicing clients in family law. Their clients would benefit by having client manuals and process and substantive law articles. If I had a chapter on civil litigation, lawyers who did not practice family law would probably skip over chapter 5 and read the civil litigation chapter, when what I really want is that all the specific practice areas chapters be read, especially chapter 5, where I have presented the most types of service applications.

A criminal lawyer pointed out to me that a significant difference with criminal law is that the lawyer, at certain points in the process, does not want to know all the facts that their client could tell them; therefore, the detailed questionnaires would not be appropriate for criminal law. He also said that as there is little paperwork and many criminal law clients are in jail, a client manual would not be necessary or convenient. I still think criminal law lawyers could benefit from service applications presented in this book. I would suggest that criminal lawyers could confirm more in writing to their clients many of the process aspects of their case rather than just relying on oral discussions. They could have articles about the many common sections of their jurisdiction's Criminal Code which their clients are charged with violating. I also believe criminal lawyers would benefit from some service applications, such as a comprehensive website. It was pointed out to me by criminal lawyers that justifiably their clients are very result-oriented and not so concerned about the service aspect but I am sure they would appreciate better service to get through the difficult process of being charged with a criminal offence. Cell phones are generally banned from jails (though they are the most smuggled item into jail), but an electronic manual may be useful for relatives of an incarcerated person, or the incarcerated client may be able to access their manual under prison supervision. And then there is the fact that many people who are charged with a criminal offense are out on bail, so they would have access to their manual.

I interviewed lawyers who practice real estate and corporate law. I have not dealt nearly so much with those two areas as with my own three areas of practice: family law, wills and powers of attorney law, and administration of estates law. I have not provided precedents for areas other than my practice areas, but I believe innovative legal service applications with modifications still apply to other practice areas.

Many of the lawyers I spoke to who practiced corporate law and civil litigation who represented institutional clients said their clients read next to nothing they provided them. The lawyers wrote reporting letters primarily to cover themselves and not for the benefit of their clients. They said their clients would not need anything more than their current level of service. They were not even interested in a client manual. I accept that in my practice areas of law, especially family law, clients have a greater need for service applications than in other areas of law. But there is still a need for all practice areas to use innovative legal service applications like those presented in this book. Those lawyers who say there is no need, and their clients, do not know what they are missing. Clients will benefit from their lawyer providing process and substantive articles and having a client manual to organize their file. Applications that improve communications will reduce complaints and negligence claims. Since these suggested applications, once established, are not overly time-consuming or expensive for the lawyer or the client, lawyers should give clients the option to avail themselves of some or all of the applications offered.

I have not included every application that could apply to specific practice areas in chapters 5 to 9. If there was not much to add to what I wrote in this chapter, which contained all the applications, I wrote very little about the application in a specific practice area. Numerous applications apply to all areas of practice. I did not repeat them when discussing some practice areas. Many applications apply to a particular practice area but need appropriate modification, so I did not always include them. I kept the subsection numbering in the specific practice areas the same as this chapter for easy referencing; therefore, the numbering of the section is not sequential. I recommend that lawyers read chapter 4 and all the practice area chapters, even if they do not practice in those areas because they may suggest an application that lawyers can formulate for their practice areas.

5

Family Law Service Applications

Family law deals with legal matters that follow a separation between spouses, which usually, but not always, leads to a divorce. Prenuptial agreements are also part of family law, as are adoption law and child protection law practices. I will not be discussing the latter two areas, but I will deal with prenuptial agreements, which in Canada we refer to as marriage contracts when marriage is involved, and cohabitation agreements when parties are living together but not married.

Marital breakdown clients would rate many of my application elements as very important, perhaps more than in any other practice area. These clients, therefore, could benefit from many of the applications set out in this book. The family law client is generally a first-time user of legal services and is going through a major, if not THE major emotional event of their life. These clients vary greatly in their needs, which are often in proportion to how bad the marital breakdown was, how far apart the parties are in resolving their issues, as well as the parties' personalities. Also, as one of my colleagues once remarked, "People going through a marital breakdown are temporarily insane." I would not go quite that far, but these clients are often not the same person they would be in normal times. Often their emotions can make them irrational. I often had to tell clients that part of my job was to take the emotion out of the case and resolve their disagreements rationally. The following are some applications that lawyers can use in marital dispute files. I provide numerous samples in the appendix because family law was my primary practice area.

5.1. The Family Law Client Manual

5.1.1 The Purpose of the Family Client Law Manual

The Family Law Client Manual satisfies several elements of the family law file. It ensures good communication and allows the clients to participate in the process and to better understand the law. The manual makes their tasks easier, provides other resources, and even shows that the lawyer is empathetic to the client's case. Also, it gives a client-friendly record of what occurred on their file.

I presented my clients with volume 1 of the Family Law Client Manual near the end of their first consultation, at which time I explained what was then in the manual and what the clients would insert in it as the file progressed.

5.1.2 Organization and Contents of the Family Law Client Manual

The manual had an index (A 5.1.2.1) showing what was in the manual's 10 sections. On my website, I had a digital copy of the manual index so clients could download it and could keep it up to date as they added documents to it. I do not believe many clients kept the index up to date, but a super-organized person could have done so. Many years ago, my legal assistant updated the index by hand for some clients when they were in my office for an appointment, but that was too laborious and not appreciated. I had considered providing an updated index every time we sent copies of documents to the client, but again, that would probably have been too much extra work for my assistant, so I never did it. If clients liked this manual aspect, they could easily handwrite or electronically keep it up to date themselves.

I inserted several pamphlets about family law produced by the provincial and federal governments in the manual's side pocket. Over the years, governments had provided me with hundreds of brochures. I culled out the irrelevant ones for the particular client coming in for their appointment.

The manual had an Introduction page (A 5.1.2.4) to explain the purpose of the manual. The manual also contained a lengthy article (A 5.12.5.1) I wrote many years ago, but that still applies to how I perceived the client-lawyer relationship in matrimonial matters. The client-lawyer relationship in a matrimonial case can be very complicated; therefore, I think it is essential to discuss each party's role and what the client and the lawyer can expect. I then had a memorandum for new clients (A 4.12.4). This all-in-one memorandum provides information on the many office policies and procedures related to clients. Topics included information about my legal assistant and what she could and could not do for clients, how to communicate with the office, storage of files, and a list of my free services for clients during and after their file is closed.

Finally, in the Introduction section, I had an article on Client Expectations (A 5.12.5.2). It is essential to manage clients' expectations related to the result, the cost, and the timing of a matrimonial matter.

In section 2 of my Family Law Client Manual, I wrote several articles to help clients better understand the family law process. I started with an article defining many legal terms with which clients may not be familiar (A 5.12.2). There are, in my opinion, six different methods of resolving a marital dispute; I wrote an article about all these processes explaining what they involved and the advantages and disadvantages of each (A 5.12.3.1). There was also a chart of all the steps in the disputed family law process (A 5.12.3.2). I had a very long article explaining these individual steps. Because it is lengthy and as the procedure will differ from jurisdiction to jurisdiction, I included in this book only parts of the article that I considered would occur in any jurisdiction (A 5.12.3.3). This article will have to be adjusted depending on the jurisdiction where lawyers practice. Though discussed at the first consultation, having the steps in order and a brief explanation is beneficial to clients.

I believe the first article I ever wrote for my manual, and the one I consider the most important, is entitled "How to Complete The Financial Statement, Forms 13 (Support) and 13.1 (Support and Property)." It is not reprinted in this book because it is much too long, and matrimonial financial statements will differ from jurisdiction to jurisdiction. It was so important to me (and should be to all family law lawyers) that I produced a six-part one-hour video (section 4.2.7) similar to the article. The video was on my website and was also posted to YouTube. The URL for my YouTube channel is https://www.youtube.com/channel/UCiUft39DIk26hjzcsj2vOMQ, or search for Lawrence Pascoe Financial Statement Videos. I also had a list of typical household items and their depreciation rate set out by an insurance company. The list would allow clients to have a better idea of what their household belongings were worth.

The following five sections would hold copies, as they became available, of the following documents: (1) letters between myself and my clients; (2) letters between myself and the other lawyers and others; (3) my client's financial statements and financial documents; (4) the other spouse's financial statements and financial documents; and (5) offers to settle, orders, and agreements.

Section 9 of the manual contained a copy of my retainer, two articles I wrote about legal fees in matrimonial matters, and a place for clients to keep their accounts.

I have included in the appendix (A 5.12.7.1) the headings of the subject matter in my long article about legal fees. After writing that article, I added a memorandum to help clients to better understand an account's format, because accounts are not simple (A 5.12.7.2).

If the court ordered a psychological assessment, I had an article about assessments for my clients to read and insert in their manual.

I wrote many articles about the current substantive law of the main areas of family law, such as custody and access, division of assets, and child and spousal support. These articles were on my website, not in the manual. Some clients would download the articles of interest and insert them in their manual. I believed my articles in section 2 of the manual were necessary because these types of process articles are not found elsewhere. Lawyers might orally explain this type of information at consultations, but they do not write about them in the public domain as they do for substantive law subjects.

If the parties could not settle the matter, one spouse would have to commence court proceedings. I would then give my clients volume 2 of my Family Law Client Manual. It had an index (A 5.1.2.2) with 10 tabbed sections. Most of the sections were for the client to conveniently file the many documents that the parties draft for court proceedings. I also wrote for these sections a memorandum to explain practical matters, such as where and when to meet at the courthouse, how to dress, what will happen, who will be present, how to act, etc. The Motion Memorandum (A 5.12.3.4) and the Questioning Memorandum (A 5.12.3.5), which are slightly different, are in this manual. I also included a map of the area around the courthouse, showing where clients could park if they had to attend a court proceeding.

I never got around to doing memorandums about going to trial. Like many family law lawyers, I went to court for many conferences and motions but did not have many trials, especially in my later years. But I suggest that lawyers who have numerous trials do an extensive memorandum about precisely what will occur at a trial and how the client should behave.

I had different manuals for prenuptial agreements (marriage contracts and cohabitation agreements) and uncontested divorces because they have fewer and simpler issues than the normal family law file. I did not give these clients the standard Family Law Client Manual, to avoid overwhelming them with information that they would not need to process their file. My memorandum on the costs and process of an uncontested divorce is found in Appendix 5.13.2. The Marriage Contract/Cohabitation Agreement Manual index is in Appendix 5.1.2.3.

5.1.3 Keeping the Family Law Client Manual up to Date

If the client received anything to be put in the manual at their appointment, I would three-hole punch it and make sure it got inserted in the right section. If they received something by mail or email, they could insert it in their manual.

5.1.4 Importance of the Family Law Client Manual

The many issues in family law and the accompanying stress most family law clients are under make it almost impossible for clients to keep all the information about their file in their head. The manual, rather than an envelope full of letters and documents, holds that information for the client in an organized fashion.

5.2 Family Law Sections of the Website

5.2.1 Importance of the Family Law Section of the Website

Many prospective family law clients choose a family law lawyer from the internet. Their legal matter is so personal that they may not want to ask friends and relatives for a referral. Even if they have a referral, clients will probably want to research their recommendations by looking at the lawyer's websites; therefore, the website can be, as it was for me, a prominent marketing tool to influence the clients' choice of lawyers.

Prospective family law clients generally want to know as soon as possible what their rights and obligations are, so short but substantive articles of what the law is for the primary family law issues should be on the website. Prospective clients want to know what information is needed to process the file which client questionnaires on the website can achieve. They want to know something about the legal process and the lawyers' fees and systems. Having all this information on the websites will significantly reduce the family law client's stress.

5.2.4 Organization of the Family Law Section of the Website

Family law is the only practice area that I broke down into two distinct sections on my website, because the separation and divorce information and process are different from the information and process for prenuptial agreements. If I had done adoptions or child welfare matters, I would have also made them separate sections.

For separation and divorce, I had five standard categories: The First-Time Client, The Law, The Process, Fees and Forms, and Resources. For marriage contract and cohabitation agreements (prenuptial agreements), and as there was not as much to write about, I combined the law and the process into one category called Articles.

5.2.5 Contents of the Family Law Section of the Website

The same level of general information a lawyer would give a client at the first appointment would be in separate articles for custody and access, child and spousal support, and the division of assets. There should also be articles for the different processes that the parties can use to resolve a matter and list each side's benefits and drawbacks. A fast-growing process is that of clients representing themselves. I discuss that briefly in my process article, but I suggest it deserves more attention than I gave it. I like what a law firm in Georgia did when they posted a one-page article enumerating the many reasons people should not represent themselves, with a summary of each reason. Upon request, that firm offered a more detailed booklet about the reasons for not doing your divorce yourself. An email providing the download of the booklet's PDF version is sent out immediately after the request. As discussed in chapter 4.2.13

in greater detail, I am not sure it is such a good idea to request the email address to get the booklet: family law clients may want to be anonymous and not want a flood of emails from a law firm not yet retained.

An essential section of the family law section of the website is "Fees and Questionnaires." Prospective family law clients can be price sensitive. Lawyers want to weed out clients who will not want to pay what they consider high fees. Some prospective clients think the lawyer will wait for payment until the end of the matter (which is a bad idea, because family lawyers will have enough bad debts without looking for trouble by financing a file). An article about fees and a copy of the retainer lawyers will ask clients to sign at the first consultation should be on the website. This subsection will reduce dealing with people who will not retain the lawyer because of the cost and payment requirements. This section can explain what the legal fees are, or the range, for particular cases.

As discussed in section 4.2.6, having client information questionnaires on the website is beneficial to lawyers and clients, especially for family law clients. I also had a very detailed questionnaire for custody and access, which I would not ask clients to complete until we knew that was a contested issue. I suggest lawyers could do the same for other issues that need more detailed facts.

Family law clients have probably never had any dealings with lawyers for such a major legal matter. Perhaps their only contact with lawyers was briefly for a house purchase or a will. They may be distraught from the separation. They may be overwhelmed with too much information. Therefore, more than any other practice area, there should be a menu for first-time clients. That submenu would link to an introductory guide that prioritizes what the newly separated person should read. Another link would be to the slideshow that will outline the agenda for their first consultation.

I had only a small resource section because I never found the time or interest to work on it. I had at one time linked to some impressive Toronto family law lawyers who had extensive resource pages. Having a useful resource page is a good idea, but it means devoting a lot of time to obtaining the material. I suggest start by just referring to a non-competing firm in another city with a helpful resource page. On my resource page, I linked to my videos, which are also on YouTube, which explain in detail how to fill out the official financial statement needed in all family law matters in Ontario.

In addition to discussing it in my reporting letter, I probably (as I did for wills) should have had an article on my website about what circumstances would necessitate a change to an agreement or court order. The article would also discuss the process to renegotiate a variation, or if the negotiations were unsuccessful, the piece would explain the court procedure.

5.2.9 Third-Period Uses of the Family Law Section of the Website

A third-period service application for this practice area was a Consent to Travel Form for separated or divorced parents to authorize the other parent to travel out of the country with the children. Border authorities required this consent to ensure one parent was not kidnapping a child. That form at one time had to be witnessed by a lawyer. I did that for free for either parent, provided they made an appointment and filled out the form entirely beforehand. What authorities require at the border changes from time to time and depends on who is on duty.

Because clients occasionally lose papers, though it is harder to misplace a large three-ringed binder, I would suggest that the family law section of the website could have information about all the possible issues that clients should follow up with after the file was closed. That would include pensions and variations. A client who knows they are supposed to do something can go back to the website to remind them of what they are to do, and, in some instances, the website is linked to the appropriate government website for further information.

5.3 The Client Monitor for Family Law

On numerous occasions, I used the client monitor, one of my favorite applications, when representing family law clients. As in all first consultations, I used the monitor to display the first consultation slideshow. Often clients would follow my note-taking on their monitor, and the odd time would want a copy of those notes.

At the first consultations, the primary question family law clients would ask was about the child and spousal support payments, particularly the amount. As, I assume, in all jurisdictions, Ontario law has complex formulas that use computer programs to calculate child and spousal support. With clients watching on their monitor, I would input into the software program the many factors that went into these calculations, such as different incomes, number of children in each party's primary care, tax deductions, and certain expenses. The client would more easily understand the effect of the factors on the amount of support payments by watching the formula produce numbers in front of their eyes instead of having me call out numbers. For each of the most likely custody scenarios and, in some cases, income, I would print out the report to insert in their client manual.

The primary and most important document in a family law matter was the 15-page financial statement. With help from my instructional article and my video on completing the financial statement, I would have clients at home, before attending their consultation, first do their best to fill the statement out themselves. At their consultation, using our monitors, we would go over their financial statements. We would usually make numerous changes so that the numbers related to assets, debts, and income were based more on the documentation they provided to prove the accuracy of the numbers than on the clients' estimates. Concerning expenses that generally had no backup documents, we would adjust them to be more realistic, so their budgets were balanced and, if not, looked for how either debts or savings might have increased or decreased. The finalizing of this task was much easier with the dual monitor system because it was a real team effort.

Reviewing and changing court documents, such as divorce applications and affidavits, was also much more manageable with a monitor than if the client had a paper draft copy in front of them. The clients then saw the changes made on the screen. Again, it was a good collaboration between the client and me.

Last, at the end of a consultation, especially the first one, clients and I would complete the family law to-do lists to document what was expected from them, from me, their spouses, and their spouses' lawyers. I would print the client's copy, and the client would insert it into their manual.

5.4 The Family Law First Consultation Slideshow

The lawyer-client relationship is significant in family law, so lawyers want to impress clients at their first consultation and instill confidence in them. There is also a lot to cover in the first family law consultation, and it is very easy in a matrimonial consultation for the client to get off track. The Family Law First Consultation Slideshow helps steer the conversation back to the listed topics when either the client or the lawyer has moved off the scheduled path. In addition, the detailed agenda of the slideshow instills confidence.

Often, I sensed that family law clients had some important matter on their minds that they were anxiously waiting to discuss with me. Until we reached that point in the first consultation, they sometimes were not listening to me closely. I would therefore often let them discuss that matter first or just out of sequence. If I did not do that, they probably were not fully absorbing what I was saying until we discussed their issue. So, as opposed to other practice areas, I did not always follow the family law agendas in order.

Family law clients were generally justifiably the most anxious clients, because they were dealing with the breakdown of their marriage. Having a copy of the slideshow of the agenda beforehand reduced their anxiety; they knew what we would be discussing and were better prepared for the consultation. These clients would often have a list of questions written out, something I encouraged them to do.

This slideshow started with reminding me to deal with preliminary first-time client matters and reviewing what the consultation would cover. It then explained the law, process, and lawyer-client relationship before gathering the facts and finding out what the client wished to be the terms of their separation agreement. I then reviewed the issues and gave my opinion based on the information I had at that time. Then we discussed the different processes that the client could use, then lawyer-client matters such as fees and retainers. Before dealing with the final topics, I had a slide with many more minor issues to review with the client. The slideshow particulars are shown in Appendix 5.4. On the website, at one time they appeared as 16 different pages.

I treated family law clients who retained me to do a marriage contract or a cohabitation agreement differently, because they had different issues and the processes differed. They had their own First Consultation Slideshow.

5.5 Family Law Client Questionnaires and Forms

There were three specific family law areas of practice that had different intake questions and information to give. For the first and most common one, a contested divorce/separation agreement, the person taking the intake information, whether a lawyer or the assistant, should convey some sympathy and empathy in their tone and language. The client may have just separated, or even if it has been some time since separation, they are likely grieving the loss of their marriage. It is different grief than if a spouse had died but may be just as painful. The lawyer should have this same tone and use words of condolences at the beginning of the first consultation, just as they should do at the start of an Administration of Estates file.

5.5.1 *Matrimonial Client Intake Forms*

Contested Divorce/Separation Agreement Intake:

I asked a question confirming that the prospective client resided in the jurisdiction where I practiced, because I did not want to drive far if I had to go to a courthouse other than the Ottawa one. Many people who work in Ottawa live outside the Ottawa judicial region. Because Ottawa is on the Ontario-Quebec border, some Quebec residents thought they could use an Ottawa lawyer, which they cannot.

I had several questions I asked which would help me decide whether I wanted to take the file. At my stage in my practice, I could be pickier about who I took on as clients. I inquired whether they were on Legal Aid, because I did not take Legal Aid except in my early years of practice. I asked whether the clients already had a lawyer and were looking to change lawyers or had fired their lawyer, both of which are not uncommon in matrimonial matters. I asked why they wanted to change lawyers. It was generally not my practice, for various good reasons, to take over a file from another lawyer; however, I sometimes offered to take over their case or give a second opinion without committing to taking on their file, as they may have had good reasons to switch lawyers. I asked if their spouses had lawyers, and if so, did they know the lawyer's name. If the spouse was self-represented or was represented by a lawyer on my list of lawyers who were very difficult to deal with, I generally did not take the case. Not surprisingly, my list of difficult lawyers was the same as that of most other lawyers in Ottawa. I did not need the aggravation of taking on problematic lawyers. I was diplomatic in advising the prospective client why I could not take the case when they mentioned their spouse's lawyer's name. I said that I did not work well with that lawyer, so it would be best to retain another lawyer. I once had to hold back while saying this excuse to a prospective client when I was yelling in my head, "because she is not of sound mind." As I was no longer going to take on hotly contested custody matters, the form asked what the major contested issues were.

Uncontested Divorce Intake Form:

I had to ensure that the prospective client's request fell into my definition of an uncontested divorce, which meant a separation agreement or previous court order required no changes. The Divorce Act residency requirement was that a person bringing the divorce had to have resided in Ontario for a continuous 12 months. I asked about the marriage certificate's whereabouts and told the client how to order one if they did not have one. My process for uncontested divorces was to obtain most of the information beforehand so that clients could sign their application for divorce at their first consultation. We would finalize anything missing on the application for divorce at the time of the appointment to have a fast and easy process.

Marriage Contracts/Cohabitation Agreements Intake Form:

The first thing I asked was the date the parties were going to get married. If the wedding date was less than four months away (which was often the case), I generally would not take on the matter. If it was less than four months, there was probably not enough time to get proper financial information and perhaps negotiate an agreement. Often, we had to discuss why I could not represent both sides. I emphasized that with separate lawyers I was protecting my client from having the agreement set aside. The same was true as to why full financial disclosure was needed.

Having a good and specific intake form was necessary to eliminate clients I could not jurisdictionally represent or did not want, at an early stage, and not after a wasted first appointment.

5.5.2 The Matrimonial Client Information Questionnaires

Basic Matrimonial Information Questionnaire: This questionnaire should be available on the law firm website to allow clients time, before the first consultation, to provide the much-needed information to process the file. So as not to overwhelm the clients at this point, lawyers should request only basic information, for which the questionnaire is long enough. In my questionnaire, I asked the client to state what they thought the disputed issues were and to rank each issue's priority, so I could know what was important to them. At their consultation, I would spend more time on higher priority issues.

Specific Issue Questionnaires: If either custody or access were contested issues, I would have my clients complete an extensive seven-page questionnaire. It would request details of each party's parenting during the marriage, from who took the children to the dentist to how each parent disciplined the children. I asked clients to fill out that questionnaire only after the first consultation when I knew custody and access were unresolved, however, many clients took it upon themselves to fill it out without my asking, even when this issue was not in dispute. Perhaps they hoped their answers to this questionnaire justified that they were the parent to have primary custody of their children.

I did not get around to having detailed client questionnaires for the other major issues, the division of assets and child and spousal support. I acquired that information in consultations. I should have started with client questionnaires to emphasize the importance of proof to validate the facts alleged. Also, finding the proof takes time, and letting the client know early to start collecting the evidence could be necessary in some cases. I requested clients to obtain immediately direct documentary evidence of financial matters. However, sometimes clients had to produce other evidence when that direct evidence was not available.

In my jurisdiction, the calculation of child and spousal support can be more complicated in some cases than completing an income tax return. Though many cases are relatively simple, like in an income tax return, there could be many credits and deductions that can change the amount of support. I attempted for years to produce a better child and spousal support questionnaire. I even harassed the software company, Divorcemate, whose product I used to calculate support, to create a comprehensive client questionnaire, but they never did. As I will discuss further in section 5.29, I asked them to write a software program similar to some of the income tax preparation software where the program asks questions to produce the amount of tax owing or, in the family law context, support amounts. Divorcemate is a great company that listens to their clients and even changed one of their working forms at my suggestion; but I would have liked a questionnaire option. Though time-consuming and not easy to produce, I think it would reduce mistakes in calculating support. Unfortunately, mistakes did occur enough that Divorcemate did write an article on common errors lawyers made in calculating support.

5.5.3 *Family Law Client Preference Questionnaire*

As I set out in detail in section 4.5.3, I had a Client Preference Questionnaire. I developed it for family law clients only. It was more about understanding clients' expectations and priorities but did include questions about their preferences regarding how they wanted me to communicate with them. I should have revised this questionnaire and used it more as an opportunity to customize the file.

5.5.4 *Lawyer and Staff and Performance Questionnaire*

I used my short performance questionnaire for all files. However, I realize now I should have had a tailored performance questionnaire for each practice area. The relationship between my clients and myself and my assistant differed depending on the type of file. I should have also had questionnaires throughout the life of the file life, such as the end of major steps in the process.

5.6 Family Law First Appointment Confirmation Letter

As discussed in section 4.6, I discussed numerous matters in my appointment confirmation letter. All the information in this letter was important. It would be impossible for a lawyer to convey all that information orally or for clients to remember it all if it were not written down. My assistant sent out this letter within a day of the client making the appointment. I wanted the client to start gathering information as soon as possible to ensure they provided the most information possible. At the first consultation, clients generally have lots of specific questions about their case. Lawyers need particular information to answer some of those questions, so the clients should be given time to assemble that information. I built a summary checklist into that letter. A comprehensive first appointment letter will instill the client's confidence in the lawyer. See Appendix 5.6 for a sample letter.

5.7 Subsequent Appointment Letters and Agendas for Family Law Clients

In one of my process articles, I did discuss what we hoped to achieve at the second matrimonial appointment if the file followed the typical path. We wanted to obtain the then-available proof of numbers to substantially complete the client's all-important financial statement substantially at this consultation. But there were other matters new and outstanding on this and further consultations. I suggest lawyers write to the clients before the appointment to remind them what they have to prepare for, based on the agenda.

5.8 Lawyer's Notes for Consultations and Telephone Calls for Family Law Clients

Using the outline feature in my practice management software, I created templates for each telephone call and consultation type. The templates generally had the following headings, which should be on any notes lawyers take:

1. Name of file
2. Date
3. Person called or met with
4. What information received
5. Advice or information given
6. What instructions given
7. What actions are now to be taken by me
8. What actions are now to be taken by the person that I was communicating with

Before making a call or having a consultation, I also filled in a section called "Purpose of the call (or consultation)"; this section ensured that I remembered to cover everything I wanted to discuss. Having these templates served several purposes: They organized a digital and readable record of my notes of that call or consultation. They prepared me for the discussion, so I would cover everything I wanted to discuss if I initiated the call. They ended in writing the next steps for me, my client, and the opposing lawyer to do. For the odd consultation upon a client's request, I would give the clients a copy of the notes. It was a copy for them of what was said. It was another record for both of us of everyone's to-dos.

5.9 Family Law To-Do Lists and Document Lists

Many participants in a matrimonial matter are required to do several tasks. Lawyers must keep track of those tasks. I suggest that a to-do-list is necessary. Besides the client's tasks, the lawyer, the opposing lawyer, the opposite spouse, perhaps experts, and the legal assistant have tasks.

The to-do list would have a column listing the standard client tasks in a matrimonial matter with the easy ability to add further tasks. If they produce it (as I did) in Excel, lawyers can add tasks easily. As well, Excel allows all the different to-do lists to be in one file but under separate tabs. There would generally be three columns to fill in beside the task itself: Date Requested, Date Provided, Date Provided to Opposing Side. I played around with this format at times, also thinking I should note how the request was made (if asked) and how the request was delivered (if asked); but I felt that other information was going too far.

This family law to-do list would be provided and explained at the client's first consultation and inserted in the client manual. It could be something the client could use and keep digitally, or it could be a form updated by the client and sent to them when updated.

There may be some overkill in my to-do list format, but there should be some documented way to keep track of all the to-dos. Reminding clients of their tasks throughout reporting letters is still going to be done but is not as effective as the client to-do list. This application was a work in progress and was not always used by me, and I am not sure how many clients used it.

Lawyers could use the same type of Excel document to keep track of the documents required from both parties in a Family Law case. I had developed such a spreadsheet but did not use it much. I relied on the court worksheet form that went along with the court's financial statement to keep track of asset and debt documentation, and I had a separate system for income documents.

5.10 Calculation of Fees Forms for Family Law Clients

Knowing the final cost of legal fees was a significant need of matrimonial clients. I tried my best, based on my experience, to provide estimates but found those estimates to be very imprecise. In section 5.13.2, I discuss the difficulty of estimating fees in family law matters and suggest that lawyers record data from their own ongoing and past files to give clients a better idea of the final costs. With a service application, I could then have produced a form with the different stages of the process and the range of fees associated with it so a client could see how much the total costs would be depending on how far the matter proceeded before being settled. This project would not apply to block fee matrimonial matters such as uncontested divorces and prenuptial agreements.

I had no spreadsheet calculating the estimated fees for the standard matrimonial dispute file, because I based my fee on an hourly rate and the disbursements, except for expert reports, which could be expensive. I would discuss the costs of those reports separately. I perhaps could have listed the court filing fees, estimated filing fees, and other disbursements for these types of files. I did list the disbursements for uncontested divorces in my Process and Fees for Uncontested Divorces Memorandum (A 5.13.2).

5.11 Client-Helpful Word Processing Software Features

Separation agreements contain numerous clauses over many pages. When looking at another lawyer's agreement, I often found it challenging to locate a specific paragraph I wanted to see. It was even more difficult for clients to find paragraphs. As a lawyer, I at least knew where in the agreement I would probably locate a paragraph, but a client would not know that. I, therefore, often used the "Table of Contents" feature and sometimes the "Index" feature of first WordPerfect and then Microsoft Word so both the clients and lawyers could more easily locate topics in the separation agreement. These features are not significant benefits but show that the lawyer is trying to make their product more client friendly.

I did not use it regularly, but some clients and the odd lawyer would use the Microsoft Word tracking function when drafting separation agreements. Some clients and lawyers find it easier to comment on proposed changes using this feature. For lawyers, it is a good feature that allows accepting changes more quickly. It is also a way to compare drafts, so a lawyer does not make changes without notice, which unfortunately has happened. Although I did not use it for separation agreements, only wills, perhaps lawyers could use the line numbering feature for draft agreements as a slightly easier method of making comments and asking questions about a draft. Again, this is not a significant benefit but shows the lawyer is keeping the client in mind.

5.12 Articles for Family Law Clients

For several reasons, lawyers should have many articles for clients in family law matters. Most matrimonial clients want to know as soon as possible what their rights and obligations are when they separate. Their separation will generally turn their life upside down, so they are anxious to know what that new life will look like. Where will the children live? What amount of support will they receive or pay? Can they stay in their home, or will it have to be sold? How will their assets be split? What is the legal process? How long will it take, and how much will it cost? There are numerous types of articles, as set out in section 4.12, that can be written or obtained from others which I will discuss.

5.12.1 Substantive Law Articles for Family Law Clients

Because clients need to know these answers quickly, brief substantive articles on the law should be posted on the website. I would suggest articles on parenting, support, assets, and procedure be at the forefront. Clients may know some law from friends and relatives who have separated, but every case is different, and there are many misconceptions of what the law is. Even after meeting with their lawyers because there are so many family law issues to comprehend, which can justifiably stress clients, it is good to have these written articles to fall back on for clients to recall what the lawyer advised them about the law and procedure.

5.12.2 Definitions and Annotations

Lawyers sometimes speak a different language, so a "Definitions" article would be helpful. I never did write it, but I suggest an annotation article for separation agreements, so clients better understand the reasoning for and meaning of the many standard clauses found in separation and prenuptial agreements. I provided a glossary of Family Law terminology in the Family Law Client Manual: it can be found in Appendix 5.12.2.

5.12.3 Legal Process Articles for Family Law Clients

As discussed in the section 5.1, I had articles about the family law legal process. "The Processes to Resolve Family Law Disputes" (A 5.12.3.1) set out the many ways clients could resolve marital disputes. I had a process chart in "Steps in a Family Law Dispute Chart" (A 5.12.3.2), and my article "The Steps in a Family Law Dispute" (A 5.12.3.3) set out the client processes in a file, from the first contact through the different consultations and possible court proceedings to the final reporting letter.

5.12.4 Law Firm Procedure Articles

I gave clients in all practice areas my New Client Memorandum (A 4.12.4) in their Family Law Client Manual.

5.12.5 Client-Lawyer Relationship and Client Expectations Articles in Family Law

The lawyer-client relationship is a complex one because of the nature of the family law file. The association will last for months and may even last for many years with numerous consultations, phone calls, and court appearances. Lawyers are also often privy to some very personal information about their clients; therefore, many years ago, I wrote a lengthy article, "The Client-Lawyer Relationship," for family law clients (A 5.12.5.1). I set out both client and lawyer roles and what each should expect and not expect from the other. I also found it necessary in more recent years to write about client expectations for matrimonial clients

(A 5.12.5.2). I wanted the client to have a reasonable expectation about the results of their case, how long it would take, and what it might cost.

5.12.6 How-to Articles

I wrote a how-to article about filling out the quite complicated government financial statement needed in every family law file, no matter what process was used to resolve the file. It was nine pages long, not counting a sample completed financial statement. Other how-to and what to expect articles were about some of the court processes, such as articles on questioning (cross-examinations) (A 5.12.3.5), motions (A 5.12.3.4), and in Ontario, the two types of pretrial settlement conferences: the case conference and the settlement conference. I got into detail, such as how to dress and where to meet. I also explained what clients should expect to transpire at these steps. If I had done more trial work, I would have done an article to prepare clients for trial.

5.12.7 Legal Fees and Billing Articles

The Family Law Client Manual should have an article answering all the standard questions clients may have about legal costs (A 5.12.7.1) and an article on understanding account statements (A 5.12.7.2). An important aspect to explain to matrimonial clients is that part of the lawyer's job in these matters is to keep the costs down but that the lawyer has lots of work to do in a matrimonial matter. I explain in my article in the manual the ways both clients and lawyers can keep client costs down. Often in matrimonial matters, clients will say they just want to end the case and get it over with because of frustration and money worries. My answer is simple: clients can end it if they settle for the amount that the other side has offered. That usually ends the discussion and brings them back to reality because they do not want to accept the offer on the table.

5.12.8 Articles about Related Issues Written by Others

I finally persuaded an Ottawa family counselor to write an article for my manual about the stages of grief one goes through in a marital breakdown so clients would know what to expect. Because he was a local, clients could retain him for counseling, so this promoted him. I had, at times, some parenting articles in my manual. Still, I never, as I had hoped to do, created for clients a bibliography of valuable books about the psychological, parenting, and even financial issues that arise because of a separation. I did provide all the many free government pamphlets, which had some helpful information on these topics and family law in general.

5.12.9 *After the File Is Closed Articles for Family Law*

Besides an article about prenuptial agreements, I did not write any after-the-fact matrimonial articles except for my memorandum about uncontested divorces for those clients who obtained just a separation agreement and were not obtaining a divorce right away. I put that after-the-fact type information in my reporting letters. In retrospect, I could have also written articles entitled "When and How to Vary Child and Spousal Support Payments," "What Happens When Your Former Spouse or Your Child Wants to Change the Parenting Agreement," "What to Do When Your Former Spouse Stops Paying Support," and "When and How to Apply for a Government or Private Pension Division." Besides being good articles for marketing purposes, I think a separate article in the client manual in which the lawyer can get into greater detail than in a reporting letter would benefit clients.

5.12.10 *Promotional and Informational Articles for Family Law*

On my website front page, in addition to a few testimonials, which I dislike, but marketing experts claim work to get new clients, I had a lengthy explanation of "Why Choose Me?" I describe it in detail in section 4.2.3.

I would suggest lawyers write, for all areas of law, an article I never got around to doing in family law, which would discuss why a person should not represent themselves, whether in litigious matters or legal matters where there is no opposing party. Many people think they can save money and do as good a job as a lawyer if they were representing themselves. As a lawyer, I am probably biased in thinking that is not the case, but I do believe the old saying, "A lawyer who represents himself has a fool for a client." This article could explain that it is not just the substantive legal knowledge needed to handle a matrimonial matter but also the lawyer's knowledge of the processes and their training in negotiating, so essential in family law. And most importantly, the lawyer will take the emotions out of the representation and represent the client on a more rational basis. However, having said that, I once had a court motion where I thought the other side represented herself much better than I represented her husband. I learned never to underestimate the ability of a self-represented client. The informational aspect of these articles would also cover why legal services are needed. There could be an article on why a written separation agreement is needed rather than relying on an oral agreement. To quote another well-known saying, "A verbal agreement is not worth the paper it is written on." I also had an article on when and why a client might need a prenuptial agreement.

5.13 Legal Fees in Family Law Matters

For several reasons, legal fees are probably more of a concern to clients in family law matters than in other practice areas. They are nondiscretionary and unexpected. Clients may not be able to afford the costs and may have to borrow the funds. The final costs are more unpredictable, because they have a wide range of possibilities if the parties contest the matter, wider still if the dispute proceeds to court. In section 4.13, I discussed the many issues in the subject of legal fees. A major service aspect of this subject of fees is superior communication with the client. These communications should be done directly and in writing. The beginning of the file must always include a discussion of costs. The Family Law Client Manual should have an article answering all the standard questions clients may have about legal costs (A 5.12.7.1) and an article on understanding account statements (A 5.1.2.7.2). An important aspect to explain to matrimonial clients is that part of the lawyer's job in these matters is to keep the costs down but that the lawyer has lots of work to do, and it costs what it costs. Among many other topics, I explained in my article how clients could keep their costs down and how I tried to keep their costs lower.

Setting a fixed legal fee in contested matrimonial matters was an area that I, like most lawyers, did not consider thoroughly enough. I could not create a better method than an hourly rate based on the local market rate for my years of practice. I combined the fixed-fee method and hourly rate method for marriage contracts/cohabitation agreements (prenuptial agreements). There I could predict pretty accurately how much time I would spend on those files, and I believed the value of such an agreement was greater than just the time spent.

5.13.1 Estimate of Fees

Knowing the final cost of legal fees was a major need of matrimonial clients. I tried my best based on experience to give estimates but found those estimates to be very imprecise. In section 5.10.10, I discussed the difficulty of estimating fees in family law matters and suggested that lawyers record data from their own ongoing and past files to give clients a better idea of the final costs. This project would not apply to block fee matrimonial matters such as uncontested divorces and prenuptial agreements. In the case of uncontested divorces, I had a memorandum that set out the legal fees, disbursements, procedure, and timing for this service. I defined what I considered to be an uncontested divorce (A 5.13.2).

5.13.2 Tax Deductibility of Certain Legal Fees

In section 4.13.5, I discussed the fact that some fees in matrimonial matters were tax-deductible. In addition, I discussed the details in section 4.13.5 of a process to ensure clients could easily take advantage of this tax break, which could be substantial.

5.13.3 Retainers

A written retainer in matrimonial matters is necessary, so there is no misunderstanding about how a lawyer will charge the client. The retainer should set out the types of disbursements and taxes the client is responsible for, in addition to the lawyer's fee. The retainer should make it clear the lawyer is not a bank and that unless the lawyer and client have made arrangements, such as using a credit card, the lawyer must have money in trust to complete the next phase of work. As stated in section 4.13.6, lawyers can also use retainers to discuss other matters. In my last couple of years of practice, when I decided not to do court work, my family law retainer stated that if the case did not settle and court action was necessary, the client would have to retain another lawyer. I agreed to help find and brief the lawyer who would take over. I never charged for briefing the other lawyer. I believe I lost only one prospective client by having this proviso, because many people were looking for lawyers who would be attempting to settle out of court. I added a clause about halfway through my practice that would terminate my retainer if I refused to follow my client's instructions for professional reasons, such as not accepting an offer that was not just reasonable but one which was so good that "it could not be refused." I believe I had to use this clause only once. The following is a good story I often tell.

I had a client that many people did not like. That group included his wife's father, who intensely disliked his son-in-law. The other lawyer, an assertive litigation type, told me that the wealthy father-in-law, who was paying his daughter's legal fees, had instructed him to spend as much money as he needed to fight my client aggressively. After I was successful at a temporary motion, and my client continued to behave poorly, I received a telephone call from the wife's lawyer. The father-in-law and daughter had had enough with my client and just badly wanted to get rid of him. So they changed tactics and made an offer to settle far more generous than my client would have ever received in court. When my client refused the offer, I fired him as allowed by my retainer. I wrote off part of his last account for his new lawyer to get up to speed on the file, but it was worth it to get rid of this client that I never liked. I thanked the opposing lawyer for making that offer which allowed me to get off that case.

I never minded taking on a difficult case to win, but I would not argue a case impossible to win. To do so would hurt my credibility with my fellow lawyers and with judges for future dealings. My clients were in charge of instructing me, but only to a point. I very much disliked dealing with lawyers who did just what their clients asked them to without controlling irrational and aggressive positions.

5.13.4 Unbundled Legal Services in Family Law Matters

With the number of self-represented clients high and growing in family law, more lawyers now offer unbundled legal services (also known as limited scope representation). In section 4.13.7, I explained that because there are risks for the lawyers who provide such services, my law society and insurers produced rules and information, including information about the risks and precedents in unbundled services, I believed that at my stage in life the risks in family law of providing unbundled services were greater than the rewards, but I foresee younger lawyers having to offer this service. My strong advice would be to follow the rules closely and take proper precautions. That means mainly having a clear and comprehensive retainer so that the clients understand what the lawyer is and is not doing as well as ensuring getting all the facts.

5.14 Free Follow-Up Legal Services for Family Law Clients

I put in my matrimonial reporting letters my policy on providing follow up family law services. Some clients might feel hesitant about call ing their lawyers on minor matters after the file is over, as they might worry about receiving another account. Therefore, I made it clear that if I provided service after the file was closed, there would be no charge, provided that I spent less than half an hour on the phone with clients and did not have to write any letters or have an office appointment. As discussed, I did not charge for Consent to Travel Forms, which once were required when one separated party wanted to take their children for a vacation outside of the country. I would not charge for simple computer calculations for an updated child or spousal support, though clients could usually figure these out themselves using the government or some other websites that had free calculators for simple cases. And as I did for all clients, I did not charge for swearing affidavits, which I did not have to draft for items like insurance claims.

5.15 Letters to Affected Nonclients

I can think only of two people, other than the client, to contact once a matrimonial file is complete. Canadian law does not require the applicant of a divorce procedure to serve the opposing lawyer or opposing spouse with a copy of the certificate of divorce, which is the final document in divorce proceedings. The divorce application and divorce judgement, but not the certificate of divorce, must be served on the opposing spouse. I always did provide the certificate of divorce out of courtesy to the other lawyer. I even offered to get a certified copy of the certificate of divorce (which both parties would need for remarriage) if the other side sent me the court disbursement cost in advance. It was a preemptive tactic; the opposing spouse would phone my office looking for a copy of the certificate of divorce on many occasions, years later.

5.16 Following Up with Clients after the File Is Closed

There are several issues that lawyers can follow up with former family law clients that would be of service to their clients and might generate business for the lawyer. Quite often, a matrimonial matter gets settled with a separation agreement with no divorce obtained at the time. There may be no rush to get the divorce for pension, health plan, costs, or psychological reasons. There is also a one-year waiting period in Ontario before a party can obtain a divorce if based on separation. Lawyers can bring forward (BF) their calendars to when clients can apply for a divorce and then remind clients.

Lawyers can annually remind clients that their agreement allows for a change of child and spousal support annually and then offer their services to determine that support if their clients need help with their calculations. The same may also apply to the obligation to have life insurance for the security of child support. The amount required may be able to be varied as set out in the agreement. The need for life insurance decreases every year as the children and spouse get older. Lawyers can remind clients that they were to complete the transfer of credits or money for government or private pension plans.

While offering these services, lawyers can remind clients that they should have a prenuptial agreement if they are about to or have cohabited or married. Lawyers should also remind clients they should update their wills and powers of attorney. To encourage my clients to update, I offered a 20 percent discount on a matrimonial client's costs to draft wills and powers of attorney if they retained me to do so within six months of their final matrimonial account.

5.17 Providing Clients Resource Information for Family Law

Lawyers can benefit their family law clients by providing them with information about professionals who deal with the many ancillary non-legal issues that may arise when couples separate. I always told my family law clients that no matter how well they thought they were handling the emotional aspect of their separation, they should consult with a counselor alone for their own benefit. This counseling was not marriage counseling or counseling concerning the children but counseling for themselves. Most would say they were okay because family and friends were supporting them. But I still pushed this type of counseling and provided them with the name of a counselor I knew or would look for other ones. As I stated in section 5.12.8, I included in my manual an article about the stages of grief one goes through in a marital breakdown. Of course, if there were a chance of reconciliation, I would help my client find an appropriate marriage counselor or child psychologist if there was a need for that. Though I bought some books about the emotional aspect of separating, I should have but never did put together a list of books they might find helpful to read. I suggest putting together a divorce and single parent support groups list.

Newly separated people may also need help concerning their finances, such as investing or budgeting. They may not have been the spouse who looked after the finances and may never have filled out a tax return before. In the card section of their manual were the business cards of my investment counselor and accountant. I said they had better know what they were doing because they were looking after my money. I would recommend a life insurance agent and a real estate agent on occasion. Having these recommendations from someone they trusted could be helpful to family law clients who had enough on their plates without being stressed about asking around about real estate agents or financial counselors.

5.18 Reporting Letters for Family Law Clients

Lawyers should use reporting letters with clients, not only after the file is finished but also after or sometimes even before every major stage of a marital dispute. These letters are more significant for family law clients because it is often almost impossible for clients to absorb the many issues, information, and advice given to them, not to mention the misunderstandings that can arise between what the lawyer and client said to each other.

Immediately after their first matrimonial consultation, I generally wrote my clients a nine-page letter confirming what they were seeking and the advice that I gave them for the major issues of the case. In doing so, I reiterated the main principles of law that applied to their case. I was also able to detail issues that we may not have spent much time on at the interview. I discussed taxation, government benefits, estate and death benefit, matrimonial homeownership, credit cards, limitation periods, counseling, and ongoing disclosure requirements. I also reminded my clients of the process and what everyone's to-dos were. This letter, though quite lengthy, contained many standard precedent paragraphs and easy subjects to write about, so it took me little time to dictate (and my assistant to produce).

Though I generally reported to clients after major stages in the process, I did not formalize or have standard reporting letters before or after these stages. I would now consider it a good idea after a case I had where a client did not fully understand the other side's position, which I thought I had explained well enough orally. I also think reminding the client beforehand what the process is about and afterward of what exactly happened are a good idea and can be done in reporting letters.

I, like many lawyers, had a very long final reporting letter that generally contained a fully signed separation agreement. I discussed all the major substantive clauses of the agreement but put them in simpler language. I would discuss the future actions that they would or might have to take, such as pension splits, tax payments, enforcement, and variations. I advised what portion of their legal fees were tax-deductible. I reminded them, if appropriate, to update their wills and powers of attorney and, as previously mentioned, gave them a discount on that cost if they retained me to update their will within six months of the reporting letter. I reminded them when they could apply for a divorce. If they were thinking of cohabiting with a new partner or remarrying, I suggested considering a prenuptial agreement. I reminded them of my free follow-up services generally and specifically for matrimonial matters. I also asked them to complete my lawyer performance questionnaire, which they could do online.

5.19 Social Media for Family Law Clients

Family law lawyers might want to be on social media to drive their clients, who are followers/subscribers, to the firm's website because a firm lawyer has written something new for the website. Another reason to be on social media is that prospective clients use these various programs to find lawyers. The social media site would then point these prospective clients to the firm's website to learn more about the law firm and the law. The social media site would be useful for staying in touch with former clients so as to ensure that the law firm is on the clients' minds to return or refer the firm to family and friends, should they have the opportunity to do so.

The social media platform is a way to announce something related to family law, such as a new good book on parenting or a guest speaker coming to their town. It could also be used as a reminder to follow up on changing support, which generally happens each June in Canada because the previous year's taxes have been government approved by then.

As explained in detail in section 4.27, I had videos on my website on how to fill out our court's financial statement, but I also put them on YouTube for marketing purposes and to help improve my website's search engine optimization. People use YouTube a lot to be visually shown how to do practically anything. I use YouTube all the time to learn about technology and find instructions on how to clean my vacuum cleaner. I would never have figured out how to set up the board to play Catan with my grandson without YouTube.

5.20 Client Newsletters for Family Law

A family law e-newsletter was not a big priority for me because family law clients were not generally repeat clients. My clients generally got divorced only once, so there was no great need to stay in touch with them with updates to the law, which probably would not apply to a closed file. If I were going to do a family law newsletter, I would follow my suggestions in section 4.20, and my content would be, besides some changes in the law, a reminder of some of the follow-ups in the client reporting letter.

5.21 Advertising on Radio and Television for Family Law Clients

As mentioned in section 4.21, I did for a short period advertise my family law practice on the radio. I did not receive much business from it but learned the valuable lesson that people want substance over style. My information radio ad received much more of a response than my ad with dramatic music and sounds of a couple breaking up. There is not much advertising in family law because the advertising costs do not justify the returns the way they do for personal injury law.

5.22 Radio, Television, and Public Speaking Appearances for Family Law Clients

I was on a cable family law phone-in show a couple of times. Neither time did it generate any business. A few clients saw me as they were channel surfing. I did impress these clients because I was asked to be on the show. So that helped my credibility as a lawyer who probably knew his Family Law for those very few clients who had watched me. As mentioned in section 4.22, I suggest this is a service to clients and a marketing opportunity if these appearances are recorded and posted to the website and YouTube.

5.23 Physical Applications for Family Law Clients

The main physical application for all practice areas is the client manual. For the Family Law Client Manual, probably more than any other client manual, the lawyers will email clients material on an ongoing basis to insert into their manuals. Therefore, I provided my clients who needed one, a high-quality three-hole-punch for this area of practice, unless it was just a prenuptial agreement or an uncontested divorce file, as there would be much less need for one in those files. See section 4.23.1 for other advantages of providing the three-hole-punch.

5.25 Legal Software Programs for Family Law

Family law lawyers need dedicated software for the two major tasks: drafting court documents and calculating support. Dedicated family law software is necessary for the support calculations because the formulas are so complicated. Some lawyers just still fill in standard court documents using their word processor program for the drafting. Even if their process works well, they do not have the significant feature of having a software company that will always provide updates when the law changes. There were frequent changes to the court forms when I practiced. A good software company like the one I used, Divorcemate Software Inc., had excellent client support and was also a good resource for information about practicing family law. Throughout the years, in various cities, it also offered very inexpensive seminars about using their products. I used to attend as the calculation of support component of the law, and their program became very complicated in some fact situations. I was amazed that only about 20 percent of the participants in these seminars were lawyers. Most were competent legal assistants, but I think lawyers should know how to work these programs. I either did the support calculations with my clients watching on their client monitor or went through the calculation process if I had worked on the analysis before the consultation.

I investigated but never used nor ever saw another lawyer use child custody and visitation software. This type of software seems to be used more by clients than lawyers, though it looks beneficial for both. I think lawyers should check out the different companies' software offerings for this subject and explain the benefits clients might receive from using it. Besides developing child custody and visitation terms, the programs produce calendars, calculate total time, enhance communications between parents, and record notes and expenses. If lawyers are not going to use these programs, they should at least advise their clients of the programs' existence and their benefits.

5.26 Decision Making Formula for Family Law Clients

Family law has come a long way because the formulas for statutory division of assets and for support reduce the arguing in marital disputes, but governments have still left a lot for lawyers to argue about. Unfortunately, in my opinion, they have also left too much discretion to judges, and there is still the issue of what are the facts upon which the judge should decide the case. So many family law clients must decide what settlement terms to accept when there is a disagreement on how to resolve some or all issues. Should they accept their spouse's offer? Should they pursue the matter further with a more generous offer? Should they go to court and let a judge decide? Sometimes that decision is easy to make because the other side has a weak case and is just trying to bully their spouse into a settlement—many were bullies and got their way throughout the marriage, so they think they can also be bullies in the separation process. Lawyers know that bullies can get lucky, so they must factor in, like as in horse races, long shots can win. Sometimes, the law is uncertain, and the judge's discretion is very broad for some issues, so the result is far from predictable.

I did not get around to formalizing it into a detailed process, but I had a list of criteria for my clients to consider, which I discussed with them when considering settlement:

- **a.** What was the opinion of the settlement conference judge? (This criterion is dependent on whether it was a proper settlement conference.)[1]
- **b.** What, based on my advice, was the possible range of outcomes and the likelihood they could each occur?
- **c.** What was the weighted average of the possible outcomes?
- **d.** Can the client financially live with the settlement proposal in the short and long term?
- **e.** Can the client emotionally live with the settlement proposal in the long term?
- **f.** What are the legal costs of proceeding further?

---

[1] I was involved in a case where I represented a former spouse in a support case. The other side's spouse had an aggressive litigator who I felt was making unrealistic demands of my client. We attended a settlement conference. The judge announced that she had just been recently appointed as a judge and had not practiced family law for many years. She said that therefore, the parties might not want to hear her opinions. I mistakenly said that we would like her opinion because I thought she would have the common sense to see through the other side's weak argument and the case law he was presenting in favor of his client was not applicable. I was wrong. She got taken in by the other lawyer's argument and suggested my client pay much more than he should, in my opinion. The other lawyer then made an offer based on their claim backed up by the judge's opinion and requested a significant amount in costs. I advised my client to go to court. He heard the judge say she had not practiced family law, and perhaps her opinion was not worth hearing. My client proceeded to a court hearing with another lawyer I recommended where an experienced judge found in my client's favor and against the former spouse. Interestingly, the former spouse went bankrupt, and her lawyer lost thousands of dollars in fees he could then not collect. Justice was served both for my client and the opposing lawyer.

g. What are the emotional costs of proceeding?
h. Can the client afford to lose if you proceed?
i. Is the opposing spouse at their bottom line?
j. Can the opposing spouse afford to lose if they proceed?
k. Are there advantages of having a settlement as opposed to a court-ordered result? Studies have shown that when parties settle, it reduces the possibilities of further disputes compared to when there are court-ordered terms.

Depending on the case and the client, some criteria were more important than others. In the end, as discussed in section 4.26, the clients decide from a gut feeling, taking all these criteria into account. Fortunately, the choice was often not hard, because it was not worth the gamble considering the costs and odds, so the parties generally settled. That settlement was not as good as perhaps it should or would have been if the client had gone to court but was acceptable. Other times, the other side's case was so weak that letting a judge decide was the best option. I believe the decision to settle process could be more formalized and decided on in a mathematical manner. I would have liked to have invented the Pascoe Settlement Algorithm.

5.27 Communications with Family Law Clients

5.27.1 Checking in with Clients

Family law clients are usually anxious to have the matter resolved quickly, and some get stressed when it appears nothing is happening on their files. Lawyers themselves or their assistants should contact clients even if there is nothing to report other than that they are still waiting for a reply. That could be accompanied by a copy of the follow-up letter to the other side if they are awaiting a response and a promised time, deadline, or reasonable time has passed.

5.27.2 Automatically Sending Copies of Received and Sent Written Material to Clients

Because family law clients are anxious to receive news of anything happening, I tried generally to send them as soon as possible by email any written matter I received on their file. If I did not get a chance to review it or take a quick look, my assistant or I would state that in the covering letter with the copies. If, as was sometimes the case, I believed it necessary for me to explain something in the material that would upset the client (like telling my client the other side's claim was not to be taken seriously), I would wait until I could phone or write my client before sending off their copy. If the material came in while I was out of the office, I left it to my assistant to decide whether she should send it out or wait for me to comment on it first.

5.27.3 Providing Clients with Copies of Court Arguments

As discussed in section 4.27.3, as a person who likes to be prepared and cannot read their own handwriting, I always had my arguments typed up for any court hearing, including settlement conferences. I could not rely just on handwritten point form notes. But this script was not just for me: I would give a copy of the arguments to the client before the hearing so I could get their feedback. Sometimes they would correct something I was going to say or want me to add something. I warned clients that depending on the judge and the way the hearing was going, I might not strictly keep to the script. The clients felt they were participating in the process more and had a record of what I argued on their behalf.

5.27.7 Drafting Letters in Front of Clients

After the first matrimonial consultation, generally, the next step is that lawyers write a letter to the spouse or spouse's lawyer concerning several matters. The lawyer advises that the client has retained the lawyer and that further contact about the legal case must go through the lawyer. If not represented, the other spouse is advised to get a lawyer and provide financial disclosure. Sometimes also stated, subject to financial disclosure, is the client's position generally on major issues.

I almost always dictated that letter in front of clients near the end of their first consultation to speed things along. I included everything the client wanted in that letter. I had client participation, and I ensured the letter had the tone the client thought appropriate. Clients often asked me to add or subtract something that I dictated, or they requested that I change the letter's tone. I also at time used this same application during a telephone call with a client. I let the client listen in as I dictated a letter.

5.28 Flowcharts

There are so many steps that might occur in a matrimonial dispute before it is resolved that I had a simple listing of those steps, which I found easier to do than to try and create a more formal-looking flow chart (A 5.12.3.2).

5.29 Inventing New Innovative Processes for Family Law Clients

During my time practicing family law in Ontario, the Family Courts invented an entirely new process to deal with family law disputes. Also, lawyers and others established, by my count, four new procedures for family law disputes: family law mediation, collaborative family law, private settlement conference (also known as five-way conferences), and limited scope representation (unbundled legal services). Then there are combinations and variations of those processes, such as collaborative law lite, which some people called the process when agreed that the original collaborative lawyers did not have to remove themselves from the case if the parties did not settle.

Though none of these processes is perfect, they are all useful, including the traditional lawyer-lawyer negotiating and court proceedings. Which process is better depends on the nature of the parties and the nature of the case. There is still room to find other procedures that may better resolve some family law cases than any of the many methods now in use.

Software companies have done excellent work producing programs in family law not just for document assembly but for the complicated child and spousal support calculations. As my company of choice, Divorcemate had excellent client service, a great product, and added valuable material about family law not related to its product. However, I do have one complaint, which I had voiced to them on a few occasions. If I had the time and were a tech-savvy programmer, I would have remedied it myself. The calculation of the amount of support can involve just a few inputs of information. But in many cases, even for lower-income payors, there are numerous inputs, some of which I have seen lawyers forget to input, such as the amount that their clients paid in union dues and medical insurance. They generally made a minimal difference in the amount of support, but still, they were factors that the formula took into account. I suggested to Divorcemate that as some of the personal income tax software programs do, their program could ask questions about the parties in a logical order to fill out the inputs into the program. This process would be a better quality control than just leaving it up to lawyers to put in the information they thought was appropriate. I do my income tax return using software programs. Last year I changed programs and opted for a slightly cheaper one. It did not have the question-and-answer format. I am switching back to the more expensive program next year because I am not as comfortable with the one where I am responsible for figuring out all my possible inputs.[2]

In section 4.28 I discussed Minnesota lawyer Stuart Webb inventing collaborative family law.

In 2015 Toronto lawyer Brahm Siegel presented a paper to Ontario family law lawyers entitled "The Compact: A Proposed New Way Forward for Marriage Contracts & Cohabitation Agreements." Siegel was perturbed by the high number of these agreements challenged in the courts and by the unwillingness of some family law lawyers to take on a prenuptial agreement file. The risks for lawyers were not worth the remuneration they received for drafting these types of agreements; therefore, he created a new process for a prenuptial agreement matter

---

[2] As the law changed, the software to calculate the amount of support also changed, usually making the software better. But from one of the transitions to the new version of the program, Divorcemate decided to remove a form they had developed called the "Net Family Property Worksheet." It was not a court-prescribed form but a very helpful form to keep track of what documentation supported the parties' claims and showed the differences between each party's position for each asset and debt in the division of property calculation. Family law lawyers did not widely use it, but I did in every matrimonial file. When I saw this worksheet was not in the updated program, I phoned to complain. Divorcemate told me by that time that only about five people had requested its reinstatement. I assume some others later complained. I wrote Divorcemate formally, asking them to put back the form in their program. I also suggested some minor improvements to their form. Divorcemate accepted my modifications, and in one of their subsequent updates put the updated form back in their program. Lawyers started using the form more. It became so valuable that later the Ontario Family Law Rules required it in court proceedings. The government made it a prescribed court form with a minor change, renaming it "Comparison of Net Family Property Statements."

that he believed would reduce challenges. He produced seven rules to follow:

1. No work is to be started unless the wedding is at least four months away.
2. Each party must have its own lawyer from the outset.
3. Each party provides a financial disclosure brief before any negotiations begin.
4. There must be at least one four-way without prejudice meeting.
5. The lawyers fully report to the clients in writing after the four-way meeting.
6. A term sheet is prepared and approved before the lawyers draft the agreement.
7. The lawyers draft the agreement, and the parties sign it with specific key clauses Mr. Siegel created.

Those clauses that Siegel drafted dealt with two specific issues if a party challenged the validity of the prenuptial agreement. He had clauses confirming that the parties believed the agreement was fair concerning both support and property and could not be set aside for being unconscionable. He had clauses setting forth a simpler legal process resolving the challenge, including a clause that would have the procedure first decide whether the court should set aside the agreement before making the parties spend time and money on the terms of a set-aside agreement.

This was one of the most innovative practical applications I had ever seen a lawyer produce. I adopted most of his rules and used his clauses for prenuptial agreements and, with modifications, for separation agreements.

5.30 Other Applications for Family Law Clients

5.30.6 Ensuring a Fair Settlement for Both Parties

My next suggestion is not really an innovative legal service application, but I could not write about the practice of family law without expressing my opinion about how aggressively some lawyers practice family law. Lawyers are taught that they should do anything within their powers to get the best possible result for their clients. I realized early in my practice that in family law that was not exactly right. If a settlement or court order is not fair for both parties, there can be bad consequences. The party that does not get a fair result (and I do not mean a result they wanted but one obviously within the reasonable range) can take several actions. If they feel so aggrieved, and they cannot live with the result, they can to some extent breach the agreement and make it difficult for the spouse receiving asset or support money to collect. This is especially true if they are self-employed. They can move to vary the agreement every time they have the slightest chance and, in some cases, argue every year about the calculations used to determine support. They can use the children by either asking to change where the children reside, or worse, they can try to alienate the children from the other parent.

If the parties have children, they will have to deal with each other for the rest of their lives, though sometimes in just minor ways. It is important that they get along after the file is closed. A way to ensure that is to make and accept reasonable settlement proposals. I am not saying to give in to unfair demands but do not be over-aggressive in arguing unreasonable positions. Often this is explained that one must start high to get where they want to be; but I do not buy that excuse. To obtain a settlement, parties may have to compromise and can start at a high, but within the possible range position, but should not ask for the moon and the sky as an opening position and pursue an unfair result. I blame some judges and mediators for not being harder on these over-aggressive lawyers and not chastising them for making outrageous claims.

I believed this theory very early in my career and remember being ridiculed by a fellow lawyer for it. I finally felt vindicated about 20 years later when one of the top family law lawyers in the country wrote an article for a legal newspaper stating the same theory. Unfortunately, even with the use of more mediation and collaborative law, too many lawyers are still over-aggressive.

I will get off my soapbox now.

6

Wills and Powers of Attorney Law Service Applications

My wills and powers of attorney practice area dealt with drafting and executing wills and powers of attorney and included some estate planning that complemented the wills and powers of attorney. The estate planning also involved dealing with how assets are registered, whether in one name only or more than one name, whether jointly or in tenancy in common. This practice area also included the designations of beneficiaries for life insurance and other financial instruments that allow for beneficiary designations. Estate planning also entailed trusts and, perhaps, tax planning. Except for simple testamentary trusts, I left the tax planning and sophisticated trusts to lawyers specializing in those fields. I did deal with methods to reduce probate fees.

One part of this practice area I thought lawyers very much neglected and which I wrote an article on and included quite prominently in my discussions with clients is what I called "Preparing for An Easier Administration of an Estate." Having a will ensures the executor distributes the person's estate to the desired people, but the administration of the estate should also be set up so that the executors can easily administer and at the least cost. Therefore, as will be discussed, a significant application found in my Wills and Powers of Attorney Manual allows the will-maker to leave proper up-to-date instructions and information about their estate to be available for their executor. It was, therefore, an area ripe for innovative services after the primary legal services of drafting and executing wills and powers of attorney.

6.1 The Wills and Powers of Attorney Client Manual

6.1.1 Purposes of the Wills and Powers of Attorney Client Manual

The Wills and Powers of Attorney Client Manual was unlike my other client manuals. This practice area dealt with a very short-term lawyer-client relationship. The Wills and Powers of Attorney Client Manual was most helpful to clients in the third service period after the file was closed. Many executors told me they were thankful that there was a Wills and Powers of Attorney Manual as it made their job much easier. It also made them feel more assured that they had found every asset the deceased owned, and they did not have to spend time looking for investments or insurance policies. Many people leave their financial affairs in a bit of a mess for their executors. However, I did have one client who went beyond the completed forms in the manual. He had typed up letters to all his asset holders and insurance companies ready for his wife to mail when he died. He just left a blank space for his wife to write in the date he died. I was surprised he did not stamp the envelopes, but I guess he was unsure what the postage amount would be when he died.

6.1.2 Organization and Contents of the Wills and Powers of Attorney Client Manual

There is little correspondence between the lawyer and the client in this type of file. My first section of the manual contained just the final reporting letter and perhaps other minor correspondence. I preceded this, as I did in all my manuals, with a manual index (A 6.1.2.1). The index had descriptions of the 10 tabbed sections. The second tab contained a true copy of the will. The third tab had copies of letters I wrote to executors and attorneys, which I will discuss later in this chapter. The fourth tab contained memoranda, such as my standard New Client Memorandum for all clients (A 4.12.4), and had two essential memoranda related to wills that I did not want just hidden away in a long reporting letter.

Those memoranda contained my policies for storing wills and powers of attorney and retrieving them from storage. Like all manuals, this one included articles of interest about the law.

The lead article was entitled "The Purposes and Plain Meanings of Clauses Contained in a Will." There is probably more legalese in a will than in any other document that lawyers draft. Wills also contain clauses dealing with archaic legal principles such as the Law Against Perpetuities and Accumulations. When even I had to read my article to remind myself what some clauses meant and what their purpose was, how would clients understand them? Besides being helpful to the clients' understanding, this article for them considerably reduced my time explaining each clause's meaning and purpose. Since most lawyers charge a fixed rate for Wills, this article was also financially beneficial to me as it saved me time. I explained to my clients that wills were long, and lawyers made simple matters longer than necessary because lawyers originally got paid by the word. I did, however, many years ago, as per an article I read on making wills more readable, change such phrases as "I nominate, constitute, and appoint" to just the acceptable "I appoint."

Though I had articles on my website about powers of attorney, I never wrote an article annotating the powers of attorney clauses. In Ontario, the continuing power of property and the power of attorney for personal care are relatively new compared to wills, the language is much more understandable, but a detailed article would benefit clients. I did have an article about powers of attorney and their use because clients generally misunderstand them.

As I explained to my clients, it may be their death, but it was not their funeral; the law made it clear that the executor, not the family nor even the deceased, decides the funeral and burial arrangements. So I suggested clients keep up to date their funeral and burial instructions on my specific form in their manual. If they decided to change their minds, then without changing their will, they could change their instructions. They could also go into much more detail on this form about their funeral and burial if they wished. I would state their wish in their wills for clients who strongly preferred being cremated, reminding them it was not binding on the executor to follow their instructions on that matter. I said their remedy against their executor for not following their direction was that they would "haunt" them.

I had two more instruction forms. One form was for clients to list people, with their contact information, who the executor should notify about their death, such as relatives, friends, clubs, and professional organizations. The other was a form about personal belongings. The personal belongings instructions specifically stated they were not binding. If it was a significant asset, I advised it should be in the will. But if they wanted particular beneficiaries or people not named beneficiaries in the will to receive smaller personal items, this was the place to state those wishes. That way, if a parent named specific children to inherit specific items (such as jewelry) and these items were not in existence at the time of death, the executor could then even things up by giving them more money or other items. These instructions could change without also changing the will. I advised clients that this was a section of the manual where they should write further instructions to their beneficiaries, such as how they hoped the beneficiaries would use their inheritance or how the custodians should raise their children. When my children were younger, my wife wrote an essay to our named custodians about raising our children if we died simultaneously.

I had a section for information forms where the clients were to keep up-to-date details of their assets, location of documents, and personal advisors. I also had a plastic cardholder sheet where I suggested they have their personal advisors' business cards (I just happened to slip my card in first). I had a crucial to-do list section, which I will detail later in this chapter then a section for their Retainer and account, and finally, the last section for notes. In Appendix 6.1.2.2, I have the instructions and information from client forms and the location of documents.

In the manual side pocket, I put the client's original copies of the powers of attorney (I kept a copy for myself in case they lost them; multiple originals are allowed). I reminded clients not to put the powers of attorney in their safety deposit box as the attorneys would not have access to them, unlike executors who would access their safety deposit box on death by showing a death certificate. I included in the side pocket information about organ donation from our provincial government and a Law Firm Performance Questionnaire.

6.1.3 Keeping the Wills and Powers of Attorney Client Manual up to Date

I gave the Wills and Powers of Attorney Client Manual to my clients at the end of their first consultation and told them to bring it back to their signing appointment. We would insert the reporting letter, copy of the will, and up-to-date index at that signing appointment. I told them this manual should be kept at home on their coffee table or bookshelf so that when their body was found in the morning, the executor would find the manual easily and be well prepared to administer the estate. For some strange reason, most clients said they would not be keeping their manual on their coffee table, even though that would be good advertising for me.

I advised my clients to review and keep up to date the information inserted in the manuals. On my website, I provided refills of all these forms so clients could update the forms periodically. When I realized that some of my clients would die after my retirement, I planned on providing a digital copy of these forms for them to use so they would not have to rely on using my website.

6.1.4 The Importance of the Wills and Powers of Attorney Client Manual

Though it was only anecdotal evidence, I received many compliments from both clients and executors about the manual. Executors specifically said their job was made much easier because the deceased during their lifetime kept the direction and information forms up to date. I had a file where two children who had been named the executors were arguing about their recently deceased mother's burial. One wanted cremation, and the other did not. In the middle of the argument, one daughter said, "Oh yes, the manual." They went running to their mother's Wills and Powers of Attorney Manual to find that the mother had written out precise burial instructions, which they then followed (not cremation). The executors also told me that the mother had listed in her manual several bank accounts about which they knew nothing. Many parents and adult children do not want to talk about burials and finances, so having the information in the manual allows the parents to leave instructions and information without talking about it during their lifetime. There is the other theory that they should speak beforehand, but I think those who talk before are in the minority.

The manual contained information to let the client better understand the law, but its most beneficial element was to prepare for the will's future use. Besides the instruction and information forms, it contained articles about the future. That included an article about when to change a will and when the law automatically changes the will. Those changes were the divorce or marriage, though the law in Ontario has changed since I stopped practicing. As well, I had my favorite article, "Preparing for an Easier Administration of an Estate."

6.2 Wills and Powers of Attorney Law Section of the Website

6.2.1 Why the Wills and Powers of Attorney Website Section Is Important

Many people will use the internet to find lawyers to draft their wills and powers of attorney. Therefore, only posting on a website that the lawyer offers this service as most firms do is not enough to take advantage of this excellent marketing opportunity. Lawyers can do this marketing by using their websites to educate prospective clients about the law, the lawyer's process, and the costs. For a second-period service application, the website could also include the information forms the clients must complete; hence, lawyers would have all the facts they need to advise clients and draft the documents. However, this practice area probably offers the most opportunity to use the website for their third-period services. Section 6.2.9 sets out those many applications.

Numerous clients told me they chose me to do their wills and powers of attorney because they liked my website, particularly because I was willing to provide so much free information. They said that impressed them about me. I was amazed that some clients came from across town when I would think the location would be an important consideration for choosing a lawyer to draft wills and powers of attorney.

The Wills and Powers of Attorney website section with its third-period service applications is an excellent way to show clients that the lawyer wants to keep up a relationship and provide free information and services after the file is closed.

6.2.4 Organization of the Wills and Powers of Attorney Website Section

As I did with most of my practice area sections on my website, I had four headings: The Law, Fees & Forms, Resources, and First-Time Client. The First-Time Client is essential for all practice areas when there is a lot of information provided by a lawyer; clients can be overwhelmed with information. I find that is a problem with many of the big law firm websites. That First-Time Client heading points the client to just the essential material they should review that crosses all headers.

I also had a section entitled "Time to Review." It dealt with reviewing one's will, because people often realized that they should check their will if there were personal changes in their lives.

6.2.5 *Content of the Wills and Powers of Attorney Website Section*

As discussed in section 4.2.5, this practice area had all the standard articles and forms about the law, process, questionnaires and fees, resources, and first-time clients. I also did have an article, I believe the first article I ever produced, entitled "Reasons for Making a Will," which I wrote to convince people who were only considering that they should have a will to actually take steps to have one made for themselves. A few years ago, according to a survey in Ontario, only 43 percent of adults had wills. I do not know the percentage now, but I do not imagine it has dramatically risen. With the advent of do-it-yourself will kits in a paper, software, or online form, I suggest an article entitled "Reasons a Lawyer Should Draft Your Will." I know a lawyer who says he wants to start a class action suit against the will kit companies because he has seen so many mistakes when clients have used these kits to try and do it themselves. Do-it-yourself wills have errors not just in the drafting but also with the proper execution of the wills and powers of attorney. My limited research shows that lawyers should write a more comprehensive article than what I have seen posted by some firms on this subject.

Concerning fees, if someone is on a legal website looking for information about wills and powers of attorney, there is an excellent chance they are interested in knowing the cost. Since, to my knowledge, most lawyers charge a set fee for this service, why the lawyers rarely post their prices on their websites is a great mystery to me. If the lawyer's fees are at the low end, they will obtain the people just looking for the lowest cost. If the price is in the middle range, within the client's budget, and the rest of the website is impressive, the client will probably choose that lawyer. If the fees are high, but the experience and the website are good, clients will choose that lawyer, believing they will get a superior product (though that will not always be the case). Years ago, some houses were listed for sale without revealing the asking price. I never see that practice anymore; people want to know the price before spending any more of their precious time than necessary.

6.2.9 *Third-Period Uses of the Wills and Powers of Attorney Section of Websites*

Lawyers should use the website for their third-period service by offering refills of forms to be kept up to date in their client manuals. The website can have articles reminding clients about the firm's practice of storing and retrieving wills and powers of attorney and pointing out when clients usually update them. This information is, of course, in their manual, but clients misplace manuals or find it easier to search on the website.

I have outlined in section 6.1.2 the many instructions and important forms that are in the manual and set out in detail in Appendix 6.1.2.2.

6.3 The Client Monitor for Wills and Powers of Attorney

I used the client monitor in two significant ways for wills and powers of attorney. As in other practice areas, I had a slideshow of the agenda for the first wills and powers of attorney consultation. Second, using the monitor, my client and I completed the important Wills and Powers of Attorney Checklist at the end of their first consultation using the monitor.

6.4 The Wills and Powers of Attorney First Consultation Slideshow

As in other practice areas, first consultation slideshows served valuable functions. Wills and powers of attorney clients were not as anxious as family law or administration of estate clients but still having the agenda in the form of the slide show was comforting. It identified issues the clients may not have thought were relevant to drafting wills and powers of attorney, allowing them to prepare for the discussion. Along with my checklist, the slideshow ensured that I covered everything I thought should be discussed.

The slides were quite detailed, starting with a reminder to obtain the proper photo identification and sign a statement that I had obtained this. I then outlined the purpose of the consultation and what we would discuss. Then there were several slides highlighting the many issues and decisions clients must make. I followed this with a slide discussing the rules when a lawyer acts for both spouses which is almost always the case for married couples. Then there were slides to finalize the interview, including introducing the client manual. The slideshow is set out in Appendix 6.4 in a table format.

6.5 Wills and Powers of Attorney Client Questionnaires and Forms

6.5.1 *Client Intake Form for Wills and Powers of Attorney*

I had two sections in my Client Intake Form devoted to wills and powers of attorney clients. One was for clients who were having me draft their wills for the first time, and one was for returning clients who just wanted minor revisions to the wills and powers of attorney that I had previously drafted. If they had wills and powers of attorney prepared by another lawyer, we treated them as first-time wills and powers of attorney clients. In both cases, we advised clients in the intake what my process and costs were. After obtaining the client's name and contact information, we made an appointment time. I sent out a confirmation letter the same day, which also reminded the clients to fill out all the forms which were linked to my website and return them to me before their appointment, so I had time to review them.

6.5.2 *The Wills and Powers of Attorney Law Questionnaires*

Before the first consultation, to keep the number of appointments to just a first consultation and a signing appointment, clients had to fill out detailed information about themselves, their family, beneficiaries, assets, and suggested decisions to put in the wills and powers of attorney. Those forms were on my website. As mentioned in section 6.5.1, they were listed and linked from the appointment confirmation letter to the website. They could be sent directly from the website to my office. Some of the information for these forms the client had to find, and some required thought, so clients need to download the forms and complete them at home and prior to their appointment. Doing so is more efficient than waiting to complete them at the lawyer's office.

For those clients who were updating their wills, besides asking for an updated Asset Information Form, I had a separate questionnaire asking what the changes were to their wills and powers of attorney and why were they making the changes. The "why" was especially important if the client was making significant changes. A person now cut out of the will might later challenge the will. If I thought there was a competency or undue influence issue, I had my lawyer's special questionnaire that I filled out for the file. In later years, I sometimes also put right in the will why someone who would normally be in the will was not in it. I think that is a better practice than just having notes recording the client's wishes.

6.6 The Wills and Powers of Attorney First Appointment Confirmation Letter

This letter followed the format letter set out in section 4.6 and related it to wills and powers of attorney questionnaires and checklists. It is similar to the first appointment letter for matrimonial clients found in Appendix 5.1. However, I did not suggest a family member be present for the consultation. Often, adult children brought their elderly parents into the office. I would let the children sit in on most of the meetings because they were of help but, near the end, asked them to leave while I had time with the client alone to confirm there was no undue influence.

6.7 Appointment for Signing Wills and Powers of Attorney Letters

My process for my wills and powers of attorney files was to confirm at the end of the first consultation the signing appointment date and time. Unless the clients were not available, it was always two weeks from the first consultation. In my early years, when I did not set a signing date at the first consultation, I found everyone, including me, took their time, and we wasted time following up and arranging a signing date.

Within a few days of the first consultation, I required the clients to get back to me with missing information or answers to what they wanted in their wills if they needed time to think. I promised to draft their wills and powers of attorney and send them out to them within a week, well in time for them to review them and get back to me with changes or questions. I told clients they could not wait until their appointment to tell me if I misspelled their cousin's name. Some clients who reviewed their wills only on the day of the signing meeting would still ask for changes at their appointment. But I had warned them that if they did so, they would spend time sitting in the waiting room waiting for my assistant to make the changes for all the copies and reprint originals and make copies. One year the winner of my contest to suggest a way to improve my practice suggested that in my letter with the draft documents, the requirement to not wait until the signing appointment to make changes be in bold capitals. I did so, which probably helped reduce the problem, but I should also have increased the font size.

6.8 Wills and Powers of Attorney Consultation and Telephone Notes

For wills and powers of attorney consultations, I mainly had a lawyer questionnaire/checklist for me to complete. It had questions for me to record the answers needed for drafting the wills and powers of attorney and a list of information I wanted to provide. I had a separate questionnaire when the will was slightly different from usual, such as when a child who was not receiving equally with other siblings might challenge the will. I did have separate notes I would make after reviewing the client questionnaires if there were some specific questions I wanted to remember to ask. For this practice area, I believe the questionnaires and checklists worked best.

6.9 Wills and Powers of Attorney To-Do List

Near the end of the first consultation of a wills and powers of attorney client, the client and I, using our monitors, would go through the client's wills and powers of attorney to-do list. These were standard tasks that clients might or might not have had to do or that might have already been done. I suggested the clients do them relatively soon, but not all were necessary to do before signing their wills and powers of attorney. I originally had this checklist of to-do's in a Microsoft Word table, but then found it easier to use Excel as that software made it slightly easier to add tasks to the standard ones. That list could also be in the same Excel file with the lawyer and assistant to-do lists, but in a different tab.

I asked clients to check that their deeds were correctly registered, which meant the deeds said "joint tenancy" as that is what was they generally should have wanted. The clients were to check that all insurance and assets that could name a beneficiary did so. Clients were to change their investments to be in joint names if that was appropriate. I asked clients to confirm that proposed executors, attorneys, custodians, and their alternates agreed to do the job they were named to do. Clients were to finalize the asset information questionnaire if they had not done so. They were to provide email addresses of the executors, attorneys, and their alternates, so, as will be discussed, I would be writing after the wills and powers of attorneys were signed. I asked them to complete the Lawyer Performance Questionnaire. If they were holding on to their former original will, I reminded them to destroy it after signing the new will. Finally, at that first consultation, even though they might have to get back to me with further instructions, we made an appointment to sign the wills and powers of attorney generally in two weeks, and we set and recorded that appointment on the form.

We went through each task and noted whether it had to be done, because some were not necessary or had already been done. There was a column for the client to mark a task done once they completed it. I then printed out the Wills and Powers of Attorney To-Do List, and the client inserted it in their Wills and Powers of Attorney Manual. Most clients would bring their to-do list to their signing appointment to show me they had completed their list, but as I told them, it was not my responsibility to check their homework.

Having this Wills and Powers of Attorney To-Do list made my clients' tasks easier to remember and understand than taking notes or waiting for a reporting letter from me listing their to-do's. It increased the possibility clients would complete some of these critical tasks such as confirming that designated beneficiaries were made for their insurance policies and other investments that allowed beneficiaries to be named and verifying that ownership of properties was correct. I insisted that clients check their documents rather than assume that they had named their spouse a beneficiary. Early on in my career, I had files where clients thought their home was in joint tenancy and that each other was named their beneficiary of Registered Retirement Savings Plans, but their assumptions were wrong in both cases. In Appendix 6.9, I have this checklist in a table format.

6.10 Calculating Fees for Wills and Powers of Attorney

Because I did not do sophisticated estate planning, my wills and powers of attorney practice lent itself to having fixed fees rather than charging on an hourly basis. I, therefore, had a chart (posted on my website) of set fixed fees. It listed all the combinations of one person and a couple (two-thirds the cost of two singles) for wills with and without powers of attorney, powers of attorney alone, and the price if the client was only making a change to a previous will or power of attorney that I had drafted for them. I also had a special discounted price for matrimonial clients. I did add the proviso that if I spent more than a certain amount of time on the file, I could charge extra based on my hourly rate, but in my 42 years of practice, I do not believe I did that more than a handful of times. I did spend more time than usual on occasions but did not bother charging extra, because I wanted it to be known I would not easily deviate from the fixed fee. As discussed more fully in section 6.2.2, I strongly suggest that lawyers post to their websites their fees for wills and powers of attorney, as a service to clients.

6.11 Client-Helpful Word Processing Software Features for Wills and Powers of Attorney

I always used the feature of numbering every fifth line in draft wills that I sent to clients. When clients emailed or phoned me with questions, they always referred to the line number rather than saying "on page 6, third paragraph from the bottom second sentence." This application was a minor matter but just more manageable for clients to pinpoint the location of their questions. It shows the lawyer is trying to make life easier for the client. I considered but never used the table of contents feature for wills and powers of attorney as my wills and powers of attorney were not as long as separation agreements. Still, it would not be unreasonable for lawyers to create tables of contents for wills and powers of attorney so clients can later more easily find something in their documents.

6.12 Articles for Wills and Powers of Attorney Clients

Lawyers should have many articles for their wills and powers of attorney practice. Lawyers usually charge on a fixed fee basis, so they should not have to spend as much time going over the many concepts if the clients, as requested, have read the articles. These articles are also a written reminder of what the lawyer discussed.

More than any other area of law, there is a need in wills and powers of attorney for promotional/informational articles, because having wills and powers of attorney is discretionary: fewer than 50 percent of people of the age of majority and therefore able to have wills do so. It is also an area where people think there is no need for a lawyer to do their wills and powers of attorney because they can do it themselves. There should be articles like "The Reason for Having a Will" and "Why a Lawyer Should Draft Your Will."

One of the most useful, if not the most useful, article I ever wrote was "The Plain Meaning and Purposes of Will Clauses." I went through every standard clause in a will and explained in plain language what it meant and why it was needed in the will. Lawyers also love standard long precedent clauses even if they no longer remember why they are there. Most questions from clients after receiving the draft wills dealt with why I put in a specific trustee power in the will and what a particular clause meant. I would answer briefly but also refer them to my article. Without the article, I am sure I would have had many more questions from clients.

A useful accompaniment to that article could be a list of definitions of some words and phrases in the wills that most clients have heard but were not sure of their meaning.

Wills and powers of attorney practices offer more after-the-fact articles on subjects needing more attention than just being part of a long reporting letter. I, therefore, had articles entitled "Changing Your Will," "Preparing for an Easier Administration of an Estate," "Retrieving Your Will," "Storage of Wills and Powers of Attorney," and "Gifts and Inheritance for Children."

Also useful for this practice area are articles about the process and articles written by other resource people. If there is more sophisticated estate planning, a tax expert or tax accountant could write something. I did have an article, "Estate Planning for the Average Canadian." Still, there were many other issues I could have written about that I never got around to doing. Articles like "Who to Choose as Your Executor," "Instructions to Leave Your Children about How you Wish Them to Spend Their Inheritance," and "Ensuring Your Will Will Not Be Contested," to name a few.

For describing all the steps from start to finish to process a wills and powers of attorney file for this book, I took my own advice and produced in table format, rather than trying to do a flow chart, to explain my process and timing. It is in Appendix 6.12.

6.13 Legal Fees for Wills and Powers of Attorney

6.13.1 Determining Fees in Wills and Powers of Attorney Matters

As discussed in sections 6.2.2 and 6.10, I suggest that legal fees for wills and powers of attorney should be charged using the fixed fee method. There are several reasons for doing this. Some clients will decide whether to have wills and powers of attorney made based on what the fixed fee is. Clients will often choose which lawyer to retain based on the costs. It is a legal service most clients expect lawyers will charge on a fixed fee basis. The amount of time and work to be done for a wills and powers of attorney file is quite predictable, and with the safety valve of saying that if the file takes more time than normal, it will cost more, the lawyers are assured of receiving a fair fee for their work. Though my prices for wills and powers of attorney seemed to be just below the mid-level of what lawyers in Ottawa charged, I was happy with my fee schedule because my articles and processes reduced my workload on the file. Some lawyers told me I should have increased my fees. Perhaps if I had done so, my revenue from this practice area would have increased, even though the number of files would have gone down, but it would have reduced the possibility of obtaining the estate work when the client died. I am not saying that wills and powers of attorney should be used as a loss leader to get estate work. That was relevant many years ago when lawyers' fees for estate work were higher, and it was more likely lawyers would get the estate work when they drafted the will. But for me, and I assume for most lawyers who do administration of estates work, most of my estate work came from the executors of wills I drafted, so drafting more wills was important.

My fees for this practice area were not based just on my hourly rate times the expected amount of time. Periodically, my assistant would call other law firms to see what they were charging. She would pretend she wanted to retain a lawyer to draft her and her husband's wills. I found the annual published surveys on fees by the Canadian Bar Association did not reflect my local market's prices as geographical areas were too big and the number of participants too small. It was more accurate surveying my local competition. I then set my fixed fee based on a combination of the local market fees and what I felt was fair to me based on the time I would usually take on the file. I emphasized to clients that they were getting more value from me than from other firms by pointing out my value-added applications such as the client manual, the many articles, and my follow-up services.

6.13.2 Discussing Wills and Powers of Attorney Fees with Clients

There should be little time spent discussing lawyer's fees with clients if the lawyer posted the price on their website, the price was confirmed in the intake process, and the price is set out in the signed retainer. The only exception occurs when the lawyer believes it would be fair to charge more because of the extraordinary time taken to complete the file. In that case, the lawyer must show how much extra time was taken and why, and calculate the higher charge.

6.13.3 Ensuring Getting Paid for Wills and Powers of Attorney

I believe I had only one bad debt during all my years of practice for an unpaid will and powers of attorney file; however, I did have a few files where I had to chase people to attend their second appointment to sign up their wills and powers of attorney and then sometimes pursue a fee for half the service. In later years, I decided to get paid by check or by credit card authorization at the end of the first consultation. That practice reduced any possibility of not getting paid something if the client changed their mind and did not complete the file; it also lessened the work and time taken at the signing consultation.

6.13.6 Retainers

For most of my practice, I did not have clients sign retainers for wills and powers of attorney files. Then I realized I needed couples to sign a Consent to Act for Both Parties anyway and later sign a direction where their wills and powers of attorney would be held in safekeeping on my retirement. I then developed a written retainer to include these items. I also added to that document what the fee would be and when paid, along with confirmation it was the client's responsibility to provide me with correct information. I wanted to make it clear that I was not responsible for reviewing property deeds and insurance policies. I also added acknowledging my limitations on tax planning and the rule about marriage and revocation again as a reminder. See Appendix 6.13.6 for a sample retainer.

6.13.7 Unbundled Legal Services for Wills and Powers of Attorney

At times, prospective clients asked me to review the wills they had drafted and perhaps witness their execution for a small fee. I refused to do either. I told them the reality was that it would take me more hours and therefore cost more to review and comment on their client-produced will than if we used my process. I also was not going to take part in the execution of a will that I did not produce because it would be assumed I had reviewed the document, which I would not be doing.

6.14 The Pricing and Process for Changes to Wills and Powers of Attorney

Wills and powers of attorney are generally not a once-in-a-lifetime matter for most clients. Clients typically make wills and powers of attorney when they start having children. When their children become responsible adults, clients generally change their wills, making their adult children their executors, and perhaps adding something for grandchildren.

If one spouse dies, a client may or may not change their will; there is probably no need because one spouse predeceasing the other is taken into account in their own will. However, if a client marries, they may need a new will if their will is automatically revoked on marriage unless their will states it is made in contemplation of marriage. That was the law in Ontario and may still be in other jurisdictions. Even if not revoked, the circumstances may have changed when marrying so that a new will might be appropriate.

Often when the second time clients retained me to update their wills and powers of attorney, their changes were minor, such as just making their children executors now that they were adults. I, therefore, had a special process and rate for these wills and powers of attorney. The process was that the clients had to complete my online Change of Wills and Powers of Attorney Client Questionnaire and submit a new, up-to-date Will Asset Questionnaire. The former questionnaire asked what the changes were and why the clients were making them. I would draft the new wills and powers of attorney based on the form and a short telephone conversation to confirm the facts and instructions if I believed there was no need for a full in-office consultation. I then had one signing appointment and charged two-thirds the cost of what I would charge a first-time client. These clients generally received the newly updated client manual if it had been some time since I drafted their first will. This offer was not available to people changing wills that another lawyer had drafted, because they would not have had my first-time consultation. Other lawyers, to my knowledge, do not offer a discount for return clients doing simple changes, but I see it as a good follow-up service to clients and is a fair price to both clients and lawyers. My Law Society requirement on my retirement to contact clients whose wills and powers of attorney were in my safekeeping was costly; but the large number of clients who decided to take advantage of my updated wills and powers of attorney process and fee before I retired more than made up for that cost.

To encourage matrimonial clients to change their wills and powers of attorney, I offered them a 20 percent discount if they had me draft their wills and powers of attorney within six months of completing their matrimonial file—not that many clients took me up on my offer.

As discussed in section 4.30.5, The Ontario Bar Association has a campaign where November is "Make A Will Month." A local cable channel interviewed me. I do not think too many people were watching, but I felt honored to be in the same waiting room as a very famous Canadian writer and historian who was being interviewed just before I was. I learned from that experience of offering a sale price that people will make wills and powers of attorney when they are ready to do so, and lawyers cannot push them even with incentives and persuasion. I found that many will clients said they wanted a will because they were going on a vacation, were having a serious operation, or someone close to them had died prematurely. Those are events beyond a lawyer's control.

6.15 Letters to Affected Nonclients

6.15.1 Letters to Executors and Attorneys

After clients signed their wills and powers of attorney, with their permission, I emailed the executors, the attorneys (unless they were the spouses), and their alternates, letters that served several functions. In the letter, I advised these people where the original wills and powers of attorney were kept for safekeeping, so they find them when needed. That place was usually in my office safe, but if the clients kept their wills themselves, I had the client advise me which bank's safety deposit box they were in or where else they were keeping them. These letters also told executors and attorneys about the Wills and Powers of Attorney Manual and what type of instructions and information they would find there. That would allow the executors and attorneys to know important details and directions, such as the clients' burial instructions. The letter also had links to some of my articles on my website, which set out executors' and attorneys' duties and some detailed articles on administering an estate. These articles informed them of their responsibilities and brought home the importance and the seriousness of their future positions. It was also good marketing for me to have a better chance of having the executors hire me when the time came, and it also got my name spread as a wills and powers of attorney lawyer.

I once got a call from an executor of a client who had recently passed away. He still had the executor letter I had sent him many years before. He, therefore, knew I had the original will, so he made an appointment with me about applying for probate and administering the client's estate. We started the process, but just before we were to apply for probate, he called to say he had found a more recent will drafted by a lawyer close to the deceased's home. The only change from the will I had prepared was that the deceased had made some small bequests to grandchildren. Like all lawyers I know, the new lawyer, who held on to the new original will, had not done an executor letter to the executors. So, the executor did not know about this new will and found it only by accident when going through the deceased's papers (the other lawyer did not have a Wills and Powers of Attorney Client Manual to put on the coffee table). As the executor had started administering the estate process with me, he picked up the original will from the other lawyer, delivered it to me, and I proceeded with the matter.

This letter is a simple application that costs lawyers no time, as it is a standard letter sent out by the support staff; but it is of value to the client, the executors, attorneys, and even the lawyer. I have attached a copy of my standard letter in Appendix A 6.15.1.

6.15.2 Letters to Former Lawyers

If a client had done a previous will with another lawyer, and that lawyer had it in safekeeping, after the client signed their new will that I drafted, I sent a letter to their former lawyer. In that letter, I attached a direction signed by my client advising the lawyer that my client had signed a new will and they should send the old will and powers of attorney to my client for destruction.

I did this for two purposes: firstly, as shown by the story I wrote in section 6.15.1, it is dangerous to have old wills in existence, because those wills might be mistakenly thought of as valid. Second, it is unfair that the previous lawyer has to hold on to an obsolete will. When I retired, my Law Society required that I contact, or at least document my attempt to contact, any of my clients whose wills or powers of attorney (even if the powers of attorney were just a second original copy) that I had in my possession. This requirement was an enormous undertaking that required hiring an additional temporary secretary. I found that many clients, especially those who had moved out of Ottawa, had done new wills. I also discovered that many clients had died many years ago, so presumably had done new wills. I could not find numerous clients though I tried through various types of searches, and finally, as required by the Law Society, I had to send a letter to a last known address. This process was a costly and time-consuming endeavor. If my fellow lawyers had had the courtesy to write me, they could have reduced my time and money spent.

And as in the story in section 6.15.1, if the new lawyer had written me when she updated my client's will, she would have obtained the estate file. This letter is a simple application that costs lawyers no time. Like the letters to the executors, it is a form letter prepared by the support staff which is of value to all parties. It is a common courtesy to fellow lawyers.

6.16 Following Up with Clients after the File Is Closed

I did not do so, but perhaps some clients would consider it to be a small "moment" if three months after they executed a will, they received a phone call or an email asking whether they completed their Wills and Powers of Attorney To-Do list. Had they checked with their insurance company and have it in writing that they had the correct beneficiary? Had they changed their bank accounts to be registered jointly?

I once wrote some clients five years after they executed their wills. I read somewhere that wills should be reviewed every five years. The government had also changed the law concerning powers of attorney. I did not receive any responses. As discussed in section 6.14, a lawyer will not easily persuade people to obtain or update their wills. Perhaps instead of five years, I should have waited to send such a letter when the youngest child turned 21, so it was time to change who the executors were. I am not sure even that would work to persuade clients to update their wills.

6.17 Providing Clients Resource Information for Wills and Powers of Attorney

For other resources for wills and the administration of estates, I refer clients to the website of Hull and Hull, a Toronto wills and estates law firm. When I last counted, it had 157 links to other resources. Their website also had many original podcasts, newsletters, and webinars. It was an excellent resource for lawyers also. I did not have a bibliography of books, but if I did, it would include a book my financial advisor gave me about why and how to discuss one's will and finances with adult children. I could have tried, but I am sure I would not have been successful (based on how hard it was to get a local psychologist to talk about divorce counseling) in having a local life insurance agent discuss the need for life insurance and the different types of it.

6.18 Reporting Letters for Wills and Powers of Attorney Clients

As I had a will and powers of attorney retainer, there was no need for an engagement-type letter, but I suggest that one is appropriate if the lawyer does not use a retainer for this practice area. The letter would have similar information as in the retainer; it is just not signed by the client. My article "The Purposes and Plain Meaning of Clauses Contained in A Will" greatly benefited clients when I was sending out the draft copies of wills to clients. But perhaps I could have summarized an explanation of the bequest clauses in plain language in this letter or, as I suggest later, produced some flowchart of the bequests.

The final reporting letter is important to confirm several matters, including where the original will is being kept. I suggest reading a copy of my reporting letter in Appendix 6.18; it has the many other matters that the client needs to be aware of that are often not found in reporting letters, including common misconceptions. As I suggest for all practice areas, this reporting should point out that the lawyer/client relationship has technically come to an end and that therefore, it is not the lawyer's obligation to advise former clients of changes in the law that may affect them. Lawyers can suggest that clients keep in touch by signing on to their lawyer's social media platforms and call if they hear or read something in the media they believe affects them.

6.19/6.20 Social Media and Newsletters for Wills and Powers of Attorney Clients

As explained in section 4.19, though, social media is used more for promotional purposes. In the wills and powers of attorney area, it can be useful to announce changes to the law. At the time of my writing this book, Ontario is changing the law about wills automatically being revoked on marriage. I would suggest that laws about medical directives will be changing in the future, and lawyers could publicize that via social media. If enough clients were interested, perhaps a blog that clients sign up to receive could discuss interesting topics in this practice area. I think a blog and a newsletter devoted only to wills and powers of attorney are just not worth doing for the small law firm.

6.21 Radio and Television Advertising for Wills and Powers of Attorney Clients

I have not observed many lawyers doing radio or television ads to promote wills and powers of attorney. I believe this is because the rate of return for the money spent on these advertisements does not make it worthwhile. It is not like personal injury law, where just one client obtained from an ad could make a considerable return. Radio and television ads are for the high-fee practice areas of law and not for the low-fee or mid-fee high-volume practice areas. My radio ads years ago were not worth the cost for the number of will clients I received, and they about broke even for my family law and administration of estates practice because radio ads produced only a few well-paying clients.

6.22 Radio, Television, and Public Speaking Appearances for Wills and Powers of Attorney Clients

Over the years, I often spoke to various groups on the basic law of wills and powers of attorney and promoted my processes and my Wills and Powers of Attorney Client Manual. The groups varied from faith groups to company lunchtime speakers. I did it mainly because I enjoyed the experience, but I often obtained some business that made it worthwhile. Speaking to government retirement programs was very lucrative for a lawyer I know: he did a lot of talks for many years to government retirees, so he had an audience focused on the subject matter. I suggest that lawyers who do public speaking, after getting permission, record these sessions. They would not show the audience or would record the audio only. They would then post the talks on their website and YouTube channel. Every time I spoke to a group, I would amend my resume to add another group to my list of speaking engagements. I did not do the same for the few times I was interviewed on television, but I have seen lawyers' resumes on websites where they have listed their television appearances. Besides providing basic information to prospective clients and promoting themselves, these speaking engagements increase the confidence prospective and current clients have in their lawyer's competency.

6.23 Physical Applications for Wills and Powers of Attorney Clients

The client manual is the major physical application. I used to have pens with my name printed on them. I would have clients use them to sign their wills and powers of attorney. I would let them keep the pens and jokingly say it was like when the President of the United States signs a bill into law and hands out the pens he signed the documents with to those involved in the legislation. However, pens do not last too long, so I moved to the longer-life refrigerator magnets to remind clients I was their lawyer.

6.24 Proper Thank-Yous to Referrals Sources for Wills and Powers of Attorney Clients

Wills and powers of attorney files are ones where clients have no trouble referring their lawyer friends and relatives. It is a legal service every person will need in their lifetime, so lawyers should thank referral sources properly, as discussed in section 4.24. At the signing appointments, lawyers should remind clients that referrals are appreciated.

6.25 Legal Software Programs for Wills and Powers of Attorney

As discussed in section 6.11, features in Microsoft Word or any word processing software can benefit clients, and as suggested in section 4.9, Excel or any spreadsheet software is useful for to-do lists.

There was no dedicated wills and powers of attorney software on the market that I wanted to purchase while I practiced. I, like many lawyers, found that using my word processor software was good enough to turn out wills and powers of attorney. Unfortunately, it was not until soon after I retired that a wills and powers of attorney software program was available that I would have bought had I planned to continue practicing. It is called "eState Planner. It was developed by the Toronto law firm of Hull and Hull. It started as a program to collect information for drafting wills and powers of attorney and grew to draft those documents. What I like about the program is the innovative client service aspect whereby the program produces for clients very visual reports about their assets and disposition of the estate and detailed reports about the beneficiaries.

The company also has a solid client service support system for using their program and practicing in this area of law.

6.26 Decision Making for Wills and Powers of Attorney Clients

Clients have to decide who will obtain what assets and when, and who will administer the estate. Making those decisions is generally very easy, but sometimes there are exceptions, and sometimes I had to advise why the client's choice could create problems. Often, clients would want to appoint the oldest of their children to be the sole alternate executor of their estate if their spouse was not alive. I would persuade them to name all their children after telling them of a case I had. In that file, as sole executor, the oldest child took advantage of his younger sister by valuing all the valuable assets at a low price and taking them for himself but valued the less valuable assets at a higher price and giving them to the sister. Sole executors can charge hefty fees for doing very little, which is unfair to the other children. Even if the executor does not take advantage of the other children, there may be a perception they did. And naming only one child as executor can result in psychological damage: a child not named an executor might have one more feeling that "Mom always liked my oldest brother the best." Perhaps an article in this practice area would be appropriate to set out the decisions that clients have to make, the possible choices, with their pros and cons, and the most common result based on the lawyer's experience (based on keeping track of previous files' choices).

6.27 Communications with Wills and Powers of Attorney Clients

The client-lawyer relationship in this practice area will not last very long or entail more than two consultations and maybe one phone call; nor will it generally involve an urgent response. However, communications are critical for ensuring that the client has provided, and the lawyer has received and processed all the relevant facts. As well, it is essential that the client understands the will and powers of attorney they signed. This is where the reports of the people, assets, and dispositions of the assets produced by dedicated software like eState Planner or lawyer-produced homegrown forms would be beneficial. These reports would ensure that the facts are correct and that the client understands the dispositive provisions of the will.

Because wills and powers of attorney individual files are generally not big money makers for lawyers, and lawyers charge on a flat fee, they may tend to rush the consultations and not encourage clients to ask questions. Some lawyers, I think, mistakenly have their assistants responsible for the intake of information, and some have their assistants handle the execution of the wills and powers of attorney appointments. These are times where clients may want to ask questions.

6.28 Flowcharts

Short of buying a program like eState Planner, I would suggest try using the flowchart features of Microsoft Word or Excel, which might visually show how the dispositions of assets will flow depending on who is alive at the time of death. My observation, however, is that rather than a flowchart for the process of the many steps in a wills and powers of attorney file, the use of a table as in Appendix 6.12 is better.

6.29 Inventing New Processes for Wills and Powers of Attorney Clients

As discussed in section 6.25, the relatively small law firm of Hull and Hull (19 lawyers), as opposed to a technology company, invented eState Planner to visually present information to clients. I do not suggest lawyers start producing major original software, but when they see something they believe can be improved upon, they should not hesitate to invent a new way of doing something. My Wills and Powers of Attorney Client Manual is a prime example.

6.30 Other Applications for Wills and Powers of Attorney Clients

6.30.1 Safekeeping of Wills and Powers of Attorney Documents and Assets

At present, 70 percent of lawyers in Ontario, generally at no charge, hold in safekeeping their clients' original wills. Lawyers do this as a service to their clients. Bank safety deposit boxes cost $5 a year at one time (and were then even tax-deductible in Canada); but their costs went up, and fewer original documents, like stock certificates, were used, so the average person no longer required a safety deposit box. The lawyer's office seemed, therefore, to be the safest place for wills. I checked out those home safes and discovered they were not very fireproof. As one Ottawa lawyer suggested, it was probably safer to put the will in Tupperware and store that in a freezer. The freezer is more fireproof than a home safe.

Lawyers offered to hold on to the wills in the hope they would get the estate work in the future. The thought was that if a lawyer held on to the will, the executors would retain that lawyer to do the legal work to administer the estate. As I kept good statistics of where my files came from, I discovered this theory is still correct. I do not believe the chances of getting the estate work by safekeeping the will are as great as they once were, but it is still worth holding on to the wills for clients.

Lawyers should have written will retainers that state clients are obligated to advise if they do a new will with another lawyer. Clients would also consent in advance that the lawyer upon retirement can pass on their will to another law firm. The retainer could also state that the lawyer could dispose of their will if the lawyer discovered that the client had died five years ago and no one came forward looking for the will. That would be because the client had probably done a new will but did not advise the lawyer.

Whether I held on to the original will or not, it was my practice that I kept a client's second original power of attorney in safekeeping. I believed that it was a good backup: if the client lost their power of attorney, I would have a copy for them to use. I think having an original copy of a lost power of attorney helped out only three times in 42 years. So, if I were back in practice, I probably would not hold on to the original power of attorney, even though it was crucial for the client in one of those three cases that I had an original copy. The lawyer should retain a digital copy.

When I retired, my Law Society obligated me to contact all my clients whose original will was in my office safe. I also had to contact those clients. I had a second copy of their original power of attorney. Yes, that was even though those clients would have their own original power of attorney. I discovered several unexpected things: Some clients who held on to their own wills had no idea where they had stored them. They, like many people, closed their safety deposit boxes as banks raised their fees

(I believe, to discourage their customers from having a box). Clients brought their wills home, and some lost them. So, it is a good service for lawyers to safekeep their clients' wills. I also discovered that many clients did new wills years later with other lawyers but did not advise me to dispose of their old will that I was holding in my safe.

The good news is that I discovered from this "find the client project" that many clients neglected to update their wills and powers of attorney. In the months leading up to my retirement, I had such a flood of clients wanting to update their wills that I had to have a cutoff date before retirement, after which I could no longer take on clients to update their wills. I had been told that my income would drastically decrease in the few months before retirement, but the contrary was true. Some clients do not update their wills as they should; therefore, lawyers should write to clients years after the wills are executed to see if updating is advisable. A possible reason could be that according to the lawyer's records, the children were now of age and should be the executors and attorneys.

6.30.5 Wills and Powers of Attorney Sales

As discussed in detail in section 4.30, I did not think it inappropriate to offer a discount on the cost of wills and powers of attorney during November, which is "Make A Will Month" in Ontario.

7

Administration of Estates Law Service Applications

The administration of estates practice area deals with advising clients what they have to do when a person who has died has named the client as the sole executor or co-executor. (In Ontario, the word "executor" has been replaced with the term "estate trustee." However, the term "executor" is still commonly used, and I will use it in this book.) Also, if the estate established trusts, the executor or executors generally become the trustees of those estates, so they must manage the trust. I told my clients that administrating an estate was not brain surgery but did have many little tasks that had to be completed. My first and foremost job was to advise my clients based on the will, and the assets in the estate, what they had to do themselves or have me or someone else do.

I found that some clients wanted to do as much as possible themselves and others as little as possible, preferring to let our office or others do the work. As will be discussed, I set up my fee structure in this practice area based on charging for the specific tasks I did, allowing clients who wanted to do a lot of the work themselves to do so and, in the process, save money. Thus, this practice area lent itself perfectly to an unbundled fee arrangement. I divided the tasks into three categories: (1) tasks lawyers generally do, (2) tasks clients generally do, and (3) tasks either the lawyer or the client could do (the client deciding who would do it).

This practice area required a very organized file to keep track of the many jobs and perhaps the many people involved, such as each financial institution the deceased dealt with and perhaps several beneficiaries.[1] The executor must keep meticulous records to account to the beneficiaries, the federal government for income tax, and provincial government for probate fees.

I do not include in this practice contested estate matters. That area is a specialty of litigation. I did not do this type of law except for a few cases in my early years of practice. Doing family law was emotional enough, and I found contested estate matters between a brother and sister or a child and a second spouse were more vicious than between separated spouses.

Though it was a sad time for the client, I tried to use a little humor so as to not have the consultation become too solemn an affair. My clients all seemed to laugh (or at least smile) when I mentioned, when it often occurred, that it was good planning for the deceased to die early in the month because they were entitled to the whole month's pension payment, or that if they died early in the year, it was good income tax planning.

7.1 The Administration of Estates Manual

7.1.1 Purposes of the Administration of Estates Manual

Like all client manuals, the Administration of Estates Manual contained general information for my clients. It held copies and originals of the essential court documents and correspondence between my clients and me. Importantly, it also kept on an ongoing basis the detailed accounting of the estate bank account for which the client was responsible. I also

[1] I once had an estate where the deceased had no children, so she left her estate to many generally described relatives such as cousins, nieces, nephews, grandnieces, and grandnephews. The lawyer who drafted the will never asked for the names of the beneficiaries. Nor did he ask how many beneficiaries there might be. It was a small estate that ended up being divided among 72 beneficiaries. I suggest lawyers should know who and how many beneficiaries there might be.

gave a second binder to the client when the file closed, which contained more detailed information and documents about the estate's assets.

7.1.2 Organization and Contents of the Administration of Estates Manual

The first volume of the Administration of Estates Manual had, as set out in the Administration of Estates Manual index (Appendix 7.1.2.1), 10 tabbed sections. The first section had, like all my manuals, my New Client Memorandum and then my Administration of Estates article briefly explaining what must be done to properly administer an estate. I also had a much longer article, "Tasks and Fee Schedule in Administration of Estates," where I set out in some detail the many tasks that might be needed to administer the estate, the costs, and who would typically be responsible for each. I accompanied that article with the Estate Tasks and Fees spreadsheet, which my client and I completed at the first interview and inserted in the manual. It only briefly set out the tasks but confirmed who was doing each and what it would cost (A 7.10).

I inserted in this manual an excellent two-page article about grieving, written by a psychotherapist. I never did, but I probably should have found out more about local grief counselors and support groups.

When the Ontario government decided to set up a bureaucracy to ensure that executors paid the correct amount of probate fees, it became necessary to keep perfect records of the estate's value if the government were to question the amount paid. My assistant maintained that information and documentation in a second manual. Keeping copies of the documentary proof showing that the amounts used for the probate calculation were accurate was quite important. This second manual was given to the client when the file closed so that the client would be prepared if the probate police knocked on their door.

The primary manual had a detailed estate bank account ledger. During the estate administration, the executor would receive several checks from various sources, and they would write checks for expenses on behalf of the estate. When it came time to do an accounting so the executor could distribute the estate, we needed this record of receipts and expenses to do the accounts. The executor would often come to their appointment to put together the accounts, bringing only a bank statement or bank book. However, the bank statement or bank book had only the date and the amount of the transaction. Many times, the client could not remember what the transaction was about as they might not yet have gotten back canceled checks, or they might have withdrawn cash to pay for something. I, therefore, developed a bank account ledger to record who a check was from or to whom it was paid and for what purpose, in addition to the date and the amount. The clients kept this ledger in the manual and updated it every time there was a transaction in the estate bank account.

The manual contained sample letters for the client to write to several government agencies that required notification when anyone died. I also had memoranda on minor tasks that clients could do themselves, such as transferring a motor vehicle license, searching for unclaimed money with the Bank of Canada, and searching for a life insurance policy.

I had one tab dedicated to the Estate Information Return, which was the initial stage of checking that the executor paid the correct probate fees. This tab had a checklist of information required to complete the Estate Information Return, the government's guide to completing the Estate Information Return, and a sample estate information return. We assured clients that filing this return was something they could do; if they still required my assistant to do it, she would, but we would charge a fee.

Finally, there was a section for an Estate Client To-Do list. This list was in addition to the Estate Tasks and Fees spreadsheet. It contained small tasks that arose from the first consultation (A 7.9).

7.1.3 Keeping the Administration of Estates Manual up to Date

Clients would not receive much correspondence from our office to put in the manual aside from reporting letters. The essential insert in their manuals was the ongoing information about activities in the estate bank account.

7.1.4 Why the Administration of Estates Manuals Are Important

Like all manuals, besides having articles of interest, it was a well-organized client-friendly copy of their file. I will again emphasize the importance of keeping track of estate accounting. The manual provided a system and a place for clients to report that accounting. The second manual with proof of numbers made the client secure, knowing they would have no worries if the government audited their file.

7.2 Administration of Estates Section of the Website

7.2.1 Why the Administration of Estates Website Section Is Important

Unlike other practice areas of law, in the administration of estates the requirement to obtain a lawyer to advise what an executor does to administer an estate comes about very quickly. That need may arise because of a sudden death, though even when a death is inevitably soon, executors do not start thinking about which lawyer they will retain to handle the estate. Then when death occurs, executors on some issues have to act fast and may have many questions. They want answers right away. Executors do not have time to ask for referrals and shop around. That is why they often use the lawyer who drafted the will, though they probably know nothing about that lawyer. They also turn to websites and look to find the information they need quickly. So again, the website is a valuable marketing tool.

Like the other practice areas, the website will also have information that will reduce clients' stress, and it will have information questionnaires that let the clients know what information the lawyer needs from them.

7.2.4 Organization of the Administration of Estates Website Section

My Administration of Estates drop-down menu contained The First-Time Client, Articles, Fees and Forms, and Resources. In the First-Time Client section, I pointed out a common misconception among many people that the lawyer who prepared the will should be the lawyer to do the legal work regarding the administration of the estate. Any lawyer can represent the executor.

7.2.5 Content of the Administration of Estates Website Section

This section was relatively straightforward and not so large as the website sections of other practice areas. The questionnaires collected the information needed, and the articles and forms outlined what the executor had to do to administer an estate and how much it would cost. Some people think a lawyer is not needed when the first spouse dies as most assets are in joint ownership or if the other spouse is specifically named in the investment or insurance documents as the designated beneficiary. There is much less to do, but an executor should consult a lawyer to discuss a few particular tasks, such as changing the homeownership and ensuring they complete everything to administer the estate. I wrote a brief article called "Administering A Simple Estate" to point out these few tasks for those estates.

7.3 The Client Monitor for the Administration of Estates

I used the client's monitor in numerous ways for the administration of estates file's first consultation. As in all practice areas, there was a comprehensive First Consultation Slideshow because there are so many issues that can arise in the administration of an estate (A 7.4). Using the monitor, the clients and I would also complete the asset information form in an Excel spreadsheet (A 7.3.2). We would input the type of ownership, present value, date of death value, probate value, beneficiary, and whether, at that time, the client had documentary proof. As it was a spreadsheet, it would then automatically calculate the estimated probate fee. At their first consultation, most clients were anxious or at least curious about how much the probate fee would be. With the form and the monitor, they could see how I calculated the probate fee.

The major item on the agenda of this consultation was deciding what tasks were needed to administer the estate and who would do them. Again, I used the Excel spreadsheet (A 7.10) to enumerate the tasks, mark which of us would do each one, and insert the fee. Similarly, the spreadsheet being in Excel, the total cost was automatically calculated.

As there were documents associated with these tasks for the clients to obtain, no matter who was performing them, there was a sheet in the Excel spreadsheet (A 7.9) for the client to mark what documents they were to obtain and what tasks they would next have to do. Like the tasks form and the asset information form, this form was printed out for the client to insert into their manual after being filled out with the lawyer.

Working with the clients completing these forms using the client monitor was more efficient and quicker than without a monitor. In addition, this application had the client participating in the process more than without a monitor.

7.4 The First Consultation Slideshow for Administration of Estates

The administration of estate files often contained many minor matters, many of them not legal but practical. Therefore, having the First Consultation Slideshow for this practice area was beneficial: it ensured that I discussed everything with the client. Having clients know the agenda in advance alerted them to topics they might not have considered (A 7.4).

7.5 Client Questionnaires and Forms for Administration of Estates

7.5.1 Client Intake Forms for Administration of Estates

Lawyers and their staff must never forget that the reason that their office is opening an administration of estate file is that someone has died. The executor, who is most probably a close family member, will be grieving that death. Therefore, lawyers should express their condolences at the first contact by phone and the first in-person contact and recognize this file is not just a business transaction. The lawyers' and firms' tone should show sympathy and empathy.

Concerning the actual intake form, after ensuring that the person calling is the executor and therefore has the authority, it has to be confirmed that the deceased was resident in the jurisdiction where the lawyer practices. The location of the original will must also be confirmed. The client should be encouraged to ask any pressing questions that cannot wait until their first consultation. The lawyer will confirm by the appointment date that the client will complete the forms about the estate on the website. The lawyer will confirm that date with links to the forms in a First Appointment Confirmation Letter, which the firm will send out right away. As the fees in this practice area are more complicated, lawyers should point clients to their website for information about fees stated on the website rather than discussing them in that phone call.

7.5.2 Client Information Questionnaires for Administration of Estates

I had two administration of estate information forms I assume all lawyers would have. One asked for particulars about the deceased, the death, the will, executors, and beneficiaries, and the other requested details about the estate assets.

7.6 First Appointment Confirmation Letter for Administration of Estates

This letter followed the format letter set out in section 4.6, relating it to the administration of estates files. I also suggested they check the Bank of Canada website to see if they had any record of dormant bank accounts. I provided the link to that site.

7.9 Administration of Estates To-Do and Document Lists

As discussed in section 7.1.2, there were two types of client to-do lists for administration of estate files. First, the overall main tasks, as explained in section 7.10, were listed in a form in Excel that confirmed what major tasks had to be completed, who was doing them, and what the costs would be. Second, the smaller to-do list detailed the tasks the client needed to do themselves as well as tasks that helped me in my work. My clients and I completed that second form at the end of the first consultation (A 7.9).

When the Ontario government required an Estate Information Return, I believed it was the lawyer's job to ensure that all documentation related to the estate's value was obtained and in an organized state. Therefore, a second volume containing just asset information was kept by my assistant. It was given to the client when the file was closed. It was available if there was an audit of the estate's value for probate purposes.

7.10 Calculation of Estimated Fees Form for Administration of Estates

My administration of estates practice was one where I used both fixed fees and unbundled fees to benefit my clients. This practice area lent itself to unbundled fees because there were so many tasks that the clients could do and that would not jeopardize what I was doing.

I could charge a flat fee for my services because I could realistically estimate the time it would almost always take because the tasks were more in my control. Where I could not control the time to complete a task, I had a proviso in my retainer, which I hardly ever used, to charge on an hourly rate after spending unanticipated extra hours on the task.

One of my favorite applications that I invented was an Excel spreadsheet (A 7.10) listing the many possible tasks that a lawyer might perform when representing an executor. In that column, I briefly described the tasks and stated my fixed fee associated with that task. I alone could perform some of those tasks, like apply to the court for probate, but others, like applying for Canada Pension Benefit, the executor could do if they chose, to reduce their costs. Therefore, next to the task list column, I had two columns in which the executor, with my advice, would tell me to identify who would perform the task. In the final column, I would insert the fee for each task I would be responsible for doing, and at the bottom of this fourth column Excel totaled the fees. I charged a small percentage based on the estate's assets for larger estates over a specific probate value. I included that additional fee formula on a spreadsheet. That amount was inserted as part of the fee and added in for a total cost. The probate fee calculation to the court was made on the Asset Information Form, though it could have been, as it once was, on this Tasks and Fees Form. Like the To-Do list, the Tasks and Fees form is printed out at the client's appointment and put in the client manual. It was also a form I used when I calculated the final fee: I would look at what was actually done and add in any extra lawyer or legal assistant time. Also, at the end of the file, the estate's value was finalized, making the fee calculation precise.

7.12 Articles for Administration of Estates Clients

For this practice area, I never felt the need to have many legal articles because the nature of the matter was not that complex. The facts that I needed were very straightforward. The law and the legal process were not complicated. There was no need to make major decisions or negotiate with another lawyer. Also, other than confirming who did what tasks, there was no complex lawyer-client relationship. I generally met with clients only two or three times because the clients dealt mainly with my assistant on the phone. I always admitted to my clients on their file

I was just "the front man," and my assistant did all the work after the first consultation. Therefore, I could generally answer all of my clients' questions and concerns at their first consultation. An article that I should have written would be on executor compensation.

I did, however, have a general article, "The Administration of Estates," which briefly explained what had to be done to administer an estate, starting with arranging the funeral. Besides being available on my website, that article had been sent to them when my clients originally executed their wills with me. I also had on my website a simple guide for what to do when death occurs. I had also placed that in the client's original Wills and Powers of Attorney Client Manual, which the executor would have found right after death. In the Administration of Estates Client Manual, I had an article about tasks and fees, which contained a little more detail about the many tasks found in my Tasks and Fees Form. Finally, I had a two-page article written by a grief counselor, though I assume the funeral homes would also provide that information.

When the first spouse passes away, if the couple had everything in joint ownership or named each other as beneficiaries, there may be little to do to administer the estate. But there are some actions, so I wrote an article entitled "Administration of a Simple Estate" to point out that there were still some tasks to be done in that simple situation and that I charged only a low set fee. Hence, there was no worry about high costs just to consult with me to ensure the surviving spouse competently administered the estate. It was sort of like my "Why Need a Lawyer?" article but only for simple estates. As my fee structure set out that clients could do a lot of the work themselves and just have me explain what had to be done, I am not sure a "Why Need a Lawyer?" article is essential for this practice area, but it would not hurt.

My article "The Administration of An Estate" and memo "What to Do When Death Occurs" were good first-period services. Perhaps with the will client's permission, though found in the Wills and Powers of Attorney Client Manual, I should have also sent to the executors when the will was signed, my article, "Preparing for an Easier Administration of an Estate." That way, the executors could remind the Will makers to keep up to date in their manuals their assets, debts, information, and instructions, to ensure the executor's job would be made easier.

7.13 Legal Fees in Administration of Estate Files

How lawyers determine their fees for administration of estate files has significantly changed since I started my practice. In the late 1970s, our local county law association set fees based on the estate's value. Those fees could be very lucrative for the amount of work the lawyers performed. That is why many law firms charged very little for wills, sometimes at loss leader prices. Lawyers often sold their practices based on the number of wills they were holding in their vaults because the expectation was so high that if a lawyer were holding on to the will, they would obtain the higher-paying estate work. Lawyers replaced those fee tariffs with an hourly rate method. That is an unfair way to charge for estates if the legal assistant works a lot on estate files. The assistants would then have to log their time and charge at their hourly rate.

As explained in section 7.10, I believed charging fees based on fixed prices and offering unbundled services was perfect for administration of estate files. I, therefore, satisfied two significant needs of clients. In section 7.10, I also explained the process of how I would calculate the fee.

For many years, I, like most lawyers, did not get clients to sign a retainer for administration of estate matters; but in later years, I developed a simple one for several reasons. I hoped that clients would read and take more seriously documents they signed more than having reporting letters written later on and perhaps not read carefully, if at all. If there was a lawyer/client conflict later, I believed a signed document was more substantial evidence than a reporting letter. The administration of estates retainer contained specific tasks, not on the task list that the executor and not the lawyer was responsible for, such as the burial and all income tax matters. It also confirmed, with client signatures, that the tasks and fees form listed how the fees would be determined. I have my sample retainer in Appendix 7.6.

Unlike family law, in administration of estates slow-paying clients and bad debts were not a problem. When I had clients attend the bank to obtain the certified check needed to pay the court probate fees, I also asked them to have the bank write out a check in trust for me for the estimated legal fees. That way, I did not have to ask the executor for money or worry about being paid when I rendered the account, and

I avoided the credit card fee, as many of my clients very often paid by credit card.

7.15 Letters to Affected Nonclients

At one time, Ontario did not require that executors provide the will or portions of it to all the beneficiaries when applying for probate. However, I always suggested the executors have me give the will to the beneficiaries even if not required by their Rules of Practice or if they did not have to because there was no need for probate. If lawyers do not provide copies, they will be inundated with beneficiaries asking to see the will and asking when they will get their money. I suggest the letter to them say that they should inquire about when they will receive their bequest to the executor and not to the law office, because the beneficiaries are not the lawyer's clients. Lawyers will keep the executors up to date on the timing.

7.17 Providing Clients Resource Information for Administration of Estates

Executors are responsible for finalizing the income tax of the deceased. Though in Canada the final tax return (the terminal tax return) is the same as a regular yearly return, there are numerous differences in taxation in the final year. There may be more tax paid, but there are rules for the possibilities of saving tax. I, therefore, suggested to my clients that they use an accountant who deals with estates rather than perhaps their accountant or the deceased's accountant unless they are familiar with the intricacies of tax on death. I had thought of writing an article about all the different ways a good accountant could save taxes when dealing with the estate; that would have made my clients more aware of the need to get an expert's help. Some clients believed that they could do the terminal year tax return themselves because the return was similar, but I inserted my accountant's business card in their client manual because the law is not similar. I sent my accountants several estate clients, so I knew they had the expertise to do the final returns and apply for the final tax clearance certificate.

My manual contained an article on grief, but I never did, as I hoped to do, more than that to help clients deal with grief, such as recommending local grief counselors and local support groups. Funeral homes generally do provide this information but having recommendations from lawyers would not only be helpful; it would also show that lawyers were sympathetic and understood what the clients were going through.

7.18 Reporting Administration of Estates Letters

I generally had three reporting letters for administration of estate files: first, after the initial consultation, second, after I obtained probate, and last, when the estate was substantially or entirely complete. These letters had the same format: they confirmed the status (including who is doing what) of the completed and uncompleted tasks. They were basically checklists.

7.25 Legal Software Programs for Administration of Estates

I used a dedicated administration of estates program, which made it much easier for my assistant to prepare all the forms necessary for the file. It also ensured I had the up-to-date forms required by the court. The program's accounting documents, which showed the inputs and outputs from the estate and the calculation determining what part of the residue named beneficiaries would receive, were in an easier format for clients to follow than an accounting presented on a nondedicated administration of estates program. I think these dedicated programs could produce more reports specially designed for clients.

7.27 Communications with Administration of Estate Clients

7.27.1 Checking in with Clients

Sometimes estates came to a standstill waiting for information, such as when there was a long wait to receive clearance from the Canada Revenue Agency. During these, even though expected, periods, lawyers should have a system for checking in on the clients just to let them know they have not forgotten about them.

8

Residential Real Estate Law Service Applications

This practice area deals with purchasing and selling residential houses and condominiums. It also deals with the financing of the purchase and with refinancing a home to allow clients to take out equity in their houses. The relationship between the lawyers and the clients is not long term, nor are there many client/lawyer interactions. Clients probably deal with the legal assistant more than the lawyer unless there are problems with the real estate transaction. Lawyers would typically meet with clients for the essential initial consultation and the signing appointment. Though clients, especially first-time buyers, might be a little stressed and worried about what is probably the biggest financial transaction of their lives, they have fewer needs than family law clients. They do not need the lawyer to be overly empathetic. They are not worried about speed because the parties have already set the timing by agreeing on the closing date before the lawyer generally gets retained. They do not need to be part of the process or heavily knowledgeable about the law; however, they probably should know more about the law than they think they need to know. I believe most clients' significant need revolves around costs, especially in purchases. They want to know all the costs involved, not just the legal fees, because the total disbursements are significant. As many are first-time buyers, they need to know the process. The lawyer should inform them of all the nonlegal tasks that they and other participants like the real estate agent does.

In terms of percentage of gross claim costs, according to a Law Pro 2019 report, in Ontario, real estate is second only to litigation for the area of law with the highest number of negligence claims. It had been that way for the previous 20 years. And when it comes to complaints, according to the Law Society of Ontario, real estate again is second only to litigation in the number of complaints. And like all practice areas except perhaps criminal law, the major causes of malpractice and complaints are not a lack of legal knowledge (only 7 percent of complaints in 2019 for real estate) but rather poor practice management issues such as communications (41 percent).

Like all the corporate lawyers I interviewed, real estate lawyers believe that their clients read hardly anything they give them, including reporting letters. As a result, they think they do not require any innovative legal service applications, even the basic client manual. However, I think the nature of the negligence claims and complaints shows that lawyers should change and adopt some innovative service applications.

I also believe that a real estate transaction is more of a commodity than are other legal services. Lawyers with a reputation for excellent service and an informative and transparent website that sets out fees will stand out from the crowd and attract more clients. Real estate lawyers should compete on service and not on price. I would suspect lawyers who compete on price may cut corners to make money and are the ones most likely to be sued and have complaints against them.

8.1 The Residential Real Estate Purchase Client Manual

A home purchasing file is different from a home sale file, so I suggest two separate manuals for the purchase and the sale. I will discuss the purchase file, as it is more complicated than the sale file.

8.1.1 The Purposes of the Residential Real Estate Manual

Like all client manuals, the main purposes of the Real Estate Manual are to provide information for the client and hold letters and documentation. Many real estate lawyers bind up in booklet form their final reporting letter attaching the relevant documents of the real estate transaction necessary for the client to have, such as the deed and the mortgage. I believe lawyers should give the manual at the first consultation and that it should be, like other manuals, in the form of a solid, substantial three-ring binder that will not be shoved in a drawer somewhere but be on a bookcase so less likely to be lost. Clients will need the deed and mortgage for a long time compared with other practice area manuals, so clients should store them well.

8.1.2 Organization and Contents of the Residential Real Estate Manual

The organization of this manual would have the basic sections of an index: an introduction section; an article section; and sections to hold letters, documents, the retainer, accounts, notes, and to-do lists. It might also be convenient to use this manual on an ongoing basis to keep the client's homeowner's insurance, property tax bills, warranties on appliances (both those that came at the time buying the house and future purchases). I would suggest the client also keep the new homeowner's warranty information in the manual. These separate subjects would have a separate tab for easier access.

8.1.3 Keeping the Residential Real Estate Manual up to Date

Unlike other practice area manuals, the real estate manual will get most of the documentation at the end of the file, some by email. This is more so now with the changes that the COVID-19 pandemic has brought about. Keeping information in digital form is acceptable for short-term use, but as personal computers are not always backed up and as technology changes, it is not guaranteed that in 10 years, one could easily find the reporting letter and documentation concerning a house purchase if they are in digital form. Since the deed and the mortgage will be needed for a long time and are original documents, I suggest lawyers mail them with a printed reporting letter. The reporting letter would be three-hole-punched with the deed and mortgage put in the manual's side pockets.

8.1.4 Why Residential Real Estate Manuals Are Important

Like all manuals, articles in the real estate manual are written reminders of information the lawyer gave the client and can provide more information not always discussed in a consultation. Manuals are important because they better ensure the lawyer's original documentation given to the client will be found and be easily accessible. In addition, the client can use the manual to store other essential information about the house, such as insurance, property taxes, and warranties.

8.2 Real Estate Sections of the Website

8.2.1 The Importance of the Real Estate Section on the Website

The real estate section of a lawyer's website can be a significant marketing tool. Because legal real estate services are much like a commodity, lawyers can use their websites to make themselves stand out from other lawyers. I believe that lawyers can start doing that by posting their fees and the disbursements involved in a real estate transaction and include valuable articles to help clients before and after the purchase and sale agreement is signed.

8.2.5 Content of the Real Estate Section on the Website

Because lawyers' fees in real estate matters are almost always on a block fee basis (with the reasonable proviso that unexpected extra work is based on an hourly basis), I do not understand why lawyers do not generally post their real estate fees prominently on their websites. It benefits prospective clients who want to know what the cost will be and does not waste the lawyer's time talking to shoppers looking for the lowest price. Posting all the possible disbursements that clients may be unaware of is also helpful to clients, especially clients on a tight budget.

Most clients retain their lawyers after signing their Purchase and Sale Agreement, so it would significantly benefit prospective clients to know some legal matters before signing:

1. They should know that the purchase and sale agreement is the most important document they will sign, and their rights and obligations flow from it.
2. They should know that if they make oral side deals with the other party, they should be put in writing and be part of the agreement.

3. They should be aware of the possible need for the conditional clauses of obtaining financing and a home inspection.
4. They should know the roles of the agent and the lawyer.

Unfortunately, clients do not discover some of these issues until after the agreement is signed; but some clients do know it is best to consult a lawyer before signing the contract, or they make it a condition of the agreement that a lawyer approves it within five days of signing. Real estate agents discuss some of these topics but cannot be relied upon always to do so. Lawyers could probably provide this information in one article. The challenge is to get that information to the clients before they sign the agreement. That is more of an advertising and promotional issue; however, lawyers can inform their existing clients and the clients of other lawyers in the firm by having these articles on the firm's website and printed copies in the waiting room. Many years ago, I approached the other lawyers in my firm to push their clients to retain me to do wills for them. I provided reasons why clients in that practice area should have wills. Unfortunately, I could not convince the criminal lawyer to tell his clients they should have a will just in case they lost their case and went to jail.

To attract real estate clients, a good website will include free and valuable information on topics such as fees, processes, and time frames. I understand that clients still have their moving van at their house at 9:00 a.m., expecting to get their keys first thing in the morning. Clients have to be told and reminded that they should not expect the keys at that time. As well, articles about home insurance and the transfer of utilities would be helpful to clients.

Like the websites for all practice areas, the website can contain a client information questionnaire to save the lawyer's time and ensure that the client collects all the pertinent information. In addition, like all practice areas, the website can post a slide show of what occurs at the first consultation, so that clients can be prepared and less anxious, knowing what they will be discussing.

I would suggest that the website could have links to related websites, though more preferably, lawyers should write their own short articles explicitly written for the website about such issues as the real estate agent's role, home inspections, financing, and new home warranties. See section 8.12 for other common topics, and look at other lawyer's websites to see what other lawyers are writing about; though these are now written usually as blogs they post to their websites.

The website could have an article about relevant warranty periods as an after-the-transaction service for clients who purchase new homes.

My hope is that rather than just saying their firm does real estate transactions, all of this information that lawyers can put on the website will impress clients who are deciding which lawyer to choose. Some law firms have real estate blogs that are very short and sometimes discuss specialized issues that do not apply to the general transaction, so they are of little interest or help to the prospective client. Lawyers should separate those specialized articles from those that will be of interest to the prospective client.

8.3 The Client Monitor for Residential Real Estate

Perhaps there is not so much use for the client monitor in real estate files as in a family law file, but there are enough benefits to make it worthwhile for lawyers to use.

Like all practice areas, real estate should have a slideshow of the agenda of the first consultation. Real estate Client To-Do Forms can be put on the screen to be filled out with the client before they are printed. Calculations of fees and disbursements (especially a land transfer tax) could be in a spreadsheet that the lawyers would use in a client monitor and then printed for the client. If there were land survey issues, perhaps having the survey on a screen would make it easier to follow: lawyers move the cursor to places of interest on the survey.

8.4 The Residential Real Estate First Consultation Slideshow

As in all first consultations, there is a lot to discuss. Having a first consultation slideshow lets the client know beforehand what to expect and ensures that lawyers cover everything during the consultation.

8.5 Client Questionnaires and Forms for Residential Real Estate

The main purposes of all intake forms are to obtain basic contact information, confirm that there is no conflict in representing the client, ensure no jurisdictional issues, and confirm that the lawyer wants to take the case. For example, a lawyer may not feel comfortable dealing with rural and cottage property or multi-unit apartments but rather wants the more uncomplicated family home transaction; if so, at the initial stage, the intake form must have these questions on it. If, as suggested, the lawyer posted the fees and disbursements on the website, the client should confirm on their intake that they understand what the fees and disbursements are. It is important to know what stage the client is at: Has the agreement been signed? Have the conditions been met? How and when will the lawyer obtain the agreement? The client will then be directed to the lawyer's website to fill out a more detailed client information questionnaire. Clients would send that questionnaire from the website and print out one for themselves to bring into the first consultation, which the lawyer will schedule depending on the stage of the transaction.

Lawyers could use the other forms as explained in section 4.5 of this book after modifying them for a real estate file.

8.9 To-Do Lists and Document Lists for Residential Real Estate

8.9.1 Client To-Do List for Residential Real Estate

I think it is worth repeating my theory about to-do lists. Though lawyers will remind clients what everyone's tasks are in confirmation letters, I suggest separate to-do lists in table format or Excel, with places to indicate the to-do and done dates. That format stands out more and customizes the tasks for each file. To-do lists are more comprehensive when completed together with the client on their monitor at the consultation.

8.9.2 Lawyer's, Legal Assistant's, and Others' To-Do Lists for Residential Real Estate

I do not think clients appreciate how much work the lawyer's office has to do in a real estate transaction. They are unaware of all the lawyer's, legal assistant's, and others' tasks. Besides being beneficial for the lawyer and legal assistant to follow, having their to-do lists available to clients lets clients understand how much is being done on their behalf and advises them when the task is completed. If the firm is using a client portal, clients can check on the status of the file. If there is no portal, the to-do lists, just one Excel file, can be sent periodically to the client when the lawyer, assistant, or other side completes some tasks. The client might be wondering whether a task has been completed yet.

8.9.3 Document List for Residential Real Estate

At the signing consultation, lawyers provide clients with numerous documents. After explanations, sometimes very brief, especially if the lawyer tells the client that it is a standard document in all files, the client signs them. The documents are generally never seen again until they are found as attachments to the final reporting letter, which the lawyer may deliver much later. Lawyers generally give clients time to read over these documents, as well as the documents the other side will be signing and paperwork not signed, such as the statement of adjustments. Still, for some clients, it is not enough time to fully digest everything.

I suggest giving clients beforehand articles that generally describe these standard documents' plain meaning and purpose. This application would benefit the clients and perhaps reduce the number of questions at the appointment.

Lawyers could have a system of listing the documents and their status, like the to-do list in Excel, which would be more valuable than just making them a list of enclosures.

8.10 Calculation of Fees, Disbursements, and Other Expenses for Residential Real Estate

Real estate clients must know for financing and planning purposes the total cost of a real estate transaction. First-time buyers may not be aware of the many costs that are involved when buying a house. The lawyer's fees are just one cost and a minor component of the total costs in the scheme of things. Lawyers should make clients aware of the land transfer taxes and all the mandatory and possible disbursements, which can be substantial. There may be a need for a property land survey, a home inspection report, mortgage insurance, and title insurance, all of which are not inexpensive. At the first consultation, I suggest using a spreadsheet program like Excel; these costs are calculated and totaled with the client using the client monitor and then printed for the client to put in their client manual. I think it would also be helpful for clients if, in another spreadsheet, the lawyers and client review other nonlegal expenses. These would be ones that the lawyer or the client have already costed, such as the costs of movers, new window coverings, and appliances. Both these spreadsheets could be sent to the client in digital form to allow clients to change them as expenses are finalized and, perhaps, new ones added. Even though it is not a legal service, helping clients with their home buying budget is an added minor application that lawyers can easily provide.

8.12 Articles for Clients for Residential Real Estate

In residential real estate there is no shortage of articles that lawyers can write for their clients, which can be placed in the client manual and on the lawyers' websites.

Following the topics set out in section 4.12, I would suggest some of these would be appropriate:

- **a.** Substantive Law Articles: The Agreement of Purchase and Sale, The Statement of Adjustments, Undertakings in Real Estate Transactions, Land Surveys, Joint or Tenancy in Common Ownership and with Whom, Title Insurance, Condominiums
- **b.** Definitions and Annotations: Definitions of Terms in Real Estate Transactions, Annotations of the Clauses in the Standard Agreement of Purchase and Sale, The Annotated Mortgage
- **c.** Legal Process Articles: The Timeline and Steps in a Real Estate Transaction, The Role of Client in a Real Estate Transaction, The Role of the Real Estate Agent in a Real Estate Transaction
- **d.** Law Firm Procedures Article: The Role of the Lawyer in a Real Estate Purchase, The Role of the Lawyer in a Real Estate Sale
- **e.** Legal Fees and Billing: List of All Legal Fees, Taxes, and Disbursements
- **f.** Articles Written by Other Local Related Service Providers: The Home Building Inspection

g. After the Fact, Third-Period Articles: New Home Warranties
h. Promotional but Informational Articles: Why Use Me as Your Real Estate Lawyer?

I suggest looking on websites for other articles of interest but do not put in the manual topics that might interest only very few clients, and do not have those articles on the website in the same section as the standard topics.

8.13 Legal Fees for Residential Real Estate Transactions

As discussed in sections 4.2.5 and 8.2.5, lawyers should post their legal fees, possible taxes, and disbursements on their website, so that clients know what they will be for planning purposes. However, many lawyers say they do not post their fees because prospective clients will shop for the lowest fees. These lawyers claim they obtain clients because when clients call them, they convince the prospective clients that their fees may not be the lowest, but they offer excellent service and do more than the bargain-basement-priced real estate lawyers. I suggest that the prospective client is better served with an informative website (articles, checklists, questionnaires). In addition, lawyers with reasonable prices will not get the shopper anyway, so they will not waste their time trying to sell them on the better service argument.

8.14 Free Follow-up Legal Services in Residential Real Estate

Besides the general free services suggested in section 4.14, mostly related to swearing affidavits, I suggest lawyers let clients know they can call with questions after the transaction has closed, without worrying about being charged. For example, perhaps the other side took some light fixtures they had no right to have, but the clients did not want to bother or pay for their lawyer to pursue the matter. All it would take would be a phone call to the other lawyer to explain to their clients they had no right to take the fixtures and ask that they bring them back. That example, and others, such as the appliances not working, could be issues lawyers could tell the clients in advance to look out for and assure them there would be no legal cost to deal with these issues unless court action is necessary.

8.15 Letters to Affected Nonclients

After a real estate transaction is completed, someone must notify the tax authorities and the utility companies. The new owners are noted on their files, and the utility companies should take final readings and send the final account to the previous owners. As well, lawyers should remind clients to contact the post office and government authorities that require notification of address changes immediately after a move. If they are to be done by owners, these notifications should be put on the client's Real Estate Client To-Do list.

Sometimes the lawyers do this, and sometimes the clients do as the utilities will deal only will clients and not accept a lawyer's letter. In any scenario, lawyers should assist clients with this task. Movesnap is a company that has a program that helps clients do these notifications and helps with other moving tasks. Lawyers can retain that company for all their clients rather than try and do that work themselves. Real estate agents also use the program for their clients. If they are to be done by owners, these notifications should be put on the client's Real Estate Client To-Do List. It is probably little known that in Ontario, a person must notify the Department of Motor Vehicles of a change of address within six days of the change.

8.16 Following Up with Clients after the File Is Closed

I suggest that after closing a purchase, lawyers could write their clients to confirm that everything is okay. Was there damage caused by the vendors moving out? Are the appliances working? Were all the specific items agreed to be left in the home there? Lawyers will look better being proactive and not waiting until the client calls them. Perhaps, as will be discussed in section 8.14, clients will be hesitant to call.

8.17 Providing Clients Resource Information for Residential Real Estate

It would be innovative if law firm websites had some basic articles, perhaps by local businesses, about the many aspects of household management, from maintaining the heating and air conditioning equipment to gardening. For example, new home buyers might want to know their responsibilities concerning snow removal and maintaining their lawn (or what they can do when the neighbor never weeds their lawn). Likewise, purchasers who are new to the jurisdiction might be interested in knowing relevant local government numbers and websites such as the all-important garbage rules.

8.18 Reporting Letters for Residential Real Estate

If lawyers are not going to use a client manual, then I suggest that their final reporting letter be packaged nicely, with spiral bindings or placed in a plastic cover at least. The reporting letter should stand out from being just an ordinary letter, so that it will be easily found in the future.

8.23 Physical Applications for Residential Real Estate

Besides the client manual or binding of the reporting letter, another physical application for real estate matters could be keychains with the law firm's name on them. They are an everyday item that can last a lifetime. They do not run out of ink. They are often misplaced, but clients usually find them. Or, to steal an idea from a Canadian charity, perhaps if they are lost, the back of the key chain would ask the finder to arrange to return the key chain to the law office. If clients lose their keys, they can call the office to see if someone turned them in. This is a moment-innovative application that a lawyer could simply swipe from a nonlegal business.

9

Corporate Law Service Applications

Corporate law, sometimes called business law or commercial law, involves legal work such as incorporating companies, drafting shareholders' agreements and partnership agreements, and representing buyers and sellers of businesses. It also deals with commercial leasing, financing issues, employment contracts, licensing applications, debt collections, and aspects of estate planning. In addition, there could be some dispute resolution work that would be turned over to commercial litigators if not resolved. Thus, there are a lot of areas of work for a corporate lawyer in a small firm.

Corporate lawyers must remember that their business is helping clients with the many legal matters that deal with the critical matter of their client's livelihood. Of course, the client-lawyer relationship will differ depending on the client and what stage of their business they are in. Many clients will lean heavily on their lawyer for advice, not just on legal matters but also on business matters. It is also one of the very few practice areas where the relationship most probably will be ongoing. Clients generally do only one or two wills in their lifetime, the same for real estate transactions and divorces. But they probably need to use the services of their corporate lawyer on numerous occasions and probably at least annually for filing requirements. Therefore, good corporate lawyers are empathetic and ensure good communications with their clients. I also believe that, as in all long-term relationships, an excellent first impression is important.

According to Law Pro (from 2008 to 2018) though not the highest number of negligence claims, corporate/commercial malpractice claims had the highest average cost per claim. Communication issues comprised 40 percent of the claims, including failing to follow their clients' instructions and failing to specify what services the lawyer would perform and what the client would do. Therefore, putting things in writing, having client to-do lists, and ensuring the client reads the material, are essential. Unfortunately, corporate lawyers I talked to say their clients read next to nothing sent to them.

9.1 The Corporate Client Manual

As in family law, there are many different legal services corporate lawyers provide their clients. As for family law clients, where I had a slightly different manual for marriage contracts than I did when clients separated, I would suggest different manuals for buying a business than for incorporating a business.

The corporate law manuals would be organized like the other manuals: there would be an introduction section, an article section, a section to hold letters, a section to keep documents, a section relating to the retainer and accounts, and a section for notes and to-do lists. There might also be a section related to after the file is closed, such as government filing requirements and information about other corporate law issues with which the lawyer could help the client. Finally, there might be a section for related but nonlegal documents such as articles about managing a new business. Lawyers might want to divide the letters and documents section based on the source of the letter or document. As I will discuss in section 9.30.1, a duplication of the corporate minute book could be kept in the manual as well.

9.2 Corporate Law Section of the Website

There is much to say about websites, as per my discussions in section 4.2. Those discussions also apply to the corporate law section of the websites, so I will not repeat them all.

9.2.1 *Why the Corporate Law Section of a Website Is Important*

I do not know how many corporate law clients pick their lawyers based on websites. I suspect it does not occur as often as in other practice areas. Personal recommendations would be more critical for corporate law because the lawyer-client relationship could be a long one covering many issues. But that should not stop corporate lawyers from having robust websites to serve their clients in the second and third periods. Having such a website might convince clients to choose a corporate lawyer for various reasons. If the lawyer provides some free information, it may be important to someone starting a business when keeping costs down is a concern. It shows that the lawyer keeps up with the times and is not having just a glorified brochure website that says they have experience and how great the firm is. And there is still the marketing opportunity of having articles on why a person needs a lawyer and should not try to do it themselves, and why they should choose that particular law firm.

As discussed at the beginning of this chapter, a corporate lawyer might perform several different types of work: some lawyers will specialize or have a large part of their practice devoted to franchising law or buying and selling dental practices. In such cases, a robust website would be invaluable for marketing purposes because prospective clients will search for law firms with a specialty in the type of work they need doing.

9.2.4 *How Should the Corporate Law Section of a Website Be Organized?*

I suggest lawyers organize the corporate law section a little differently than set out in section 4.2.4. I like the basic structure of having five subsections: (1) First-Time Client, (2) The Law, (3) The Process, (4) Fees and Forms, and (5) Resources. But there are many different corporate law specialty issues, more than most other practice areas. So, as I did for family law, where I separated "Separation and Divorce" from "Marriage Contracts and Cohabitation Agreements" (prenuptial agreements), I suggest the same for the corporate law section, but using subsections. So "Starting Up a Business" would be a subsection category of Corporate

Law, as would "Landlord and Tenant" or "Franchise Law." I suggest these subcategories also be separated, with the first part primarily sticking to articles on the basics of the subject area. The website would still have the more specialized news and up-to-date articles, which often appeared on their blog but then were republished on the website.

Most lawyers' websites may have very long and helpful blog articles but do not organize them for a prospective client to easily find. Instead, lawyers dump them on their websites, all under a specific practice area. The only organization is the order of the date they were written, with the last one first. I do not think that is the right way to place them on the website.

In almost all websites, the opening page of a particular practice area lists all the things the firm's lawyers can do in that practice area. Perhaps I should have had an introduction subsection to go along with the five subsections previously suggested, which would list what I could do in that practice area. But I thought it was evident that separation and divorce dealt with obtaining a divorce and a separation agreement and would deal with custody, support, and assets and did not need to be spelled out.

9.2.8 Resource Pages for Corporate Law

As corporate clients are often looking for some business advice in addition to legal advice, the corporate section of the website could have a variety of links to relevant business resources, such as government sites. It could have articles written by local experts; for example, a local accountant could discuss the impact of taxes when a business incorporates. A human resources firm could discuss the main employment issues relevant to a small business. The website could list information or just the names of other businesses that the client might need to employ. Some lawyers do not like to recommend other service providers such as accountants or financial advisors in case there is a dispute between the client and the recommended person. I would suggest making it clear that it is a limited recommendation and that the lawyer is not responsible if something goes wrong. Or lawyers could recommend not one but a few people and ask the client to check them out. If the lawyer has more than one accountant as their own client, they may worry that the one not writing the article will be slighted.

9.2.9 Third-Period Uses of Corporate Law Websites

Most family law clients or wills and powers of attorney clients will probably use a lawyer's services only once or twice in their lifetime. However, corporate clients will more likely need a lawyer much more often. For example, there might be the annual filing requirements a lawyer may do for their client. There are also many legal situations for which a corporate client will need a lawyer. Therefore, having some after-the-fact services on the website is advisable to increase the service to clients, impress them, and remind them who their lawyer is. Clients do not visit their lawyer's website weekly looking for new articles. Announcing a recent article is where social media and newsletters can drive clients to the website to read the latest article, hear about a change in the law (such as a change to employer obligations to their employees), review a new service application, and see any other updates on the website.

I suggest using a client email mailing list to announce the new article, application, or office news. It could be called a bulletin. A newsletter connotes something sent periodically and having more than one piece of information. Clients have to subscribe to a blog, and Facebook posts can get lost among the many other postings, so I think the email bulletin is the best delivery source.

9.2.11 Promoting Corporate Clients

With permission, of course, sometimes businesses list the corporate clients they have represented. I would think that some law firms would also like to brag about major corporate clients who have retained them. The *quid pro quo* is that these businesses could write something brief about their product or services and have a link to their website. This possible application is discussed more fully in section 4.2.11.

9.3 The Client Monitor for Corporate Law Clients

As it is for all practice areas, it would be helpful to have a client's monitor to show clients the first consultation agenda (section 4.4). In addition, lawyers could use the client's monitor together with clients when making changes in negotiable documents such as shareholder, partnership, and buy and sell agreements. This application also applies to the completion of to-do lists.

9.5 Client Questionnaires and Forms for Corporate Law

As in all practice areas, "inadequate investigation" was the second-highest reason for negligence claims for lawyers practicing corporate law. Lawyers cannot rely only on their memories when questioning clients about their legal matters but should have comprehensive questionnaires that clients fill out to obtain all the facts.

9.12 Corporate Law Articles for Clients

Lawyers should organize articles on their website according to their subcategory and whether they are primarily legal or process articles that would occur in almost all situations instead of "Breaking News" or highly specialized articles.

For a suggested subcategory of "First-Time Business Owner," there could be an article on the different types of ownership—sole proprietorship, partnership, or incorporation. There could be an article about the differences between buying shares and buying assets if buying an existing business. There should be an article about franchises for those buying a franchise though franchising should probably be a subcategory. For those considering incorporating, it would be helpful to have articles about the different jurisdictions in which one could incorporate and the rights and obligations of shareholders and directors. A resource article about sources of financing would be beneficial to prospective and actual clients.

Some governments have made it easy to incorporate online, and there are do-it-yourself incorporation kits, so it is important to have an article on why one should use a lawyer to incorporate and what a lawyer will discuss with and do for the client. A good first consultation slideshow also posted to the website would help convince the prospective client to retain a lawyer. Finally, a "Why Choose Me?" article and the suggested articles should convince the client to choose that lawyer instead of other firms who have no free information on their website.

Later on, I suggest that more specialized articles annotating standard clauses in a partnership and shareholders agreement would benefit clients. Researching what other lawyers are blogging and writing about should provide numerous topics lawyers can post to their websites after they have written the primary articles.

9.13 Corporate Law Legal Fees

Good business people will be mindful of costs, so they will be looking for legal services that bill on a fixed fee basis when possible. Lawyers can provide some corporate legal work, such as incorporating a business on a block fee basis, so they should post their prices on the website. The disbursement costs, especially the registration fees to the government, should also be set out, because business people do not want to waste their time shopping around for prices—which is another reason lawyers should post their fees. If there is work that the client can do, and unbundled legal services are an option, then these options should be made available to the client.

9.14 Free Follow-up Legal Services in Corporate Law

As I did for family law, I would suggest that lawyers advise corporate clients that if they have a legal question, whether related to the legal work previously performed or to something new, they should be encouraged to call the lawyer for advice. If the time to provide the advice is less than half an hour (or more or less) and no administrative work is needed, then there will be no charge. I would keep track of the time. If a client is continually calling and the cumulative time is too high, the client can expect an account. Like all clients, corporate clients can avail themselves of the other free legal follow-up services discussed in section 4.14 and perhaps others relevant to corporate law.

9.16 Following Up with Clients after the File Is Closed

As pointed out in section 4.16, lawyers have several reasons to follow up with their clients after their file is closed. Corporate clients may have annual filing requirements with the government, which lawyers can remind them to complete. There may be other post-file client to-do's; lawyers can see whether the clients have done these. Lawyers can call to see how their clients are doing: Is the new business thriving as well as they had hoped? Because corporate clients can easily be repeat clients in the future, for maybe an unrelated corporate matter, it is essential to keep in touch with them so they remember they have a lawyer that they can turn to for help.

9.17 Providing Clients Resource Information for Corporate Law

There are many related subjects about which lawyers can suggest resource people, such as accountants and human resource companies. They can recommend websites, articles, and books that might be of interest to their business clients. They can attempt to get local resources to write articles specifically for the lawyer on subjects such as the taxation of companies compared to unincorporated sole proprietorship so that clients could have help deciding where, when, and whether to incorporate.

Providing this resource information benefits clients in all three time periods of service, and it reminds clients who their lawyer is and that that lawyer is providing some value-added service.

9.18 Reporting Letters for Corporate Law Clients

The corporate lawyers I talked to stated that their clients did not read any of their reporting letters. Some lawyers were quite vehement that these letters were not read and therefore thought a client manual was unnecessary and a waste of a corporate lawyer's time. If their clients were not going to read the vital reporting letter, why would they read the many articles provided to them? Corporate lawyers told me they wrote reporting letters only to cover themselves.

With the initial package of articles and forms for the first consultation, I surveyed my clients about my articles. I wanted to know if they were helpful, were the right length, whether they covered what the client wanted to know about and what other subject matter I could write for that practice area. For my wills and powers of attorney practice, I received many replies indicating that my articles were read and well received, but my family law and estate clients rarely filled out those surveys. I did not follow up on why they did not. I should have followed up and kept track of the precise numbers. I also should have followed up to see if those saying they read the articles thoroughly really had done so and understood them.

I gave attention to the subject of ensuring that clients read reporting letters and articles only near the end of my practicing days. However, while working on this book, I realized it was a bigger problem. I, therefore, decided to give it some thought and include it as a topic. It especially applies to corporate clients. So, please read about it in section 4.12.12.

9.19 Social Media for a Corporate Law Practice

Most businesses now realize that they need not only a website but also a Facebook page and perhaps LinkedIn and Instagram accounts. If all of a lawyer's corporate clients are on these platforms, so should their lawyers be. Again, like follow-up applications, having a Facebook page directs clients to current articles of interest on the firm's website. It also keeps the lawyer's name in the clients' minds and projects an image that the law firm keeps up with the times.

9.20 Corporate Law Client Newsletters

Lawyers want to have their corporate clients continue to use them for all their business (and personal legal needs, where applicable); therefore, they must keep up their relationship after the initial file is closed. Not every client is on Facebook, and even then, the client may not see the lawyer's post. The client may not always check their Facebook account every day, and even then, the client might not see it among the many entries posted every day. It is more assured that clients will see a corporate law email newsletter. It can include a recent article or announcement of a change in the law. It can also have some cross-selling with personal legal issues discussed, such as estate planning. The newsletter looks more like a client relationship technique than a marketing application, which a Facebook page is.

9.26 Decision Making Formula for Corporate Law Clients

Corporate clients must make many types of decisions, from the initial determination of whether to incorporate or not to determining what terms are needed to settle an employment dispute. Some decisions are easy, and some lend themselves to mostly mathematical calculations, such as whether to incorporate. But many decisions are judgment calls as the outcomes of any dispute are never certain. I have heard corporate clients complain that they expect their lawyers to use their lawyer's experience to provide more definitive guidance when making business, not just legal, decisions. They do not want the lawyer to just tell them it is a 50/50 case and that the decision is up to the client. Clients know that nothing is guaranteed and know (or should be told) that a long-shot outcome can happen; but clients rely heavily on the lawyer's opinion because the lawyer has been there before and is often in a better position to predict the outcome. There may be other considerations better known to the client of whether to settle, such as whether the client can afford the emotional and financial costs of gambling for a better settlement; but they want to know what the lawyer would do if in their shoes. They are also looking for creative solutions that the parties may not have considered. Lawyers should, as the saying goes, "think outside the box" more. Finally, I believe clients will think more highly of the lawyer who acknowledges that outcomes can be uncertain for various reasons but also definitively advises the client on what they should do.

9.27 Communications with Corporate Law Clients

It is worth repeating, because the number is so high, that 40 percent of negligence claims by corporate clients are due to failed communications. Clients complained that lawyers did not follow instructions and did not explain certain matters, including those tasks for which each was responsible.

Some communication problems would not occur if there were client manuals with to-do lists, articles, and numerous reporting letters that clients read. Lawyers should check in on clients periodically, even when nothing is happening on the file. Lawyers should send clients copies or allow clients access to every letter and document on the files. And of course, again, for some unknown reason, it has to be repeated that lawyers have to return clients' phone calls within a day or have someone in the office call to say when the lawyer can return the call. This is as important to corporate clients as it is for family law clients.

9.30 Other Applications for Corporate Law Clients

9.30.1 Safekeeping of Corporate Law Clients' Documents and Assets

Most corporate lawyers will hold on to their clients' seals and minute books because more than likely, the lawyer will be the one to update the minute books and have the client use their seal while in their lawyer's office. However, I would suggest that a duplicate copy of the minute book be kept by the client in the Corporate Client Manual.

6.20 Other Applications for Corporate Clients

6.21 Safekeeping of Corporate Documents and Assets

[illegible]

PART 4

Creating, Implementing, and Evaluating Legal Service Applications

10

Finding and Creating Innovative Legal Service Applications

It is not very difficult for lawyers to create innovative legal service applications. Lawyers can start by borrowing, stealing, or to be more polite, as Tom Peters says in his book *Thriving on Chaos*, "creatively swiping" ideas from other lawyers and businesses. I have provided in this book over 100 specific applications that might be useful to lawyers so they can start using any of them now. Lawyers should also creatively swipe ideas from other types of businesses and adapt them to their law practice; they can start with finding and then adapting applications rather than creating applications from scratch.

There are several principles to keep in mind when creating new innovative legal service applications. First, the innovative application does not have to involve technology. Technology is used in many, but far from all, of my applications. Second, as stated in my original definition in chapter 1, the application does not have to be completely new. It can be an improvement on or an enhancement of a present application. Clients like small changes more than revolutionary new ideas, so minor enhancements may be more acceptable and therefore used more. The application also does not have to be overly complicated. A simple application may be more beneficial because it is easier to use.

The process of innovating is a management science more than a creative art form, and therefore, anyone can create applications as long as they follow a process and work hard at it. As Thomas Edison said, "Genius is one percent inspiration and ninety-nine percent perspiration."

10.1 Applications from Other Lawyers and Other Businesses

Besides taking much less time than it takes to create an application from scratch, using applications that other lawyers have already invented is a good idea. As other lawyers have used, but perhaps not evaluated, those applications, they probably are worthwhile. There is nothing wrong either lawfully or ethically with copying other lawyers, provided the articles written by other lawyers are not reprinted verbatim. The legal profession has a culture where lawyers generally do share ideas to improve their legal practices, though not so much their marketing ideas. It is okay to use the topics in other lawyers' articles and questionnaires, but lawyers should use their own words in their own style of writing.

Lawyers are not overly generous with sharing their marketing techniques, so finding out precisely what other lawyers may be doing behind the scenes may be challenging; however, like mine and many others, their websites may show what articles they thought their clients would be interested in reading and what applications the firm uses. However, some lawyers' websites do not have much content because they do not want other lawyers to see what they are doing; unfortunately, that means prospective clients do not know what they are doing either. When I had clients who had previously used another lawyer, perhaps years before me, for a will or matrimonial matter, I always looked at their previous lawyer's reporting letter and other material the client may have received. I was looking to see if there was something I could copy. Some law firms, pre-internet and now, send out informational packages with articles and questionnaires when prospective clients request them. I used to ask those law firms to send those packages to me. They would not know I was a lawyer, not a prospective client. I would also sign up to receive law firm newsletters that were offered to anyone. I also looked at textbooks that had precedents for initial and reporting letters.

Creatively swiping from other nonlegal businesses is more manageable in one way and more difficult in another way. It is easier because other businesses are more open about how they operate, so their applications are exposed. But the problem is that a client's needs for legal services are much different from those of a person using a mobile phone provider. And sometimes mobile phone providers' applications seem out of place for use by lawyers—even for me. For example, I do not see lawyers offering clients points for every dollar spent on legal fees toward their next legal purchase. Nor do I think clients would think it appropriate to be given discounts to movie theatres and clothing stores the way my mobile provider does. However, it might not be too audacious for a law firm to provide discount coupons to local restaurants in the vicinity of their office or pay for parking if there is no free parking available near the law firm's office.

One of my favorite and most practical applications, the client manual, came from an application that other businesses have. The idea was really from manufacturing companies, not personal service businesses. One cannot buy even the most inexpensive electronic product without being given a manual of some form explaining how the product works. Then to my client manuals, I added the other main component of storing and organizing the paperwork on a file. I also saw how companies had videos on YouTube to explain aspects of their products, so I produced my videos "How to Fill Out a Form 13.1 Financial Statement." I have them on my website and on YouTube.

Many manufactured goods are so complicated to use, clean, and repair that their companies have to have a large customer support system to serve their customers. These primarily nonservice companies must compete based on service after the sale. These businesses are constantly introducing new and better ways to help their clients; therefore, lawyers must keep a close eye on these other businesses to see if they can adapt their unique service ideas to their practice.

10.2 Application Ideas from Clients

Clients can be a good source of ideas both from their words and by their actions. Clients know what they want and may say or show what is lacking in how lawyers are serving them. During consultations, I often had clients reach for my small scratchpads on my desk to make notes. Besides general notes, they usually wanted to write what they had to do next. I realized I should have a "notes" section in their client manual.

If they reached for the notepaper, I handed them a few 8 × 11 pieces of three-hole-punched paper, which they could write their notes on and eventually insert in their manual. Their manual came with a notes section with a few pieces of paper already in it. Their actions showed they wanted a written record of what was discussed; hence the availability of notepaper, perhaps a copy of my notes and articles about the subjects of the substantive law, the legal process, and my processes.

To obtain good ideas for service applications directly from clients, lawyers must do two things. First, they must continually ask for clients' ideas; and second, they must make it worthwhile for clients to think about and submit ideas. As I have often mentioned and discussed in more detail in section 4.5.6, it was a client, when I had a contest to suggest the best way to improve my practice, who first told me about the internet when it was in its infancy. That resulted in my having a website long before other lawyers did. There were a lot of internet users in Ottawa at that early stage. Ottawa liked to say it was "Silicon Valley North" because of the many tech companies located there and in the surrounding area. It had one of the first and largest free nets. It was rumored that Ottawa, in the early days of the internet, was the most "wired" city in the world.

10.3 Application Ideas from Negligence Claims

Lawyers' Professional Indemnity Insurance Company (Law Pro) insures all Ontario lawyers. It publishes both statistics about negligence claims as well as loss prevention advice. I assume all other insurance companies that cover lawyers would also publish the same information and have relatively the same results. By looking at the major causes of claims, lawyers can develop applications that would address those causes.

Law Pro's Family Law Claims Fact Sheets in 2019 listed several risk management tips based on the causes of negligence claims. They stated the importance of proactively controlling client expectations to significantly lower a lawyer's claims exposure. It is much harder for a lawyer to deal with a client's too-high expectations after the fact. The lawyer should therefore manage the expectations beforehand. It made me feel good that I had included questions about expectations in my Client Preference Questionnaire. I also had an article in the manual about general client expectations. However, I realize from this tip that I did not spend enough direct time in the first consultation discussing expectations, and I did not check in on expectations enough during the file's life. After every major stage in a file, I suggest using client service questionnaires that include questions about client expectations. Are their expectations being met for results and the service? Another observation to be mindful of, especially in family law, or any other litigation practice area, is that a lawyer gives a client a range of outcomes. Clients often remember or focus only on their best outcomes and set them up as their expectations. Clients also need to be reminded of the worst-case scenario.

Another risk management tip is to make sure the lawyer carefully and thoroughly explains any settlement or agreement terms. Here is where articles on legal terms and annotated agreements would be helpful, as well as a reminder to lawyers to continually ask, "Are there any questions?" and also, "Do you fully understand that clause in the agreement?" Another risk management tip is to have good to-do lists and reporting letters so that the lawyers cover every issue. The first consultation slideshow application, as well as to-do lists, can help.

A risk management tip from Law Pro suggests for wills that lawyers have a standard form with questions to ask the testator when there is the slightest suspicion of a capacity or undue influence issue. The lawyer would record the answers along with steps the lawyer took to ensure capacity and no undue influence, such as meeting with the client alone. When a parent does not include a child in their will, I suggest, as I started doing some time ago, putting in the will the reasons for not including the child. The service to clients is that lawyers are protecting clients' wishes. The lawyers also protect themselves from the beneficiaries suing the lawyer for not taking adequate steps to ensure the will is valid.

A Law Pro risk management tip for corporate commercial lawyers is to document instructions and advice. This is where the lawyer's consultation/telephone notes application and client's to-do list, or perhaps a checklist of advice of standard instructions and advice to hand out to clients for their manual, would be helpful. An advantage of these applications over a reporting letter alone is the timing: reporting letters may arrive too late and look self-serving if not done immediately after giving the advice or instructions. These separate documents also stand out more and, if signed by the client, are also more substantial evidence that the lawyer properly advised the client.

As the negligence statistics show, inadequate investigations are the second-highest reason for negligence claims. Therefore, I believe lawyers should use more detailed written questionnaires for the major standard issues of a legal matter so as to have a more thorough investigation. These questionnaires are better than just relying on the lawyers' memories each time they interview clients. A written questionnaire will also allow the client more time to remember and, therefore, will encourage more detailed answers.

10.4 Application Ideas from Client Complaints

Complaints against lawyers, like negligence claims, are time-consuming and stressful. They can be costly, especially if it goes so far that the lawyer has to hire a lawyer to defend against the complaint. Like negligence claims, the main claim is not a lack of knowledge but rather practice management issues, with communications, a service issue, being the number one complaint. Law Society continuing education programs and their statistics state that the most common complaint is that clients believe their lawyers did not keep them informed on a timely basis of the happenings on their file. Also, clients complain that their lawyers did not respond to a client inquiry in a timely fashion.

Lawyers cannot do everything immediately and do not want to fall into the trap of always trying to respond right away in detail to the latest communications; but there is no reason to keep the client waiting to look at the material the opposing side sends. When any material came in on a file, I had a policy that if I could not thoroughly review and discuss it with my client that day or the next day, my assistant would automatically email the opposing side's letter to my client. It would have a note stating that I had not yet reviewed the material but would be in touch shortly. This complaint of not being kept in touch is so important to clients that an application performed by an assistant could be to use a BF system to write clients a short nonchargeable letter to say we are still waiting to hear from the other side (section 4.27.2).

The other major client communication complaint is the failure of lawyers to respond to a client. I find it strange that lawyers must still be constantly reminded to return phone calls promptly, which to me was the same day, if the call came in the morning, or the next day, at the latest, if the call came in in the afternoon. If I could not return a telephone call promptly, I often had my assistant call to say why I could not immediately get back to the client and say when I would probably return the call. I also changed my voicemail every morning or the evening before to let my clients know my schedule, especially if I would be out of the office and not be able to return their call that day. Yes, I have made this point many times in this book, but it is so important.

My Law Society says a frequent cause of complaints, not surprisingly, is about fees. They recommend that lawyers have clear retainers, render interim accounts, and have detailed accounts. I believe lawyers could do much more, as previously discussed in section 4.13. by having more articles explaining legal fees. I also suggest having an application that can better predict the legal fees, as discussed in section 4.9 and section 5.9.

I recognized in section 3.1.5 that a major need of clients is to have their files resolved as quickly as possible. Unfortunately, lawyers are not meeting this need to many clients' satisfaction as the files' slowness is a significant client complaint. Any applications or processes that move files along more quickly would help combat this complaint.

Another frequent client complaint, seen in motor vehicle accident cases, and which I have also seen occurring in matrimonial matters, is that their lawyers often bully them into signing a settlement, usually on the courthouse steps. Clients claim they did not understand the settlement terms and believe on reflection (and, of course, after talking to friends) that they could have done better. And with all due respect, I think some judges have a role in pushing clients too much to settle on the spot. However, the lawyers are at fault for not preparing the clients to expect a last-second settlement offer and to have a strategy to deal with it beforehand. I often resisted the pressure to sign agreements at a settlement conference because I wanted to make sure the client understood the agreement and was not feeling pressured to sign. I also found these quick settlement agreements had mistakes, or they were missing some minor issues that we still had to resolve. And there was no bargaining power to deal with these minor matters if the parties had settled the main issues.

In chapter 3, I presented a Recommended Lawyer Action: "Lawyers should prioritize applications that reduce negligence claims and complaints." This element is not advantageous just to lawyers. The nature of these negligence claims and complaints shows how clients think and what they believe is important. They should therefore come first in priority, as stated in section 3.2, lawyers should recognize that what is important to lawyers may not be important to clients and what is important to clients may not be important to lawyers.

10.5 Application Ideas from List of Client Needs and Suggested Lawyer Actions

Chapter 3 sets forth some fundamental elements (Client Needs and Suggested Lawyer Actions) found in innovative legal service applications. Lawyers may think of more elements to add to this list; my list is just a starting point. Considering this list and any additions, lawyers should contemplate what application they can produce to satisfy an element. It could be an article, questionnaire, computer software program, process, physical object, or activity.

10.6 Conclusion

This chapter contains just a few basic methods of that lawyers can use to create innovative legal service applications; however, there are voluminous resources on this subject, because all businesses realize they must compete with innovative ideas in their industry. Before getting more sophisticated with focus groups and brainstorming sessions, I suggest that lawyers try my simple methods first.

The good news is that lawyers are so far behind in producing service applications they can easily copy others, and any small service improvements will make them look good, innovative, and different.

11

A Process to Implement Legal Service Applications

11.1 Proposed Steps in the Implementation Process

With the numerous ideas presented in this book, together with their own ideas, lawyers' minds will be swimming and perhaps overwhelmed with new service applications they would like to put into their practice. The question is then, "Where to begin?" I think it best if lawyers use a defined process to create and introduce applications into their law practices like the ones I have developed—and, if not my processes, then ones that they formulate themselves. The process I am now presenting in this chapter is not the one I used over my career but one I created for this book. Over my 42 years of practice, I added applications one by one, as I thought them up, primarily based on my gut feeling of client needs or if they interested me. Some lawyers may want to do the same by picking applications I have used and those they have created and slowly integrating them into their practice. I suggest a managed approach will be more productive; it will make a lawyer more focused. It will also, if lawyers use my process, start with applications with the highest value. An in-between approach could be that lawyers consider some aspects of a process and add applications across practice areas as they deem fit mostly, but not primarily, based on need.

I suggest the following steps, details of which I will discuss after listing the steps:

1. For each area of law practiced, using the form found in Appendix 11.1, which contains the list of applications that I have suggested in this book, mark on the form whether that application should be used, what value there would be if used, how long it will take to create and implement.
2. Make a list of your own applications for each practice area that you have fully or partially thought of that you believe will benefit your practice. Add these applications to the first list and complete the form noting their value and how long each would take to create and implement.
3. Mark beside each application whether you can do it quickly, in a moderate amount of time, or that it will take a long time.
4. Choose a practice area to start with after considering the principles set out hereafter in section 11.2.
5. Prioritize your list of applications for the first practice area chosen, considering the principles set out hereafter in section 11.3.
6. Work on applications in the order of priority you chose until you believe the next application on the list will take so long to do that it may be more beneficial to skip it for the time being. But if it is a high-needs application, though it may take a long time to develop, consider working on it before moving on to the next application.
7. If a new idea for an application arises from any source, add it to the original list of applications. Do not work on the new idea until the higher priority applications are completed, unless it takes almost no time to implement.
8. Review the list after adding an application and readjust the priorities if necessary.
9. After completing the first practice area, move on to the next one.
10. Rather than switching practice areas, consider implementing applications for every practice area with common applications, like the client manual, client monitor, or the New Client Memorandum. That would be appropriate if the value is high and not much time is needed to create the application.
11. Once one practice area is complete, then move on to the next prioritized practice area.

I am not trying to be overly rigid in designing this process; however, I believe there has to be some direction and focus so lawyers do not get overwhelmed preventing them from completing and implementing an application.

11.2 Choosing Which Area of Practice to Work on Applications First

As will be discussed in more detail in chapter 12, to ensure lawyers create and implement the application, it is essential to focus on one application at a time. Therefore, it is probably best to choose one practice area of law and concentrate on its applications. There are several factors to consider in selecting the practice area first. Though it may not be a certainty, it is most likely that lawyers will choose their primary law practice area. The need factor would be a major criterion to select in which practice area to start. My Client Needs and Lawyer Should Do's list would help assess what practice areas have higher client needs. Complete the Application Elements Form in Appendix 11.2 for each practice area. Lawyers could add other elements of importance. The total score would help determine what practice area they should start with and what applications should be created or introduced first. Not surprisingly, when I did this exercise, I found that family law had the highest score, followed by the administration of estates and then wills and powers of attorney. Lawyers might also consider choosing a practice area about which they may have already written articles for the public to be inserted in a manual or post to a website. Or lawyers may select areas where they have already spent time perfecting useful client questionnaires, which they can post to their website. If the proposed applications for a practice area will necessitate many hours to complete, it may be a reason to choose another practice area first; because it is important to have a sense of accomplishment. If a practice area has some applications that the lawyer could use directly or slightly modified for another practice area, they should consider choosing that area first.

11.3 Prioritizing the Order of Applications to Work on within a Practice Area

Once a lawyer chooses the first practice area to work on, she or he should prioritize the applications within that practice. This choice is made considering a variety of factors. Use the completed chart of elements in Appendix 3.2 to identify which applications are the most needed. Lawyers should look at applications that they can quickly develop because they can be easily copied or delegated to others to implement, such as indexing, line numbering, and tables of contents of documents. Lawyers can use articles previously written for a different medium (community paper or website.) Lawyers should also consider applications that were used for other practice areas. For instance, the new client memorandum will be the same for all practice areas and can stand alone even without a client manual ready for that practice area.

Finally, lawyers should consider making it a priority to work on applications that will benefit them as much as the client. Applications good for marketing or reducing negligence claims or client complaints should be considered.

I appreciate that I have provided numerous factors, so after contemplating them, go with your gut, or if that does not work, write them down and choose them blindly out of a hat—but do create a list and follow it. Plan your work, work your plan.

11.4 A Suggested Priority of Applications to Implement

Taking all the criteria outlined in section 11.3, I suggest the following priorities for any practice area: first, I would start with a client manual, even if it merely holds the letters, documentation, and accounts the client will receive over the file's lifetime, as well as a section for client notes. It should have a short introduction. Lawyers can modify my examples found in the appendix. As lawyers' biographies are probably in existence, they can be placed in the client manual. However, lawyers should redo them if they are only one paragraph, like the "dating bio" often found on websites, as I discussed in section 4.2.3. Any previously written articles still relevant should be in the client manual as well as a plastic cardholder sheet, which costs about $1, to place the lawyers' and legal assistants' business cards and the cards of any other experts for that practice area. I had business cards with my assistant's name and contact information. Legal assistants will probably be dealing with clients a lot and, in some practice areas, doing more work than the lawyer, so their valued status should at least be acknowledged to the client with an assistant's own business card. It would be nice to have a New Client Memorandum inserted in the client manual when it is first presented, but this is not essential. My example of a New Client Memorandum in Appendix 4.12.4 can be a sample that lawyers can adapt. As lawyers write more articles of interest, they can add them to the client manual.

I suggest the second priority, depending on the practice area, is the client monitor. The monitor would be a priority when the practice area involves litigation documents and agreements that clients would review and change with their lawyers. Such practice areas would be any form of litigation, especially family law. It would also be for a practice area with number-crunching, such as family law and administration of estates. I could not have practiced family law as well without the client monitor. Even when the file did not involve redrafting court documents and number crunching, I used the client monitor for to-do lists and slideshow presentations for first consultations. The slideshows are valuable applications that lawyers can start using on their website to fulfill clients' need to know their matter's process and issues.

The third priority I suggest would be implementing the many simple applications that take little or no time to create but are more of a matter of getting into the habit of doing. They would be such things as in a wills and powers of attorney practice to write to executors after the will is signed, advising where the will is being stored. If lawyers have the article already written, I would suggest that they comment on executor responsibilities with that letter. Agreements should be indexed and have a table of contents. If lawyers type out their arguments for a court appearance, they should give copies to their clients. Other applications that take little, if any, time for lawyers to create should be generated and implemented. Perhaps using my samples for ideas, first appointment letters will not be time-consuming to produce and implement. I think they are a valuable application to introduce early in the process when building up lawyers' arsenal of applications.

My next priority would be to update or create useful client questionnaires because they fulfill a high-priority need. Articles about fees and billing, another high need subject, could be produced next.

I have stated the great importance of a good law firm website. I have spent a lot of time in this book writing about websites; however, I do not suggest lawyers launch their new websites until they have enough material so that they do not look like most other lawyer websites—glorified brochures. Designing sites and writing material solely for the website is very time-consuming. As valuable as websites are, the other applications should come first. Lawyers can post much of the material from those applications as well as material written explicitly for the websites.

As discussed in chapter 3, a significant reason lawyers should create and implement service applications is that some applications will help reduce the number of complaints and negligence lawsuits against lawyers. If this is of great concern and causes stress to a lawyer, then work first on those applications that reduce negligence claims and complaints first.

11.5 Conclusion

I realize I have been all over the map with suggestions about the order in which lawyers should create and implement applications. Every lawyer has different priorities for a variety of reasons. With limited resources, especially time, lawyers cannot introduce into their practices all the service applications they have considered. Though the order of creating and implementing applications will vary from lawyer to lawyer, I suggest lawyers have a process, like the one I presented at the beginning of this chapter. It will help decide priorities. It will ensure lawyers create and implement applications and avoid the situation where too many application projects in the works delay completion of any or only a few of them.

12

Ensuring Legal Service Applications Get Created and Implemented

Some readers may find it odd to include a chapter devoted to ensuring that lawyers create and implement legal service applications. This topic seems more like a subject for a self-help book. The reason for including this subject is quite simple. Great ideas are useless if lawyers do not follow through and finish creating the applications and then put them into practice. I agree with the author of *Business Innovation for Dummies,* Alexander Hiam, when he writes that implementation is as important or sometimes more important than creating an innovative idea. Developing and implementing service applications is not typically part of a lawyer's job. I suspect some lawyers have thought of innovative lawyer service applications but have never implemented them; therefore, lawyers need to have methods to ensure they finish developing applications and put them in place.

Solo and small firm lawyers have little time to spend on application projects because they have all the office responsibilities. Associate lawyers at large firms have little time because they are expected to put in many billable hours. Large firm lawyers who are partners have limited time because they also have to put in many billable hours, do some management and marketing, and deal (argue) with their partners. So the fact that lawyers have limited time is a significant issue. Over the years there have been many books written on time management, but the solutions are much broader than just using the latest time management techniques. Theories on ensuring ideas get implemented have been the subject of many books in recent years. This chapter will briefly discuss some of the methods I used to complete more service applications. Much of what I have to say is common sense and probably used by many lawyers. Others have written numerous theories on this subject. I am presenting some techniques I used, and I want to emphasize the importance of the issue.

12.1 Focus: Do One Project at a Time

It has been a long time since I heard this story, but it is still relevant. A prominent early 20th-century industrialist hired a management consultant to advise him about how he could be more productive. The consultant recommended the industrialist make a list of 10 projects he wanted to do. The industrialist was then to do the first item on the list and not start working on the second item until he completed that first project. The industrialist was then to work on the second item. He followed the same procedure of not working on any project until he first completed the one before it. The industrialist was furious, saying, For this simple advice, I am paying you $10,000." The consultant replied, "Try it." The industrialist tried it and found to his amazement that this simple technique made him much more productive. He then happily paid the $10,000 because the advice was worth it.

In their excellent book *The 4 Disciplines of Execution,* the authors Chris McChesney, Sean Covey, and Jim Huling have a chart that says if you take on 2 to 3 projects, you will get 2 to 3 done. If you take on 4 to 10 projects, you will get 1 to 2 done, and if you take on 11 to 20 projects, you will get 0 done. Therefore, their first principle is to focus on a "Wildly Important" project and do it first. They have added prioritizing to the process, but their main point is that lawyers should not work on new applications until they have finished the first one they started.

Taking on too many projects at once was a major fault of mine. Like many people, I had too many projects I wanted to do, so I worked on many simultaneously. As a result, I fell short of getting more applications completed than if I had just focused on doing one project at a time. There was an exception: after literally years in the making, I finished my video on "Completing the Form 13.1 Financial Statement" only when

I decided not to work on any other management projects until I completed it. Besides taking on too many projects simultaneously, I also had a bad habit of buying the latest management book before finishing the book I was still reading. It was more exciting to explore a new idea than to finish reading about the one I was still learning. Lawyers must resist that natural temptation to move on to new theories or projects before finishing the ones they have started.

12.2 When to Work on Legal Service Applications

As I did, probably most lawyers work on nonfile projects at the end of a busy day. Or perhaps lawyers take service application work home, believing they will find time to work on a project after dinner and when the children are in bed. According to Daniel Pink in his book *When: The Scientific Secret of Perfect Timing*, our cognitive ability changes in a regular pattern throughout the day. I believe many people are more alert in the morning though some are night owls like Thomas Edison was. Based on Pink's theory, I changed the time of day when I worked on certain tasks. In the mornings, I found I had more brainpower to work on more challenging tasks. During the low periods, I did activities that were not as difficult mentally or forced me to find the energy, such as having client appointments.

So, I did not start my day by working on cleaning my desk and making my to-do lists but did that along with other mundane tasks at the end of the previous day. Like me, many people may often rebound after the low afternoon period, and if I did, I did more challenging tasks then.

I would suggest that a lawyer plan to work on service applications during their peak time. However, if they get that burst of energy during a usually low period, take advantage of it and do the high-energy work. I also suggest lawyers follow another principle expressed in Pink's book and espoused by others: Do the most challenging activity first.

12.3 Important but Not Urgent

There is a lot of great information in Stephen Covey's classic book *The 7 Habits of Highly Effective People.* I liked when he divided up a worker's tasks into what he calls the Time Management Matrix. He theorized that there are four categories: Urgent and Important, Not Urgent and Important, Urgent and Not Important and Not Important and Not Urgent. For example, creating service applications is important but not urgent. Unfortunately, tasks in this category do not get done so often because they are not urgent; even non-important tasks tend to get more attention than important and non-urgent tasks. Lawyers must be proactive and realize that they must make time to do these important but not urgent activities because they will be very beneficial in the long run. Therefore, lawyers should set aside time for this work. It is a simple concept but it must be accepted and used by lawyers to create innovative legal service applications.

12.4 Time Management and To-Do Lists

There are numerous books written about time management and personal to-do lists. I should know: I have many of them. I followed some time management principles as set out in this chapter, but it would be impossible to list all the different theories and systems I have read. Unfortunately, I cannot say I produced my own perfect to-do list process. I had too many to-do lists floating around on my computer and printed out in binders. However, I strongly recommend, and was pretty diligent about, writing everything down on a list. The to-do list guru David Allen, author of *Getting Things Done*, calls it "the collecting or capturing stage" of making a to-do list. Our minds can hold only so much information, and we cannot remember everything that we once put into our heads. Even if not categorizing where on the to-do lists the idea goes, writing it down ensures it will be recalled and used appropriately. It reduces the time trying to recall what you once knew and the stress caused by being upset that you cannot remember something once heard or read.

12.5 Managing Caseloads

Lawyers often take on too much work, probably more in practice areas that do not have ongoing clients or major clients that will be the source of continual business. In these one-off practice areas, lawyers are worried about where the next client will come from, even though they have good practices and referrals and their networks will always provide new clients. I knew a lawyer who was one of the best lawyers in his field, had an abundance of clients, and had an excellent referral network; yet he took on every new client possible because he was worried about obtaining new business. Too much work affected his personal life and health. I refused to take on new clients if my caseload was too high at the time, because I knew my ongoing clients would suffer, usually by my taking longer than average to complete their file. I would tell these prospective new clients I refused to take on their case because I wanted to make sure I could serve my present clients properly. Though I never measured, the effect I hoped saying that impressed them enough to wait for me or be a future referral source.

Lawyers often complain that they are overworked. There is a simple remedy for this problem. Work fewer hours. Take on fewer clients.

Follow the principle, "I can do anything, but I cannot do everything."

12.6 Kaizen: Make Small Improvements

Rome was not built in a day. A Japanese concept called *kaizen* is the theory and practice of making small improvements rather than taking on one large project. I have suggested the importance of lawyers having a superior website. A website is something lawyers can start small by just having some basic information. They can then slowly build it out each week with the addition of another article or feature. The same is true of client manuals. Lawyers can produce initial client manuals that mainly organize and hold letters and documents and then slowly add articles.

12.7 Keeping Score

A concept discussed by McChesney, Covey, and Huling in *The 4 Disciplines of Execution* is that of keeping score. Programs to lose weight have as a central component counting calories, carbohydrates, sugar, fat, protein, or whatever that particular diet program believes is the critical ingredient of reducing weight. There is a reason for this. People will act differently when they keep score and know whether they are winning or losing. They want to win. People will try harder, whether they are behind an opponent in any game or behind in the numerical goal they set for themselves when they are on a diet plan. This is the same reasoning management writers use to persuade people that they should have and measure goals.

It is not an easy task, but keeping a score works to reach goals. I was good at setting goals but not a good scorekeeper. I am sure I would have produced more applications if I had been better at keeping score. I also would have lost weight if I kept the score of what I ate.

12.8 Manage Energy and Motivation, Not Just Time

For most years of my working life, time management was a popular topic. Experts would write about and give seminars about how to manage one's time to get more done. But near the end of my career, I subscribed more to the theory as discussed in the article entitled "Manage Your Energy, Not Your Time," which was originally published in 2007 in the *Harvard Business Review* and republished in its 10 Must Reads book *On Managing Yourself*. One of the article's authors, Tony Schwartz, also wrote a book, *Be Excellent at Anything*; he has a chapter, "Sleep or Die." He and other management writers now tout that sleep is as essential as exercise and diet are for good health. Proper sleep will result in a person being more alert and able to do more complex thinking. Sleep-deprived people, which a large part of the population are, also make significant mistakes.

A significant energy drain for lawyers is stress. Amiram Elwork wrote the excellent book *Stress Management for Lawyers* that was so popular it has had three editions. The author was a psychologist who specialized in treating lawyers for many years. He points out that lawyers in some practice areas are more prone to stress than others. My primary practice area of family law is at the top of his list. I took stress management seriously, as should all lawyers.

I would also suggest that to gain energy, one must work consistently on managing motivation. And though it is obvious to say, being physically active and eating correctly also help create energy. And do not forget to floss.

12.9 Conclusion

In this chapter, I have barely scratched the surface of the theories of getting things done. Therefore, I suggest that lawyers who are serious about getting more done in their practice should read further the books or articles I have mentioned or any other of the voluminous articles and books on this subject. As well, lawyers should explore books on motivation, passion, and perseverance, which will also help ensure that service applications get created and implemented.

Being creative and producing innovative legal service applications is a management science that lawyers can learn. It is not an inherent talent that a person has when they are born. Lawyers should not beat themselves up, as I often did, if they do not follow all these numerous rules and activities. Unfortunately, I found some of the books are based on studying world-class athletes or leaders in their field of business. The average lawyer does not compete on that high level, so they do not have to follow all the principles but should be happy with doing what they can as often as possible.

13

Analytics for Application

13.1 What Is Analytics for Applications?

Analytics is the systematic collection and analysis of data to help make decisions. In my practice, I did some analysis of my services but fell far short of what I could have done now that I have had a chance to study and reflect about analytics. Lawyers gather little data other than financial numbers to evaluate their financial performance, and not on client satisfaction or product development.

Lawyers can obtain voluminous data about their website visitors from Google Analytics, which helps lawyers make decisions about the content of their law firm's website. Among other information, it is possible to obtain data about what people are searching for on Google and YouTube so lawyers can tailor the subject of articles, videos, and blogs based upon what topics people find of interest. Good webmasters can help analyze the data to make improvements to their websites. During my years of practice, I focused mainly on the data produced by my financial software, which tracked how much money I was receiving based on the different referral sources. As previously mentioned, this helped me decide whether a referral source was working. It helped me decide whether to drop or reduce the resources spent on a referral source; however, it did not tell me why a referral source was working, whereas detailed analytics such as what Google provides would have. My webmaster did take a close look at the data produced about visitors to my website and made suggestions about what to add to heavily-read articles.

Lawyers should have a comprehensive analytical program because of its benefits to them and their clients. Lawyers have a significant advantage in the analytical process compared to other businesses: they have a smaller, mostly known, and almost captive audience they can question and observe. In contrast, other businesses have thousands of anonymous buyers of their products. Lawyers also sell big-ticket products, so even small, inexpensive applications can reap significant returns because a lawyer may need to obtain only one new client from a new application to make it financially worthwhile. Making a small change affecting just a small group of people can be very beneficial for lawyers.

The process I recommend to analyze existing legal service applications is as follows:

1. Decide which highest-priority application to analyze first.
2. Decide what data needs to be collected.
3. Design the methods to obtain that data.
4. Decide when in the process to collect the data.
5. Ensure the data will be collected.
6. Collect the data.
7. Analyze the results.
8. Take action based on the analysis.

Before discussing these steps in more detail, though not in order, I will use my oldest and most beneficial analytical project as an example of this process and show the benefits I derived from it. This project analyzed many existing applications of a marketing nature at one time.

13.2 Analysis of the Website Application

Very early in my practice, I decided to analyze how well my marketing applications worked because I spent time and money using many different referral sources. It was a high-priority application because I needed more clients, and being a new lawyer in a small firm, I would have to obtain them myself. I wanted to know where best to spend my limited resources of time and money to obtain new clients, so this was a high priority. In Appendix 13.1, I have set out the many referral sources I kept track of over the years, some of which came and went.

For each file I opened, the data item collected was the reason why the client chose me as their lawyer. The method I used to collect the data was to ask my clients why they chose me as their lawyer. My assistant or I noted the referral source on their client intake form. If the source was an individual as opposed to the website or a speaking engagement, I sent a thank-you letter and placed them on my list to send a thank-you bottle of maple syrup at the winter holiday time. When the file was closed, I noted the total fee on that file. When the technology arrived in the early 1990s, my accounting program produced a report showing how much revenue each referral source generated and what percentage of total revenue that referral source represented. For many years I had to trick the program into giving me this information by disguising "referral sources" as "referring" lawyers." In later years, the legal accounting software finally woke up and produced "referral sources" and "referring lawyers" reports separately. I gathered the data without much effort. My assistant was not to open a file in the accounting system without knowing the referral source, and she was to be sure to put the correct referral code on each file opened. I tried to review the monthly reports to make sure all files billed had a proper referral code.

From these reports, I analyzed what marketing was working and what was not and then took action. The reports told me how productive the Yellow Pages advertisement was, even with the high cost of an ad, so I increased my ad's size. The report told me the radio ads brought in very little revenue, so I dropped them because they were not worth their cost. They were not overly expensive, and I did not lose money, but the cost did not equal the benefit after I considered that I had to spend time working on the files. I enjoyed making the radio ads and bringing the 8:00 a.m. news to Ottawans on a local radio station. Speaking engagements and writing articles for a local community paper did not result in much business for me, so they became a low priority. The reports showed me the high percentage of business I was getting from my website, even in the internet's early stages. That knowledge convinced me to spend more time and money developing a good website and processes to drive people to my website, otherwise known as search engine optimization.

At that time, many lawyers thought lawyer websites were a waste of their marketing dollars and their time. I remember speaking at a local lawyer technology meeting about websites as few lawyers had them.

My audience wanted to know whether websites were worth having because of the misconception that lawyers did not need one. I jokingly responded that they were not worth it, and lawyers should not spend their time having websites. I said I just liked wasting my time and money on them. I believe that misconception still exists among most lawyers.

I vacillated over having a separate referral source for returning clients and just used their original source if they returned for another matter. I later decided to record returning clients as a separate category. I believed knowing my return rate was beneficial because of my multiplier effect theory. That theory was that if I got a client from, say, my website, then because a high percentage of clients came back or referred clients to me, or did both, then obtaining that client in the first place from the website had a much higher value than it showed standing alone. Knowing my return and referral rates were high was also good for me to see that I must have been doing something right because I noticed that my clients referred clients to me and returned themselves.

I did this analysis for over 30 years and adjusted my time and money resource allocations based on these reports. When I saw the decline of business from the Yellow Pages, I spent less on ads until I stopped using them entirely. If I no longer advertised in a community paper, I dropped that category. I added a category in later years, which was slightly narrower than just "returning client." I had a category for when I obtained an estate client when I had done the deceased's will. It confirmed it was wise to have reasonably priced wills because I would eventually get the estate work. My fees for wills and powers of attorney were not the lowest, but I kept them below the average and median price charged by others, knowing I had a good chance of obtaining the well-paying estate work later in my practice.

Though almost all the data would come from clients, it is possible to open up some data gathering to prospective clients by having some questionnaires on the website and inviting visitors who may not become clients to answer questions. Because of my extensive library of articles, I had many website visitors from other parts of Ontario and even from different jurisdictions. At one point, I had a prize for a person at random who answered my legal quiz questions. One winner was from California, so I gave him money to buy tickets to a Dodgers baseball game rather than the Ottawa Senator hockey tickets I gave to locals.

13.3 What Data Should Lawyers Collect?

The type of data collected depends on whether the application is already in use or is in development. Unless it is a significant and expensive proposed application, the best way to evaluate a proposed application is to try it out, collect responses, and analyze those responses. Perhaps a focus group's feedback on the proposal is a good idea for a significantly expensive application. However, it is essential to consider that what people say and how they act can be different.

I will discuss only an application already in use. The data that I suggest may be collected based on an existing application are the following:

Do the clients use the application?

Yes, or no? Ask clients if they read the articles on the websites or in the client manual. Observe whether clients completed the questionnaires.

How valuable did the clients find the application?

Ask clients how useful the application was on a scale of 1 to 10.

If the client did not use the application, why not?

Ask the client why they did not use the Application. For example, perhaps the article was too long, not understandable, or there was just too much information.

How can the application be improved?

Ask the client how the lawyer can change the application to make it easier to use or add more information.

If it is an application the lawyer routinely uses, how often is it used?

Count the number of times the lawyer forgets to use the application or finds it is not helpful.

How valuable does the lawyer find the application?

Does the lawyer find the application saves time and/or seems valuable to the client? Rate the value.

How much time do lawyers and their staff spend using the application?

Does it take a lot of time for the lawyer to write an article?

How much money does the lawyer spend to create and maintain an application?

What does it cost for the webmaster to provide and analyze website statistics? For example, how much does a particular advertisement cost?

What revenue does an application generate?

Calculate the amount of revenue generated from certain marketing activities.

How likely will the client recommend the lawyer to others?

This question seems to be very popular and tracked heavily by some law firms and many businesses. Sometimes, it is the only question asked, as if the answer is all the lawyer needs to know. However, I do not get it. How does that question help improve client service? It is nice for the lawyer to know they did a good enough job that their client would refer clients and, alternatively, alert the lawyer they have a problem if the client says they would not refer the client. But it will be too late to do anything if the client says they would not refer if they are asked after the file is complete.

Does the client believe that the lawyer did everything to solve their problem?

Like the previous question, this is now a popular question asked, particularly by tech support departments. However, to be of value, this question must be asked at various stages of the life of the file, not only at its end.

13.4 Methods for Collecting Data

There are several methods for collecting the data needed to analyze applications. The first is to ask the client some specific questions by way of written questionnaires. I had a questionnaire on my website for each of my practice areas, where I asked questions about what my clients thought of my articles on my website, which I suggested they read before the first appointment. I asked whether the articles were too long, too short, interesting, understandable, and what other topics of interest I should write on. I asked if they had any difficulty filling out the questionnaires. I asked them whether they thought the fees set out in my fee schedule were reasonable. I reviewed their answers before their appointment if I received them beforehand, which I usually did, or at their consultation if I received them then. At their appointment, we discussed their feedback.

I also invited clients to give me oral feedback. I realize now I should have been more forceful and specific. If I spent any time discussing how to improve my practice, I would always say I was stopping the billable hour clock, so clients were not charged for time discussing my practice.

However, the feedback can actually be different from what really does take place. For example, some clients may be afraid to be critical, and their true beliefs are shown more by action than words.

Lawyers can obtain relevant data from their financial records, such as the revenue generated from a particular referral source, as well as costs for specific applications such as placing an advertisement.

A significant opportunity to collect a lot of accurate data is to have a formalized exit interview at or near each file's end with either any client who wishes to do so or with a selected number of clients. I, unfortunately, did not do this, though it was on my wish list for years. Obviously, it would be on my time, and clients would get a slight reduction in fees or a gift certificate for participating. I like the idea of a gift certificate more, so fees do not have to be adjusted, and a client can decide to do the exit interview later without my having to refund money. Lawyers should compensate clients for helping to improve their practice. I recommend a very detailed questionnaire for the clients to fill out beforehand about every service application asking most of the questions set out in section 13.3. It should take place in the office, by phone, or preferably by videoconferencing as, since COVID-19, we have become so accustomed to virtual meetings. The videoconference could be at night or on weekends, which would be more convenient for clients and would eliminate travel time to the office.

Concerning the physical data collection and analysis, sophisticated computer software can collect and sort the data. I had hoped to see, but have not seen, a legal case management software company create a survey analysis component. Those case management programs already have the information about clients and the law firm's finances, so I think it should not be that hard to produce an analytics add-on feature.

13.5 When to Collect the Data

Using my Performance Questionnaire, I formally collected data at the beginning and at the end of the file. I was always receptive and encouraged feedback throughout the file; however, I realize now I should have had a formal performance questionnaire and a specific application questionnaire at the end of each major stage of the file's life, starting with one after the critical first consultation. I think that application would resolve any lawyer-client issues. The question, *Did you feel the lawyer did everything to solve your problem?* would be more relevant. Lawyers would obtain more data because some clients will not bother filling out questionnaires after the file is over. The data obtained would be more accurate, being closer in time to the event. If a client were not using an application (e.g., hadn't read an article they probably should have), the lawyer would know and either discuss the matter orally or ask the client to read the article. Having feedback after major events would make the exit interview easier and less time-consuming; the client would already have given some information. However, they would be given the opportunity to update or change some opinions.

It is essential not to overdo the number of times lawyers ask clients to complete a survey. I do not appreciate that every time I have the slightest interaction with many companies, they ask me to complete a performance questionnaire. Lawyers should not send out performance questionnaires after each consultation but only after they finish the main steps.

13.6 How to Ensure Data Is Captured

I found that most of my wills clients filled out my Performance Questionnaires and many clients filled out the first questionnaires about my website, but many family law clients did not fill out Performance Questionnaires. I believe (hope) it was not because of not being happy with me but rather that they were fatigued from filling out questionnaires and wanting no more to do with their matrimonial matter.

Every month, I get a letter or a call from companies to see if I will answer questions about a new product or service or about political issues. Sometimes they want 20 minutes of my time. I always ask, "What is in it for me?" They say I am helping either a product or political cause, or I have a chance to win an iPad. Usually, the odds of winning the iPad are not laid out, so I suspect I would have better odds of being struck by lightning than winning an iPad I don't need anyway.

For many clients, like myself, there must be something the lawyer can offer them to encourage them to fill out these questionnaires; therefore, I suggest a prize for best ideas, a random draw for some preliminary questionnaires, and gift certificates for all clients who participate in a comprehensive extended exit interview.

For questionnaires that clients are to complete during the life of the file, lawyers can ask the client to answer the questionnaire orally, with the lawyer recording the client's answers. Their replies will go a long way to improve service to them and other clients.

13.7 In What Priority Should Application Analytics Be Applied?

My criteria for prioritizing where analytics provide the best value in applications include the following:

- **a.** how important it is to know whether the application is working because of its high resource costs, of both time and money;
- **b.** how easy it to do a cost-benefit analysis of using the application;
- **c.** how easy it is to define the data;
- **d.** how easy it is to collect the data;
- **e.** how time-consuming it is co collect the data and do the analysis;
- **f.** whether the analysis will analysis produce good ideas to improve the practice; and
- **g.** whether the data personalize the service to help the lawyer better serve that particular client.

13.8 The Benefits of Application Analytics

There are many benefits for lawyers who use application analytics in their practice. The main one is that lawyers will obtain information from their clients about whether they are using the legal service application and whether the application is working. If the application is found not to be working, then the analytics may produce information that can improve it. Improvement to a working application can also be an outcome. Perhaps the client is not using the application correctly so that the lawyer can explain it better. Alternatively, the data may show that the cost is greater than the benefit of the application, so the lawyer may decide to drop it and other applications which are not being used or are of little value to clients.

Lawyers will make better decisions using actual data rather than relying on a few anecdotal incidents and their gut feelings.

Requesting client feedback shows clients that lawyers are concerned about the service in general and about each individual client. In addition, excellent reviews allow clients to easily thank lawyers for their service and give them some positive feedback. That is something they (especially family law lawyers) need and do not get often.

As legal products are comparable and all law firms have access to the same technology, lawyers will have to compete by way of superior processes in all aspects of their practice. Using analytics to improve service applications will get lawyers used to the analytics concept and perhaps encourage them to use analytics to make other business decisions. Lawyers could analyze the many financial reports legal accounting software provides and the numerous data that website analytics produces.

Finally, I would note that none of my close colleagues in Ottawa have any performance questionnaires. I also understand that fewer than 50 percent of lawyers ask for client feedback about their services; so, what does that say about the fact that most of our profession does not care what our clients think of the quality of our services? Lawyers have to change their image. At least asking for feedback on their services is a good start.

PART 5
Conclusion

14

Closing Remarks

14.1 Introduction

Congratulations on making it this far in the book, even if you have skipped over some chapters. Though I have bought many management books over the years, I rarely made it to the end of many of them, even the good ones.

I hope you found this book useful, insightful, readable, entertaining, and motivational. I hope I have persuaded you to pursue a practice full of innovative and improved service applications for your clients. I hope you have learned some theories behind the legal service applications and the processes so you can discover, create, implement, and evaluate them. I hope you will soon implement into your practice many of the applications presented in this book or create new ones of your own. I know that not everyone will agree with some of the theories and suggestions put forth in this book, and I may be wrong, but I have presented, based on my experiences, how I see the state of legal services. I could have named the book *The World According to Pascoe* but settled on a more conventional title.

I thought I had implemented many applications throughout my law practice, but while working on this book, I discovered I had only scratched the surface of the endless possible improvements and innovations that I alone could have used. As a result, I have put forth applications that had not previously entered my mind. That is not to say that lawyers must try and implement as many new applications as possible in a short period; as previously stated, "I can do anything, just not everything." Lawyers must pace themselves, and it is better to have completed one than partially finish ten applications. Lawyers should not be discouraged when an application is a failure. Not every application is going to work. Just as lawyers lose cases in court, lawyers will have unsuccessful applications; that is part of being in business. And again, sorry for the cliché, but "What does not kill you makes you stronger."

There are a few related subjects I would like to discuss, followed by some final words.

14.2 The Importance of Reading Management Books

In the 1980s, starting for me with *In Search of Excellence*, business management books of all kinds became popular. This was not so much the case for law office management books. A friend working with a major Canadian law book publisher told me years ago that Canadian law book companies did not publish many law office management books because they did not sell. I have seen law office periodicals in Canada and the United States come and go during my years of practice; but though they are still far from the top of the best-selling lists, business books, including ones on law office management, must be selling well enough because they are still being produced. There is no shortage of material on law practice management. Numerous books and electronic magazines are being published by the American Bar Association (ABA), small publishers, and self-publishers. Then there is the large volume of material the governing law associations produce to help their members better manage their law firms. The information lawyers need to be innovative and run the law office like a good business is out there.

The main reason for lawyers to read management books is to obtain the knowledge and learn specific applications to improve their practices, but there are other good reasons. It is trite to say that the world is changing. New ways of doing things and new theories are being introduced daily by businesses as they strive to improve their product, production, or marketing to stay ahead of the competition. There seems to be more studying of human behavior, and companies are using analytics to make decisions rather than relying on long-held assumptions that may no longer be valid or were never adequately analyzed in the first place. Lawyers, therefore, need to read management and specifically (but not exclusively) law practice management books to ensure they are not falling behind but rather thriving using the latest management theories and technology.

When I read a book, I found that the author often suggested an application or minor action I had already put into practice. That reference validated what I had been doing. Besides feeling good that I had figured it out myself and put it in place, the reference motivated and inspired me to continue to produce and improve applications. Also, when reading something not related to law, I got an idea of how it could be adjusted to apply to a law practice. I hope reading this book will similarly motivate lawyers to read more general and law office management books and create and implement legal service applications.

14.3 How Can Lawyers Evolve?

In the first chapter, I discussed why lawyers collectively and individually have not evolved very much. To evolve more, I suggest the following: First, lawyers must change their culture. They must accept that they are a service business and must learn and then use standard business practices and not be such snobs about acting like a business. Interestingly, lawyers generally do not advertise their prices in advertisements or on their websites, as if it would be beneath them to talk about money upfront, but then they spend a lot of money on flashy advertisements and billboards. So, they can easily act as a business when they want.

Second, all law schools and Bar admission programs, where they still exist, should have courses on all aspects of running a business. However, as discussed in chapter 1, only about 30 percent of law schools have classes in Law Office Management, and the subject is nonexistent in Bar exams, and even then, the law school courses are generally not extensive. Most schools I surveyed do not have exams for these courses; rather, the courses are pass/fail, or students pass by just showing up to class. Bar associations and law societies' continuing education programs should increase the number of business-related courses they offer and should require lawyers to take more hours devoted to business-related classes. In addition, law school courses should employ (at the same salary as their professors) lawyers who have had years working as practicing lawyers to teach substantive classes on the practice of law. I interviewed a law school that said they used to have a law office management course but had to cancel it because they had no one to teach it. Perhaps the law school offered only a pittance to the person who would teach it. It is a known practice for universities to give part-time lecturers from the real-world small honorariums to teach rather than give them respect and the salary they deserve.

If law schools or bar associations do not offer these courses, individual lawyers should take it upon themselves to read more general business books and law practice management books and periodicals. In addition, they should join the ABA Law Practice Division and attend conferences devoted to law practice management or business conferences for business in general.

The last impediment to lawyers evolving is the toughest and yet, in some ways, the easiest to overcome. The main reason that lawyers do not spend time improving their service applications is that they claim they have no time left after producing their service and carrying out the essential law office management functions. Lawyers should set aside time, almost every day, to develop and implement applications to improve their service to clients. It may, in the short term, reduce a lawyer's total billings. I say "may" because perhaps the enjoyment of working on a new application will, in fact, produce personal energy, resulting in the lawyer working more productive hours, and perhaps, the new application will bring in more clients. More clients to choose from will result in the ability to say no to difficult potential clients who are often less profitable.

14.4 The Advantage of Using Innovative Legal Service Applications

Lawyers who create a practice with innovative legal services and improved client services have a real advantage over other lawyers and other businesses doing legal work that do not embrace innovation.

Because the legal culture frowns upon acting like a business and embracing change, many lawyers are dinosaurs who will never evolve. However, those who embrace change and have improved services will stand out to the public and attract more clients.

Many new service applications exist, so lawyers do not have to invent them but simply copy what other law firms use. Business practices cannot be copyrighted. Because law practices are very localized, no one will know if another lawyer uses an application in a city 100 miles away or even, probably, in the same town. For suitable service applications used in other types of businesses, lawyers can just modify them to suit a law practice. Finally, the legal profession lags so far behind other businesses in the client service applications that any slight improvement using applications from any source will make a lawyer look good.

14.5 Some Last Words

In the Opening Remarks to this book, I observed that lawyers have not changed and improved how they serve their clients, compared to the banking industry, another age-old conservative service business. But lawyers should compare themselves to all types of businesses, many of which have evolved tremendously. Take the automobile industry. When the car was invented in 1885, it originally comprised a little more than an open-air carriage, four wheels, a steering mechanism, a braking system, and an engine. The automobile's purpose was to travel from point A to point B. Now, 125 years later, the automobile's objective is still to get from point A to point B, but that trip has dramatically improved for the user. The automobile is enclosed with heating and air conditioning systems for comfort, automatic transmission, power steering and braking, making driving easier. There are entertainment and navigational systems, many safety features, and a control panel full of information. If there is any leftover space, the car manufacturer has inserted a cup holder, USB port, or storage space. And soon, probably most cars will be self-driving. A lot of the evolution of the automobile came from advances in automobile technology; but radios, heating systems, air conditioning, navigational systems, and cup holders were independently invented and not initially for the car. A cup holder is pretty low-tech and not sophisticated, but it is convenient. There are many ways of improving the delivery of legal services. Lawyers must just put their minds to it.

Several years ago, I spoke at the Law Society of Ontario's Annual Solo and Small Firm Conference about some innovative applications discussed in this book, such as my client manuals. The conference chair thanked me for presenting my ideas to other lawyers and asked why I was willing to share such good marketing information with other lawyers. That was a subject she said Toronto lawyers did not share. I told her there were three reasons:

1. It was part of my personal mission statement to help other lawyers improve their practice.
2. I said I had been in practice long enough to feel secure that I would still have enough work to keep me busy, even if other lawyers using my applications took potential clients away from me.
3. I reminded her that I was speaking to lawyers and, therefore, very few will get off their rear ends and do any of the things I suggested they do, so I did not fear a possible loss of business.

My wish is that many lawyers will prove me wrong about the third reason, and those reading this book will take action and do it soon. Lawyers should accept that they are in business—a noble and exceptional business—that helps people navigate through life's major and sometimes most traumatic events. Life is getting more complicated. Other businesses have risen to the challenge by inventing and improving products and services to deal with life's many changes - why should lawyers not do so also. From my experience, doing so will benefit both clients and lawyers.

Good luck, and I thank you for listening.

Resources

Allen, David. *Getting Things Done: The Art of Stress-Free Productivity.* New York: Penguin Putman Inc., 2001.

Beckwith, Harry. *Selling the Invisible.,* New York: Warner Books, 1997.

Belsky, Scott. *Making Ideas Happen: Overcoming the Obstacles Between Vision & Reality.,* New York: Penguin, 2010.

Covey, Steven. *The Seven Habits of Highly Effective People.* New York: Simon & Schuster Ltd., 1989.

Clio. *2020 Legal Trend Report.* www.clio.com

Clio. *Why Lawyers are Moving to the Cloud.* www.clio.com

Drucker, Peter F. *Innovation and Entrepreneurship: Practice and Principles.* New York: Harper & Row Publishers, 1985.

Elwork, Amiram. *Stress Management for Lawyers (3rd edition).* North Wales, Pennsylvania: Vorkell Group, 2007.

Gladwell, Malcolm. *Blink, The Power of Thinking Without Thinking.* New York: Little Brown and Company, 2005.

Harvard Business Review. On Managing Yourself. Boston: Harvard Business School Publishing Corporation, 2010.

Heath, Chip, and Dan Heath. *The Power of Moments.* New York: Simon & Schuster, 2017.

Hiam, Alexander. *Business Innovation for Dummies.* New Jersey: Wiley Publishing, Inc., 2010.

Johnson, Steve. *Where Good Ideas Come From.* New York: Riverhead Books, 2010.

Lawyer Professional Indemnity Insurance Company. *Law Pro Magazine.* May 2019

Keiningham, Timothy L., Terry G. Vavra, Lerzan Aksoy, and Henri Wallard. *Loyalty Myths: Hyped Strategies That Will Put You Out of Business and Proven Tactics That Really Work.* New Jersey: Wiley, 2005.

Kiernan, Matthew J. *Get Innovative or Get Dead.* Vancouver: Douglas and McIntyre, 1995.

McChesney, Chris, Sean Covey, and Jim Huling. *The 4 Disciplines of Execution.* New York: Free Press, 2012.

Newton, Jack. *The Client-Centered Law Firm.* London: Blue Check Publishing, 2021.

Nischwitz, Jeffrey L. *Think Again! Innovative Approaches to the Business of Law.* Chicago: American Bar Association Book Publishing, 2007.

Peters, Tom. *Thriving on Chaos: Handbook for Management Revolution,* New York: Alfred A. Knopf, Inc., 1988.

Pink, Daniel H., *When, The Scientific Secrets of Perfect Timing.* New York: Riverhead Books, 2017.

Ries, Al, and Jack Trout. *The 22 Immutable Laws of Marketing: Violate Them at Your Own Risk!,* New York: Harper Collins, 1988.

Riskin, Gerald A. *The Successful Lawyer.* Chicago: The Law Practice Management Section of the American Bar Association, 2005.

Schwartz, Tony. *Be Excellent at Anything.* New York: Free Press, 2010.

Stickdorn, Marc, and Jakob Schneider. *This is Service Design Thinking.* New Jersey: John Wiley & Sons, Inc., 2011.

Trout, Jack, and Steve Rivkin. *Differentiate or Die.* New York: John Wiley & Sons, Inc., 2000.

Ulwick, Anthony W. *What Consumers Want: Using Outcome-Driven Innovation to Create Breakthrough Products and Services.* New York: McGraw-Hill, 2005.

Appendix

The Appendix mainly contains samples of some of my applications presented in this book and used by me when I practiced or drafted for this book. They are to show the type of content and format that lawyers can use for applications. These samples should not be used directly as precedents but should be modified by lawyers to fit their particular practices and jurisdictions. Some of the applications are presented in a Microsoft Word table format when I actually used them in Excel. It was easier to present them in this book in a table format.

A 2.1 Ontario Malpractice Errors for All Practice Areas by Percentage of Claims 2009–2019

	2014	**2015**	**2017**	**2018**	**Average/4**	**Average/10**
Communications	26	28	27	26	25	32
Inadequate Investigation	21	20	23	21	21	18
Time Management	21	18	18	17	18	15
Knowing, Applying the Law	15	15	16	15	15	18
Other	4	7	6	10	6	4
Clerical Error	7	6	6	6	6	3
Conflict of Interest	2	4	4	3	3	6
Fraud	0	1	0	8	2	4

A 2.2 Ontario Malpractice by Practice Area by Percentage of Claims 2008–2018 Averages

	Wills & Estates	Family Law	Real Estate	Civil Litigation	Criminal	Corporate
Communications	28	39	41	18	36	40
Inadequate Investigation	33	9	29	15	6	18
Time Management	8	10	0	16	4	0
Knowing, Applying the Law	15	22	7	11	39	14
Other	3	9	6	6	11	15
Clerical Error	8	7	7	4	4	0
Conflict of Interest	5	4	5	0	0	13
Fraud	0	0	5	0	0	0

A 4.12.4 New Client Memorandum

LAWRENCE PASCOE NEW CLIENT MEMORANDUM

I want to introduce you to my staff and to advise you about some of my office management practices related to our lawyer/client relationship.

<u>JENNY SMITH</u>

My legal assistant is Jenny Smith. Jenny works on all my files. She looks after Wills and the Administration of Estates, as well as the Matrimonial files.

If I am unavailable to take your telephone call, please speak with Jenny. Remember, however, that she is not allowed to give legal advice. You should always email me and not Jenny with your questions. Often Jenny will send emails on my behalf. If she does, please ensure you copy me when replying to that email.

<u>COMMUNICATIONS</u>

A vital element of a good lawyer-client relationship is good communication. That is why I have developed my manual system, which provides written information and a process to ensure clients receive copies of all correspondence and documentation stored in a convenient location. My policy is that clients receive copies of all correspondence and documentation relating to their file as soon as our office receives them. I also like to do extensive reporting letters to summarize the status of my clients' files.

<u>TELEPHONE AND CELL PHONE</u>

I generally take calls between 8:30 a.m. and 5:00 p.m. if I am not with clients or have not put my phone on "Do Not Disturb" while I focus on getting some specific work done as I often do in the early mornings or after 5:00 p.m.

I try to return my calls the same day. If not, I will return the call the next day. If you call in the late afternoon, I will try to return your call that day; however, as I might be in Court in the afternoons or have clients late in the day, I cannot always return calls on the same day.

If you cannot get a hold of me and it is an emergency, please call my assistant. She will assess whether there is a need for me to get back to you as soon as possible.

As previously stated, my assistant is not allowed to provide any legal advice. You are welcome to speak with her to make appointments or to hear a status report on your file, or if you cannot reach me and believe it is an emergency.

We have a client-friendly voicemail system that allows you to leave short messages if Jenny or I am unavailable or if it is an after-hours call. My extension is 117, and Jenny's is 101. If you wish to bypass our greetings, you may press # # and leave your message.

As my wife will attest, I do not always have my cell phone on though you can try my cell phone (613-7XX-XXXX) in an emergency. It is not a reliable method of getting to me. Emails have a better chance of getting a hold of me though I do not always check my email after hours.

EMAIL AND WEBSITE

Even though I have an Apple iPhone and email at home and the office, I do not check my mail every time a message comes in.

So an email sent at 9:00 a.m. is not like a telephone call at 9:00 a.m. I may not see the email for a few hours.

Though you may email me at any time, please do not assume that I will look at it until business hours that day or the next day. If the email arrives on the weekend, I may not look at them until Monday, though I often look at my emails Sunday morning.

Email rather than long voicemails is the best way to ask small questions and give me facts rather than long voicemails. I do often answer my emails in the early morning before work.

Please do not reply to my assistant's email address unless she is asking you for something. My process is that my assistant automatically forwards you any correspondence received by my office and letters that I wrote. There have been several incidents where clients have written to me but used my assistant's email. My assistant had gone for the day, so I do not get emails that needed my immediate attention. There is a bolded reminder right in my assistant's email.

From time to time, I will review emails in the evening or early morning, in which case I may send a reply to you from my home email account. That account is pascoexxx@xxxx.com. Please try not to respond to my home account, but rather to my work account: lspascoe@xxxx.com.

Please try not to repeat the long threads of an email when it is unnecessary to do so. Just the last email that I wrote should be in the thread.

My email is checked by my staff when I am on vacation but handled only in emergencies. The same is the process for voicemail when I am on vacation.

- My email address is lspascoe@thepascoedifference.com.
- My website is http://www.thepascoedifference.com, and I invite you to visit my site as there is a lot of useful information on it.

STATUS REPORTS

Please feel free to email or phone me and ask me for a status report if you think something should be happening on your file. You do not have to wait to hear from me. There is no charge for a simple status report if that is all we discuss. If you have not heard from me by the time you think you should have, please feel free to contact my office.

Please remember that many factors that are entirely out of my control will affect how long a file will take. The court system has built-in delays; often, I am waiting for the spouse or the other lawyer to respond. It sometimes takes some time to complete a file (though not as long as it seems to see a doctor in this province).

You may not know this, but at any one time, I may have 70 open files. There may be 30 files in which I have work I can do. Therefore I cannot work on every file immediately or at the time I want. A third of my day I have found that I devote to appointments, a third to unplanned calls and emails, and only a third for planned work.

So it takes time to get work done, and therefore it takes time to complete a file when the other built-in delays by other parties are taken into account, including my own client's delays in getting me information. I attempt to get things done as soon as possible. I have implemented processes such as having good precedents and doing dictations on the spot to move a file along, but the reality is that some files simply take a lot of time to complete.

ELECTRONIC STORAGE OF FILES

It has been my practice to retain all my files rather than discard them after a certain number of years. However, after many years of practicing law, I now realize it is impractical to continue to store physical files. Therefore, I am currently scanning everything on new files. I will keep your present file electronically and a closed file for fifteen years from the file's closing.

Therefore, for at least fifteen years from when the file closed, I can provide you with documents you may require but have lost. At your last consultation, we will review your file to ensure you take back any original documentation I might still have.

FOLLOW UP SERVICES

I am pleased to tell you that I provide my clients with several free services even after completing your file. They are as follows:

- I will provide free swearing of Affidavits or Statutory Declarations for Ontario documents for my clients. You made need this for insurance claims and when one receives a bequest under a Will. I just ask that you complete your forms beforehand and you make an appointment to sign with either my assistant or me. Please do not sign the documents until your appointment.
- If I still possess them, I will provide any digital copies of any important documents such as Wills, Powers of Attorney, Court Orders, Agreements, and Certificates of Appointments, if misplaced.
- My website has replacement forms for your Will and Powers of Attorney Manuals. They are found at: http://www.thepascoedifference.com/pdfs/willmanualforms.pdf
- In matrimonial matters, I provide up to half an hour of free follow-up oral legal advice.
- My website has a sample Consent to Travel Form, which I will witness for free for a client or a client's former spouse if the client calls to make an appointment and has the form filled out.
- I will hold on to the completed Will information forms in your digital file.
- I will hold on to your Will in my fireproof safe.

- I will recommend or help you find a lawyer in Ottawa for an area of law you may need but that I do not practice.
- I am available to provide legal services to your friends and relatives.
- My comprehensive website has many articles on Family Law, Wills, Powers of Attorney, and the Administration of Estates.

OTHER AREAS OF PRACTICE

I practice in the areas of Family Law, which includes Separation and Divorce and Marriage Contracts, Wills and Powers of Attorneys, and the Administration of Estates. I do not handle Estate Litigation.

REFERRALS ARE APPRECIATED

Your referrals of family and friends (or even people you do not like) are also welcome. Word of mouth advertising is an essential element of my and any lawyer's practice. If you are happy with my services, please tell the world (and if you are not, please tell me).

CLIENT INFORMATION FORM

To continue our relationship, I will retain your detailed data to serve you better on a going-forward basis. On my website on my forms page, http://www.thepascoedifference.com/forms-general.html, I have a Change of Information Form, which I would ask that you use when any of your information changes. Alternatively, you may email my assistant with any change of contact information. It is always a good idea to ensure that your contact information remains current with us, especially if we are holding your Will.

CLIENT COMMENTS AND SUGGESTIONS

I have always been open to my clients' suggestions to improve my services and have actively sought their opinions. That is why I have had my survey contest since 1993. The winner that year was a client who suggested I learn about this new technology I had not heard about yet. He told me about "the internet." I particularly welcome client feedback as to how to improve my follow-up services. I annually award Ottawa Senators Hockey tickets for the best suggestion. If you have any questions or comments concerning my communication policy, I would be pleased to hear from you.

A 5.1.2.1 Index to Volume 1 of the Family Law Client Manual

FAMILY LAW CLIENT MANUAL PART 1

Index

Accounts
10. Notes
Other LSP Articles Manual on the Website
Custody/Access Assessments
Custody and Access
Division of Assets
Mediation
Checklist for Separation Agreements
Support
The Spousal Support Advisory Guidelines

A 5.1.2.2 Index to Volume 2 of the Family Law Client Manual

1. Client's Pleadings
1.1 Cumulative Table of Contents of Continuing Record
1.2
2. Spouse's Pleadings
2.1
3. Mandatory Information Program (MIP)
3.1 Information Memorandum
4. Client's Case Conference Material
4.1. Client's Case Conference Brief
4.2. Map of Court House Showing Parking
4.3. Memorandum to Client Attending at a Case Conference
4.4. Copy of LSP Oral Arguments
5. Spouse's Case Conference Brief
6. Client's Motion Material
6.1. Memorandum to Client Attending at a Motion
6.2. Client's Motion Material – Notice of Motion, Affidavit
6.3. Copy of LSP Oral Arguments

7. Spouse's Motion Material – Notice of Motion, Affidavit
8. Client's Settlement Conference Material
8.1. Memo to Client Attending at a Settlement Conference
8.2. Client's Settlement Conference Brief
8.3. Copy of LSP Oral Arguments
9. Spouse's Settlement Conference Brief
10. Questioning
10.1 Memorandum to Clients Regarding a Questioning
10.2 Copy of LSP Questions

A 5.1.2.3 Index to Marriage Contract/Cohabitation Agreement Manual

MARRIAGE CONTRACT/COHABITATION MANUAL INDEX

1. Introduction
1.1 Lawrence S. Pascoe New Client Memorandum
1.2 Marriage Contract Cohabitation Agreement Process
2. Letters
3. Client's Financial Statement and Financial Disclosure
4. Other side's Financial Statement and Financial Disclosure
5. Retainer and Accounts
6. Agreements (Drafts and Final)
7. Notes

A 5.1.2.4 Introduction to the Family Law Client Manual

INTRODUCTION TO THE FAMILY LAW CLIENT MANUAL VOLUME 1

I have developed a Family Law Client Manual as I believe that clients can contribute better to their case if they are fully aware of the written material that the file contains. Therefore, I give copies of all relevant documentation and letters to my clients on a timely basis.

The manual also contains information in the form of articles and memoranda written by me. They explain the law and the procedures of the various steps in the process concisely. Although I will cover many subjects orally during this case, I believe having written memoranda ensures that my clients have a written record of all important matters. Not only will this enable the client to assist in developing the case, but it will also save my time and hence, the client's money.

As I receive documentation and letters, I will send you copies. The manual will serve as a convenient place to store material. I have given you a three-hole punch if you did not have one to assist you in inserting the documents in your manual. If you wish, you may write into the index the documents you receive. Alternatively, on my website, there is an index in digital format. You can download it and then insert the names of documents digitally when you receive them.

Several articles in my Family Law packet or other articles on my website can be downloaded and put in the manual. As some of those articles may not be relevant to your case, and to help the environment, I have not reprinted them all for the manual. I have just listed them in the manual index. If you printed the whole packet as many clients do, I would suggest that you insert them in the manual.

Please bring your manual to your appointments, as I will often be adding material at your meeting.

A 5.4 Matrimonial First Consultation Slideshow

MATRIMONIAL INITIAL CONSULTATION LAWRENCE S. PASCOE
IDENTIFICATION 1. Explain need and requirement for identification 2. Obtain copy of driver's license or photo identification
INTRODUCTION (Explain what this consultation hopes to achieve) 1. Explain the basic principles of Family Law 2. Obtain basic facts 3. Understand what client wants to achieve 4. Obtain more detailed facts 5. Give basic opinion as to what client wants to achieve 6. Advise as to legal process 7. Discuss Lawyer-Client Relationship 8. Discuss Fees and Payment 9. Advise as to ancillary issues 10. Produce a letter to spouse or spouse's lawyer 11. Confirm what lawyer and client will each do next and set next appointment 12. Confirm what information and documents client must obtain
THREE MAIN ASPECTS OF CONSULTATION 1. Substantive Law 2. Process 3. Lawyer-Client Relationship
OBTAIN BASIC FACTS 1. Review and complete basic matrimonial questionnaire
ADVISE CLIENT OF BASIC LAW 1. Three areas of substantive law a. Custody and Access b. Equalization of Assets c. Child and Spousal Support 2. General principles for each area of law

OBTAIN WHAT CLIENT WANTS AND SUPPORTING FACTS 1. Obtain particulars of what relief client wants in a settlement 2. Obtain specific facts
WHAT FURTHER INFORMATION IS NEEDED FROM CLIENT TO OBTAIN RELIEF REQUESTED 1. Sign actuarial direction if a pension is to be valued 2. Provide client with a checklist of information and documentation to
REVIEW ISSUES, GIVE OPINION OF POSSIBILITY OF OBTAINING RELIEF REQUESTED 1. Record in notes the major advice given, generally what chances are to obtain relief requested based on information given
THE PROCESS 1. Advise as to the processes available to resolve the matter a. Client/Client b. Mediation c. Collaborative Law d. 5-way meeting (Mediator, clients, lawyers) e. Lawyer/Lawyer f. Court
THE LAWYER-CLIENT RELATIONSHIP 1. Discuss the lawyer-client relationship
THE FAMILY LAW CLIENT MANUAL 1. Provide and explain the Family Law Client Manual 2. Print out Client's blank Financial Statement
LEGAL FEES 1. Discuss Legal Fees - possible costs and method of payment 2. Explain written retainer 3. Explain legal fees article in manual 4. Obtain credit card authorization

ANCILLARY ISSUES 1. Reconciliation 2. Marriage counselling 3. Tax 4. Child Tax Benefit 5. Dating other people 6. Name change 7. Canada Pension Plan 8. Will, Life Insurance RRSPs. TFSAs, house ownership 9. Credit cards, bank accounts, loans 10. Limitation Periods 11. Personal counseling 12. Expectations 13. Enforcement 14. Offers and Binding Agreements
LETTER TO SPOUSE/LAWYER Draft letter to spouse or spouse's lawyer if applicable
REVIEW TO-DO'S 1. Client to-do list 2. Lawyer to-do list 3. Set next appointment date
REQUISITION TO OPEN FILE FORM 1. Complete requisitioned open file form 2. Provide LSP magnet
QUESTIONS 1. Confirm client has no further questions at this time

A 5.6 First Appointment Letter for Matrimonial Client

Date

VIA EMAIL TO:

Dear X:

Re: Your Appointment

I wish to confirm that you have an appointment with me on x, at x.

If you have a change of plans and cannot attend, please advise me as soon as you know you will not be attending. I can then rearrange my schedule to do other work. You may obtain the next available convenient appointment time. I do not charge a fee for canceled appointments but ask that clients not cancel appointments lightly and give me as much notice as possible. You may call me after hours and leave a message on my voicemail if I am not in the office. My extension is 117.

There are a few forms that I would ask you to complete before your appointment. Completing the questionnaires saves time and therefore reduces your fees. Please complete the Matrimonial Information Form and the Client Preference Questionnaire (links are below). Please fill out the forms before your appointment, submit them online or have them sent to my office at least one day before your appointment so I can review them and input the relevant information into my computer programs. If you have any difficulties using the fillable forms online, please inquire with our office as to some tips to make the forms function. **PLEASE NOTE: I highly recommend that you save a copy of your completed forms to your computer BEFORE sending them to me to ensure the information is not lost in transit.**

I suggest you look at my Separation and Divorce Introductory Guide for information about your rights, obligations, and the process. I also have on my website an overview of what happens at a first matrimonial consultation. This guide highlights what topics will be discussed and will hopefully reduce anxiety and have clients better prepared for the meeting.

At subsequent appointments, I will need tax returns and notices of assessment for the last three years, a recent pay stub, proof of the value of your assets and debts at the time of separation, and the date of marriage, so please start working on obtaining those documents now.

The Family Law Rules require that to start an action, one must file with their action their full Tax Returns for the last three years and their Notices of Assessment. These assessments are often not available, so the rules also allow one to file an "Income and Deductions Printout" from CRA. I would therefore ask that you immediately contact CRA at 1-800-959-8281, and order that "Income Deductions Printout" if you do not have your last three years of Tax Returns and Notices of Assessments. When ordering, you should have your previous Tax Return and Notice of Assessment in front of you, as CRA will ask to verify your identity. The questions would be like what is your Social Insurance Number, your address, and general information that would have been on your Tax Return. CRA says it will send out the printout immediately.

I would remind you there is a fee for the initial consultation payable at the consultation. I base my fees on my $375 an hour billing rate with a minimum of one hour for the initial consultation. If you retain me to act as your lawyer, you will provide a retainer at the end of the appointment. The amount of the retainer would depend on the work I will perform. Or I will get a credit card authorization to bill your credit card as we go along. Please read my article "Family Law Legal Fees FAQ" found on my website so there is no misunderstanding how my fees are determined. I charge for my time from my first contact with you. I would also ask that you read and be prepared to sign my written retainer if you retain me at the end of your first appointment. Please note my retainer states that "I understand that if the matter goes to court that Lawrence S. Pascoe will withdraw from the file but will help to obtain and brief a Family Law Litigation Lawyer to take over the file, to start or defend a court action." Our goal should be to settle without going to court. Most cases settle without court action, but sometimes it is necessary to start a court application. The client is best served by having a Family Law Litigation Lawyer who I will work with.

The Law Society of Ontario now requires lawyers to verify their clients' identities at the time of being retained. As such, please be sure to bring to your first appointment proof of identification in the form of photo identification such as a driver's license, passport, or photo health card.

It might also be helpful if you write a list of questions you specifically want to be answered to ensure everything is covered though I have my extensive checklist of topics to discuss. If you wish to bring a relative or friend, please do so.

I look forward to meeting you at your appointment. If an emergency cannot wait for your appointment, please call me.

Yours truly,

LAWRENCE S. PASCOE
LSP*jm

Links to Forms

Matrimonial Information Form

http://thepascoedifference.com/wptpd/wp-content/uploads/2017/02/Matrimonial_Information.pdf

Client Preference Questionnaire

http://thepascoedifference.com/wptpd/wp-content/uploads/2017/06/Client_Preference_Questionnaire.pdf

Separation & Divorce Introductory Guide

http://thepascoedifference.com/introduction-separation/

What Happens at the First Matrimonial Consultation

http://thepascoedifference.com/what-happens-at-the-first-matrimonial-consultation/

Family Law Legal Fees FAQ

http://thepascoedifference.com/family-law-legal-fees-faq/

Retainer

http://thepascoedifference.com/wptpd/wp-content/uploads/2017/05/Retainer-Matrimonial.pdf

Choosing a Lawyer Survey and Will Packet Survey

http://thepascoedifference.com/wptpd/wp-content/uploads/2017/02/Choosing_Lawyer_Survey.pdf

Family Law Client To-Do Checklist – First Consultation

Complete the Matrimonial Information Form and Client Preference Questionnaire either online or print it out to bring to the first appointment:

Review the Retainer

Review Separation and Divorce Introductory Guide

Read the presentation of the first consultation.

Start collecting the financial documents that will help support the numbers put in the Matrimonial Information Form.

Write out a list of questions for LSP that are important to you (Optional).

Complete the Survey Contest online or print it out to bring to any appointment (Optional).

Contact Revenue Canada at 1-800-959-8281 to request your last three years of the "Income Tax Return-Regular Summary" also known as the "Option C Printout," which is used instead of your actual Income Tax Returns or Notices of Assessment. The courts require three consecutive years. This summary is free and takes only up to a week to receive. Even if your case does not go to court, this information is still useful to have.

Bring to your appointment any agreements between you and your spouse such as a Marriage Contract or Draft Separation Agreement.

Bring to the appointment your Marriage Certificate if it is in your possession (you can order it if you no longer have it).

If a variation of an existing agreement or court order, then bring in that agreement or court order.

Bring to the appointment one original photo identification document (such as a driver's license, passport, or photo health card.

A 5.8 Lawyer's Notes for Consultations and Telephone Calls

1. Name of File
2. Date
3. Person called or met with
4. Purpose of call or consultation
5. What information received
6. Advice or information given
7. What instructions were given by the client
8. What actions parties and lawyers are now to do

A 5.9 To-Do List for Family Law

MATRIMONIAL CLIENT TO DO LIST	DATE REQUESTED	DATE CLIENT PROVIDED	DATE SENT TO LAWYER
QUESTIONNAIRES			
Matrimonial Questionnaire			
Client Preference Questionnaire			
Client Survey Contest			
Marriage Certificate			
Custody Access Questionnaire			
CLIENT INCOME DOCUMENTS			
Last 3 years Tax Returns			
Last 3 years Tax Notices of Assessments			
Canada Revenue Income Form			

MATRIMONIAL CLIENT TO DO LIST	DATE REQUESTED	DATE CLIENT PROVIDED	DATE SENT TO LAWYER
Last 3 Pay Stubs			
Draft Financial Statement			
ASSET DOCUMENTATION			
House Valuation			
Motor Vehicle Valuation			
Pension Information			
Severance Entitlement Letter from employer			
Vacation Entitlement Letter from employer			
Sick Leave Entitlement Letter from employer			
Bank Statements			
Investment Statements			
Household Valuations			
Jewelry Valuations			
DEBT DOCUMENTATION			
Mortgage Statement			
Loan, Line of Credit Statements			
Credit Card Statements			
Automobile Loan Statement			
OTHER			

A 5.12.2 Definitions of Legal Matrimonial Terms

DEFINITIONS OF LEGAL MATRIMONIAL TERMS

The following are short definitions of some of the legal terms found in a matrimonial case. Please ask to clarify any words you do not understand.

Action: The legal term for a lawsuit.

Affidavit: A written statement of facts made under oath and signed before a lawyer or Commissioner of Oaths (which lawyers are). It is used primarily for motions.

Affidavit of Documents: The Court document that sets out what written records a party has that are relevant to the case.

Alimony: Payment of support from one party to another. This term has been replaced by "spousal support" and does not appear in any present-day legal proceedings.

Answer: The document made in a divorce action that replies to the Application for Divorce.

Appeal: The process whereby a higher court reviews a lower court's decision. The court determines whether there was an error in law.

Applicant: The person who first brings an application under the Family Law Act or Divorce Act.

Application: The first pleading in a Divorce or under the Family Law Act.

Barrister and Solicitor: A barrister is a lawyer who goes to Court. In contrast, a solicitor is a lawyer who does legal work but does not appear in Court. In England, a lawyer is one or the other. In Canada and the United States, all lawyers are both.

Book of Authorities: A compilation of case law, statutes, and legal articles that one party's lawyer will use to argue the legal principles that the judge should consider to decide the case.

Case Conference: A mandatory hearing before a Judge to obtain an opinion (and perhaps some relief). It occurs before a party can bring a motion. See the article about the Steps in a Matrimonial Dispute for more details.

Certificate of Divorce: The document indicating a divorce has become final.

Cohabitation: Living together as spouses, whether married or not.

Cohabitation Agreement: A contract between unmarried people who agree to live together.

Contested Case: Any case in which there are one or more issues on which the parties have not agreed.

Corollary relief: In a Divorce action, it is the claim in addition to the dissolution of the marriage, such as a division of assets, support, or custody.

Costs: A sum of money the court awards to the successful party. The unsuccessful party pays them towards payment of the successful party's legal expenses.

Cross-examination: A questioning of a witness under oath by a lawyer for the opposite party. The questions are about an affidavit, application, or financial statement for an impending motion or trial. It is now called questioning.

Custody: The legal right and responsibility that the Court orders for the care, possession, and rearing of a child.

Disbursements: Expenses lawyers pay on behalf of their clients.

Divorce Order: The Court document setting forth the terms of the Divorce and setting forth on what date the Divorce becomes final.

Domestic Contract: A separation agreement, marriage contract, or cohabitation agreement.

Equalization Payment: The amount paid by one party to the other party to equalize their respective "Net Family Properties" as calculated according to the Family Law Act.

Evidence: Documents, testimony, or other material offered to the Court to prove or disprove allegations.

Ex-parte: This term has been replaced by "without notice." It is a motion giving the other party notice.

Execution: Formal signing and witnessing of a legal document.

Factum: The document of one party setting out the main facts and the statute and case law supporting their claim.

Family Law Act Application: The proceedings in which one party seeks relief for custody, equalization of assets, support, or custody, but are not asking for a Divorce.

Financial Statement: A sworn document showing the value of a party's income, expenses, property, and debts.

Joint Custody: An order giving custody to both parents; usually, this gives both parents input into decisions concerning the health, education, and welfare of the children. The children may ordinarily reside with one parent more than the other or live equally with both parents.

Judgment: A final decision of the Court handed down after a trial.

Jurisdiction: The authority of the Court to decide on an issue.

Minutes of Settlement: The written settlement agreement made when one party has started an action.

Motion: A written application to the Court for some particular relief such as temporary support, custody, or interim exclusive possession of the marital home. A judge hears it.

Net Family Property: The value of a party's property on the valuation date, less excluded property under the Family Law Act, less debts and liabilities on the valuation day, less the net worth of the party on the date of marriage (other than a matrimonial home).

Net Family Property Statement: A court document showing what one party claims are their Net Family Property and the other party's Net Family Property. It also calculates the amount argued by a party as the amount of the equalization payment.

Offer to Settle: A document formally stating all the terms upon which one party will settle a motion or the entire case. The judge does not see this document until after the Motion or Trial is decided.

Party: A person in a divorce action named as an Applicant or Respondent.

Pleading: The written documents for the Court, including the Application for Divorce, the Answer, and the Reply to the Answer.

Precedent: A court decision that judges may follow in deciding on a similar case; an example of a legal document followed in preparing another similar document.

Questioning: An oral examination under oath of the opposite party or possible trial or motion witness.

Relief: Whatever a party to Divorce or Family Law Act proceedings asks the Court to do: such as dissolve the marriage, award support, enforce a prior court order or decree, divide property, address specific behavior, dismiss the complaint of the other party, and so on.

Respondent: The party who defends the Divorce application or family Law Action brought by their spouse.

Rules of Evidence: The rules that govern the presentation and admissibility of oral and documentary evidence at court hearings.

Separation Agreement: A written agreement between two parties as to the terms of their separation.

Settlement Conference: A mandatory hearing before the trial takes place to obtain a judge's opinion about how the judge would decide to get a settlement without a trial.

Transcript: A typewritten record of testimony taken by a court reporter during Questioning or at a Trial.

Trial: A court hearing with live testimony to decide disputed issues raised by the parties.

Uncontested Divorce: A court action in which the parties have reached an agreement, and all they ask of the Court is the granting of the Divorce. Neither party must appear in Court.

Undertaking: A written promise to do something.

A 5.12.3.1 The Processes to Resolve Family Law Disputes

THE PROCESSES TO RESOLVE FAMILY LAW DISPUTES

Introduction

There are several processes that spouses may use to resolve the terms of their separation. This article briefly explains the procedures. It outlines how they work and the advantages and disadvantages of each method. There are six distinct processes; however, they are often used in combination with each other. The six are: (1) Client/Client negotiating; (2) Mediation; (3) Collaborative Law; (4) Lawyer/ Lawyer negotiating; (5) Five Way Meetings; (6) Court Proceedings.

1. Client/Client Negotiating

Often on marriage breakdown, clients will discuss what they believe are fair terms of dealing with the children, dividing up the assets, and paying support. They may or may not obtain advice from lawyers as to whether or not their agreement is fair. They may or may not put their deal into writing in the form of a Separation Agreement.

The advantage of this method is the low cost since they are not paying for lawyers. Usually, this method is faster than the other methods, and the clients have control of the process. But the major disadvantage is that the clients are not lawyers and do not know what their rights and obligations are. Therefore, they may not come to a fair settlement. If one party is more aggressive than the other, the agreement might not be appropriate. If there is no written agreement and there is spousal support, the parties can not take advantage of the overall tax breaks that spousal support provides. The Income Tax Act says these contracts must be in writing for the tax breaks.

The clients might start with this method and then retain a lawyer for advice to confirm that their agreement is fair and to have that agreement put into writing. The major problem with starting with this method is that the clients may agree to something that they think is fair, but then they discover when talking to a lawyer they have given away rights that the law provides for good reasons. These rights may be more challenging to get back in the ensuing negotiations. There is often no complete financial disclosure of assets in this process, and one party may be hiding income. I do not recommend this method as the primary method. Of course, spouses will generally talk with each other about what they expect the terms of the separation to be but should not make any agreements until talking to their lawyers.

2. Mediation

Mediation is the process when the two clients negotiate the terms of their settlement with a third-party mediator's help. The mediator is, in effect, a referee between the parties. A mediator cannot technically give legal advice. Each party in mediation will still obtain a lawyer to receive legal advice, but the lawyers will not be involved in the negotiations. The clients will negotiate with the help of a mediator. The mediator is generally trained and is often a lawyer for the financial issues and a mental health professional for the parenting issues.

An advantage of mediation is that it will most often be less costly than going to Court. The clients must be aware that it is generally more expensive than getting a settlement through lawyer negotiations and can be quite expensive if the mediation is lengthy.

Mediation can be completed relatively quickly, although genearlly not as fast as lawyer/lawyer negotiations. The time it takes is dependant on the schedules of the mediator and the clients. And clients still need to see a lawyer to be told of their rights and obligations. The lawyers must also make sure their clients understand what the agreement states.

There is a high degree of participation by the clients in the mediation process compared to the other methods. If the mediator educates the clients, often concerning parenting issues, the process can be somewhat therapeutic. A spouse has the opportunity to express their feelings in a controlled setting in front of a mediator. The mediated settlement is bound to work better in the long run than Court imposed resolutions as the parties have an interest and a say in the decision rather than having it imposed upon them.

The disadvantage of mediation is that it can be costly if the parties have difficulty resolving a resolution/agreement. The communication aspect of mediation can be a little cumbersome as each party has to go back to their lawyer for opinions. Another disadvantage is that sometimes mediation is a waste of time as one client had no intention of compromising and only used mediation in the hope that the process would result in settling on the terms that that person wanted.

A good mediator will ensure that the parties are on an equal bargaining level. Still, sometimes the more aggressive spouse will obtain a better deal for themselves by pushing their position more firmly. In my opinion, mediation is very appropriate for parenting issues but not always for contested financial issues.

3. Collaborative Law

Collaborative Law is a process invented in the 1990s by practicing lawyers to take the best of mediation, lawyer/lawyer negotiation, and client/client negotiation. In terms of time and costs, this process has significant advantages over the Court action process.

The basic concepts of Collaborative Law are as follows:

a. The parties and their lawyers use four-way meetings to discuss the terms of the Separation Agreement;
b. The parties and their lawyers commit themselves at the beginning of the process to resolve the terms of the separation cooperatively without the need to go to Court. The clients and the lawyers sign an agreement stating that if they do not resolve the matter, the clients retain other lawyers to take the case to Court.
c. The lawyers are trained in the collaborative law process and are associated with a network of collaborative law lawyers.

The advantages of Collaborative Law are many. There is a high rate of participation by the client. It is the best form of communication of all the systems because all of the parties are in the same room at one time. Misunderstandings and positions can be explained and understood. As lawyers are present, there is less chance of a spouse being aggressive and a greater chance of preparing a settlement.

Costs are lower than taking the matter to court; however, they are more costly than the lawyer/lawyer and client/client method. They are most likely, the same costs as mediation. There is less stress on the parties in knowing that if there is a breakdown of negotiations, one is not immediately going to be in Court because the parties have to seek new lawyers to start the Court action.

There is more of a commitment to resolve the matter than in mediation and lawyer/lawyer because there is bound to be more expense and time if the process fails.

Some may also say that there is far more of an interest on the lawyers' part to settle the matter because they will lose the file if there is no settlement.

Not all lawyers are collaborative law lawyers, so clients can not always use this method as both lawyers must be collaborative law lawyers.

4. Lawyer/Lawyer Negotiating

Lawyer/Lawyer negotiating is the most common method to process a marital dispute, and often the one that is the starting point. Each client retains a lawyer. Through their lawyers, the parties exchange financial information and their positions to resolve their matrimonial dispute and trade their positions regarding what the terms should be in the Separation Agreement. The lawyers will then negotiate based upon their client's instructions as to what the terms will be. After consulting with their client, one lawyer drafts the Separation Agreement. That lawyer then sends a copy of the agreement to obtain the other lawyer's comments. Lawyer/Lawyer negotiating is usually the least costly method next to the client/client process. It is generally the fastest method.

The level of client participation is not as high as mediation or collaborative law, but it still has the client control over whether to accept the agreement or not. It is not as therapeutic as mediation or collaborative law because there is no face to face discussions with the spouse. Communications may get misinterpreted because information goes from the party to the lawyer, to the other lawyer, and back to the other party.

This method should be used to start the process, and then depending on the case; the parties may switch to mediation, collaborative law, or court action.

5. Five Way Meeting

A popular way of resolving matters once the lawyer/lawyer negotiations or discussions break down is to retain a family lawyer specializing in resolving files by meeting with lawyers and clients. This Family Law Mediator will generally conduct a half-day or a whole day meeting similar to a Settlement Conference. The Lawyer Mediator will try to mediate the issues in dispute. The Lawyer Mediator will provide an independent legal opinion about what would happen if the matter went to Court. This Lawyer Mediator often will then be requested by the parties to draft the Separation Agreement. It is advantageous that the parties hear from an independent person how to resolve the matter and draft an agreement, resulting in less arguing over the contract's wording.

6. Court Proceedings

If, after lawyer/lawyer negotiations, mediation, five-way meetings, collaborative law, or client/client negotiations, the parties still cannot agree on the terms of their separation, then a Judge will have to decide those terms.

There are not many advantages to this system other than it is the method necessary when the parties cannot agree. It is very costly and can wipe out a large portion of a person's assets. It can be lengthy. It is stressful for the client. Often the losing party is not happy and will do their best to work against the decisions. However, this method is often necessary because the parties are too far apart on what they believe is a fair settlement. Sometimes court action is started just to prompt the other party to deal with the negotiations. After starting the action, or after one or two steps in the proceedings, the matter settles. Only a small percentage of Court actions proceed to trial.

Conclusion

Which process to use depends on the issues and the parties. If custody and access are in dispute, then a mental health mediator will probably be the best to use in that instance. For the client/client negotiations, mediation, and collaborative law methods, both the parties must agree; otherwise, the process will automatically default to start with lawyer/lawyer negotiating (or lawyer/opposite client negotiating if the client refuses to get a lawyer). If the parties cannot agree after lawyer/lawyer negotiations, the Court action method will be employed.

For a more detailed explanation of family law's many processes, please read my more detailed articles and government pamphlets. Visit the web sites of mediators and our local collaborative law network at www.collaborativelaw.ca to receive further information.

A 5.12.3.2 Steps in a Family Law Dispute Chart

STEPS IN A FAMILY LAW DISPUTE

1. INITIAL CONTACT BETWEEN CLIENT AND LAWYER
2. FIRST CONSULTATION
3. SECOND CONSULTATION
4. EXCHANGE OF INFORMATION BETWEEN LAWYERS
5. NEGOTIATIONS WITH SPOUSE'S LAWYER
6. <u>IF NEGOTIATIONS ARE SUCCESSFUL THEN</u> -

    6A. DRAFTING, DISCUSSING, AND SIGNING OF A SEPARATION AGREEMENT (OR MINUTES OF SETTLEMENT)

<u>IF NEGOTIATIONS ARE UNSUCCESSFUL</u>

    6B. COMMENCEMENT OF LEGAL PROCEEDINGS

    or

    6C. MEDIATION WITH CLIENTS or MEDIATION WITH CLIENTS AND LAWYERS (5 WAY MEETING) or COLLABORATIVE LAW (may start earlier)

    and/or

    6D. APPOINTMENT OF CHILDREN'S LAWYER (in disputed parenting cases)

    and/or

    6E. PSYCHOLOGICAL ASSESSMENT (in disputed parenting cases)

    and/or

    6F. OFFER TO SETTLE

    NEGOTIATIONS - If successful, then 6A

7. CASE CONFERENCE

    NEGOTIATIONS - If successful, then 6A

8. TEMPORARY MOTION - (Optional and Court must grant permission)

    NEGOTIATIONS - If successful, then 6A

9. QUESTIONING A PARTY OR WITNESS - (Optional and Court must grant permission)
   NEGOTIATIONS - If successful, then 6A
10. SETTLEMENT CONFERENCE
    NEGOTIATIONS - If successful, then 6A
11. TRIAL MANAGEMENT CONFERENCE
    NEGOTIATIONS - If successful, then 6A
12. TRIAL
13. APPEAL TO COURT OF APPEAL (If one party is not satisfied with the decision)
14. AWARDING AND SETTLING OF LEGAL COSTS

A 5.12.3.3 The Steps in Family Law Disputes Article

THE STEPS IN FAMILY LAW DISPUTES

The legal process involved in marital disputes consists of several specific steps. I will briefly outline how I view these many activities.

1. INITIAL CONTACT BETWEEN CLIENT AND LAWYER:
This step usually occurs when the client initially telephones my office. If the client wants to talk to me on the phone, I will do so for a brief period. I will complete my Client Intake Form. I ask about the general nature of the client's problem, whether the client needs immediate help, whether the other spouse has started a legal proceeding, and whether I am the right person for that client. I will advise the client about any urgent concerns. I generally discuss fees and then arrange an appointment. If he or she has not already done so, I ask the client to look at my website. I will send an appointment confirmation letter with instructions about completing questionnaires and preparing for the first consultation.

2. FIRST CONSULTATION:
This important meeting will often be the longest consultation. I will review the questionnaires from my Family Law Packet. I will obtain

further information needed to advise the client of his or her legal rights and obligations. I will explain the process to get those rights. I discuss our lawyer and client relationship by explaining our respective roles. I ask clients to tell me about their priorities. I ask what the client expects to achieve in terms of the settlement.

The client signs a written contract (retainer) agreeing to my hourly rate and provides me with money (cheque, cash, or credit card authorization) as a down payment (also called a retainer). I deposit that money into my trust account. I do not have use of the funds until I bill the client. The trust account's interest goes to the Law Society to help pay for legal aid, libraries, and research projects.

The client will usually not have all the required information and documentation. I will therefore list further information or documentation the client needs to obtain. I will provide the client with a blank court financial statement (showing the client's income, expenses, and assets). The client should complete this statement for the second consultation. My video on how to fill out this statement on my website or YouTube can help. Also in my manual is a written memorandum on how to fill out the statement.

The client and I will decide a strategy on how to proceed, whether by trying to negotiate a Separation Agreement, by starting court proceedings, or by mediating. Whether to have a psychological assessment or to involve the Ontario Government's Children's Lawyer will be discussed. I will advise on the ramifications of each option.

Even if the other spouse has already started court action, it is still possible to suggest a Settlement Agreement or mediation. At this time, there may be enough information to write to the other spouse, or the lawyer representing the spouse, with a preliminary or even final proposal. I draft that letter at this consultation in front of the client to ensure that the letter's contents and tone are acceptable to the client and to expedite matters.

I will also discuss several related topics of interest to the client, such as personal counseling, tax implications, dating other people, name changes, Canada Pension division of credits, Wills, insurance beneficiaries, and RRSP designations.

I provide the client with my Family Law Client Manual, which contains further information and a place to hold all correspondence and documents on the file. I ensure my clients receive a copy of everything of importance on his or her file.

3. SECOND CONSULTATION:
The second consultation usually takes place a week after the first meeting. At this time I will finalize the financial statement with the client. I have a second computer monitor on my desk so that my clients and I can review the financial statement together more efficiently. Information gathering will continue, and hopefully, we will complete it. I will answer new questions the client has which arise from any recent discussion with the spouse, from our first consultation, or from the client reading of material that I provided in the Family Law Client Manual. I will report to the client on any issue I had to research. The client and I will review another letter to the spouse or spouse's lawyer to reflect the position the client wants. That letter will state the client's position concerning the terms of the settlement. The letter can be conditional upon confirmation from the other spouse about their exact income and assets.

4. EXCHANGE OF INFORMATION BETWEEN LAWYERS:
To advise a client, it is necessary to know the other spouse's facts and position. We, therefore, exchange sworn financial statements and proposal letters. The Family Law Rules are very clear that if any information provided in a financial statement, affidavit, questioning, or any other method was incorrect or has changed, there is an obligation to correct that information immediately in writing.

At this early stage, it may be advisable to have one lawyer draft a Separation Agreement setting forth all the terms of the settlement, so there is no question about what all the terms are that the client is proposing down to the fine detail.

5. NEGOTIATIONS WITH SPOUSE'S LAWYER:
The purpose of this stage is to obtain quickly, cheaply, and without going to court, a Separation Agreement that sets forth the terms of the separation (custody, access, division of property, and support). Some basic rules to obtain these goals are as follows: 1) All information the other spouse is entitled to should be quickly and easily given. This information would usually include a sworn financial statement and supporting material such as pay stubs and asset documentation.

2) Make one's position clearly known. 3) Be reasonable in even the initial proposal. Too often, in my opinion, clients and their lawyers make outrageous demands that only fuel the existing animosity between the parties and reduce the likelihood of a settlement. 4) Positions taken should be based on legal rights, not on unrealistic desires.

6. DRAFTING, DISCUSSING AND SIGNING OF A SEPARATION AGREEMENT (OR MINUTES OF SETTLEMENT):

If neither party has commenced a court action and the parties have come to a tentative agreement, the next step is to complete a Separation Agreement containing all the settlement terms. If a party did start a court action, then the document to draft is called the Minutes of Settlement. Sometimes there will be both documents, with the Minutes of Settlement containing only the main terms (custody, support, and assets) and the Separation Agreement containing the many other ancillary terms.

I will discuss with the client all the terms that will go into the agreement. They include the main terms, the fine detail, such as exactly how much life insurance will be in place, the length of time for child support and higher education costs, as well as the standard release and other legal clauses that make up the agreement. I will then send the draft agreement (or signed agreement) to the spouse's lawyer for approval or further discussion of the agreement's wording. The parties will often have agreed to the main terms, but the fine details, which are generally accepted, may not be acceptable by the spouse or the other lawyer.

The other side will sign the agreement once negotiations are complete, and they return it for the client to sign if the client had not signed first. Usually, there are four copies of the agreement, one for each party and one for each lawyer.

A Separation Agreement does not have to be approved or sent to the court. Only if the spouse receiving support (payee) wants to enforce the agreement because of arrears of payments or wants the Government Family Responsibility Office to receive the payments is a separation agreement registered with the court. If Minutes of Settlement are signed, one of the lawyers will file them with the court. A judge will sign a final Order, incorporating all of the Minutes of Settlement terms.

A Separation Agreement is just as binding and enforceable as a court order. It can only be changed if there has been a material change in circumstances. A party can not ask for a change just because one of them has changed their minds. They both have to agree to changes unless there is a material change in circumstances. See Chapter 5.12.3.2 for further steps.

A 5.12.3.4 Memorandum about a Court Motion

Memorandum for a Client Attending at a Motion

1. Where to meet me at the courthouse:

Meet me at the seats to the left of the elevators as you come in from Elgin Street. This floor is considered the "main" floor, but it is the second floor of the building.

2. What time to meet:

Unless instructed otherwise, please meet me 20 minutes before the motion is scheduled time to start. That would mean meeting me generally at 9:40 for morning sessions and 1:40 for afternoon sessions unless we are given another time.

3. What if you cannot make it on time?

3.1. Call me on my cell phone at 613-797-XXXX

3.2. If you arrive only 5 minutes before the motion is scheduled to start, I will be waiting for you in the courtroom. To find out what courtroom the motion is being held in check with the Information Booth. This booth is located to the elevators' right on the "main" (2nd) floor.

4. What to wear:

4.1. I strongly recommend that you dress as if you are going to a job interview (no jeans).

5. What will happen before the motion?

5.1. I will review with you (usually with a copy of my notes) what I hope to say to the judge.

5.2. There may be necessary last-minute discussions with the other lawyer.

6. When will Your Motion be Heard?

6.1. It is impossible to predict precisely when the judge will hear your motion. We must wait until the session starts to see what number your case is on the list. There may be several cases before yours, so I strongly recommend that you count on taking either the whole morning or afternoon (depending on when your case is slotted) off from work. On busy days, I have seen morning sessions go into the afternoon as well.

7. Who will be present in the courtroom?

7.1. The judge, a court reporter, a court clerk, a court bailiff, the other lawyer in your case, along with their client. The court is "open", which means that lawyers and their clients having cases heard after your case are allowed to sit in the courtroom.

7.2. I can ask that the court clear the room of other lawyers and clients, but since it is an open court hearing, judges have been instructed by the Chief Justice not to clear the courtroom though the judge can recommend it.

8. What will happen at the motion?

It depends on the judge's process. Generally, each side will present their position on each contested issue (usually all at once as it is unlikely that the judge will listen to one issue at a time). The applicant's lawyer goes first, then the respondent's lawyer. The applicant's lawyer then has a reply to matters raised by the respondent's lawyer but cannot introduce anything new. Neither party will be allowed or asked to speak and give evidence as the motion will be decided on the material filed. The judge will either make an order right then or advise that he or she will take some time (usually a day or two) to decide and advise when the decision is ready to be picked up from the courthouse.

9. What will happen immediately after the motion?

I will meet with you outside the courtroom. I will discuss with you what the judge ordered and what everyone must now do. If the judge made no decision, I would discuss how I believe the motion went.

10. Next steps:

- draft any order the judge made
- adhere to any order the judge made
- perhaps make an offer to settle based on what the judge said if there is enough disclosure to make an offer
- prepare for the next step, which may be questioning, motion, or a settlement conference

A 5.12.3.5 Memorandum about Questioning (Cross-Examinations)

WHAT IS QUESTIONING?

- taking of testimony under oath by a court reporter
- it takes place in a small room with just the reporter, the lawyers, and the parties being questioned
- though allowed, the other party shouldn't be present as it only inhibits the party being questioned. The purpose of the Questioning is to obtain as much information from the other party as possible

PURPOSES OF A QUESTIONING:

- to learn about the other party's case, the particulars of the claim, facts, and arguments, what documentary proof will be relied upon, and what experts will be relied upon
- to learn what the other party says about your case
- to obtain admissions that support your case
- to obtain admissions that should not be changed at trial (or can be read into evidence at trial)
- to assess the credibility and character of the other party (will they make a good witness)
- to confirm that specific issues are not in dispute
- to move the case along

HOW TO CONDUCT ONESELF AT A QUESTIONING

1) Tell the truth to the best of your knowledge
   - if you do not understand the question, say so
   - if you do not know or are uncertain as to the answer, say so, do not guess
   - do not exaggerate

If you are caught in a mistake, correct yourself rather than digging a deeper hole. You are not expected to be perfect and remember everything to its fine detail.

It is easy to make a mistake.

2) Answer the question asked in a short, concise manner
   - if it can be answered "yes" or "no," do so
   - do not go on and on trying to convince the opposing lawyer of your case. You may just be providing more information for their case
3) Do not be hostile to the opposing lawyer. They are just doing their job.
4) If I say not to answer a question, do not answer it.

In Family Law, there are very few questions that the lawyer can say not to answer. The importance may be minor, but that is to be argued at trial and not at Questioning.

5) Come prepared
   - read over your affidavit and financial statement, and your spouse's affidavit. Be ready to support anything you have said. "How did you arrive at any figure in the financial statement?"
   - bring all financial papers, **pay stubs, tax returns, bank books,** evidence as to asset values
   - come dressed as though you were at the trial so that you make a good impression upon the opposing lawyer

MY ROLE

- to ensure that the other lawyer does not harass you. The opposing lawyer can ask a question in two different ways, but after that, I will state that you have already answered the question and therefore move on.

- to advise you whether or not to answer a question (as stated above, very rarely is a question not relevant)
- to decide and confirm that you will provide the undertakings asked (an undertaking is an acknowledgment that you will give more information or documentary evidence)
- to help, in only a minor way, answer some questions (particularly financial ones as I helped prepare the financial statement)

AFTER THE QUESTIONING

- you must obtain the undertakings you gave at the Questioning
- advise me if the answers you gave were inaccurate or incomplete. It is also essential to inform me as to whether circumstances have changed and whether these circumstances could affect the answers you provided me.

A 5.12.5.1 The Client and Lawyer Relationship Article

THE CLIENT AND LAWYER RELATIONSHIP

A good working relationship between the client and the lawyer, especially in family law matters, will result in a better outcome, a smoother process, a lower account, and a satisfied client. To obtain a good working relationship, both client and lawyer must recognize their own and the other's responsibilities. To help achieve this, I am setting forth what I believe are the client's and lawyer's respective roles.

THE ROLE OF THE LAWYER

1. TO ADVISE: The lawyer advises the client on how the law would apply to the client's case. As the law is not an exact science, the advice will include the range of possible outcomes if the matter is litigated and a judge has to decide the case. The lawyer will advise the client on the different arguments that can be made for and against the client and assess the probability of success and the best strategy and legal procedure to obtain the desired outcome. That strategy may range from doing nothing to taking the case to the Court of Appeal if need be. The lawyer will advise initially on the facts first given and the law at that time. As the opposing spouse's evidence becomes known,

and the lawyer assesses the Court's probable findings of the facts, that advice may change. The law is also evolving as new cases interpret the Family Law Act. Those new cases might result in a change of direction too.

2. TO NEGOTIATE A SETTLEMENT: The lawyer will negotiate on the client's behalf with the opposing spouse's lawyer or the opposite spouse, if he or she has no lawyer, to obtain a complete settlement of all the issues. During the negotiating process, the client will be consulted and expected to give the lawyer instructions about the settlement's terms, which are acceptable to the client.

3. TO DRAFT THE APPROPRIATE DOCUMENTS: If the matter settles without commencing court proceedings, the lawyer will draft a Separation Agreement. If court proceedings are needed, the lawyer will prepare the Application for Divorce and all other documents required to commence and continue a court action.

4. TO ADVOCATE: If the parties cannot settle the matter, the lawyer will argue the case at all levels - the Case Conference, Settlement Conference, motions, the trial, and the appeal. The lawyer will conduct the appropriate questioning and prepare the necessary documents.

CONDUCT THE CLIENT IS ENTITLED TO FROM THE LAWYER

1. TO PROVIDE GOOD SERVICE: This includes returning phone calls the same day they are received or the next day if the lawyer is out of the office. If the lawyer cannot return the phone call by the next day, the lawyer's assistant should call. Good service also includes receiving copies of all court documents and necessary correspondence. Significant developments in the case should be communicated by the lawyer as soon as possible. The prompt and courteous service also must be extended by all the office staff to the client.

2. TO GIVE A REALISTIC ASSESSMENT OF THE CASE: The lawyer should advise the client what the lawyer believes are the client's realistic chances of obtaining the outcome the client wants. The lawyer should not try to make the client feel better by being overly optimistic. That excessively optimistic advice may fuel a court battle that the client cannot win. That unwarranted promising approach also will result in a big letdown if that outcome is not achieved either through negotiations or through the court system. However, the

lawyer should not be overly pessimistic either. Being pessimistic is not fair to the client, as it does not allow the client to assess the case appropriately.

3. TO PROVIDE FINANCIAL ACCOUNTABILITY: The lawyer should, at the first interview, explain how the lawyer will determine the fee and when payment is expected. The lawyer should tell the client what the disbursements (money spent on the client's behalf) will be. If the fee is to be on a time basis, the account should detail the work's date, the job done, and the time it took. The statement of account will also detail the disbursements. As best the lawyer can, there should be estimates of how much the case will cost if charged on a time basis. The lawyer should send interim accounts to the client to know the amount due to the lawyer.

4. TO TAKE THE CLIENT'S INSTRUCTIONS: The lawyer must take the client's instructions. The lawyer should not try to force the client into taking a position the client does not want. On occasion, a lawyer may believe the client is willing to settle for far less than a court would order. In those situations, the lawyer should not bully the client into changing positions but instead obtain a written acknowledgment from the client that the settlement in the lawyer's opinion is unfair to the client.

5. TO HOLD THE CLIENT'S INFORMATION IN CONFIDENCE: The lawyer should hold in strict confidence all information concerning the client and not divulge any such information unless authorized by the client.

6. TO GIVE THE LAWYER'S BEST EFFORTS: The lawyer should treat each client and each file very importantly and try the their best. But it does not mean spending so much time on a file that the resulting cost is more than the matter is worth. Although what the lawyer is doing may be routine work, it is important to the client and deserves the lawyer's best efforts.

7. TO BE SENSITIVE: The lawyer must be a good listener and empathize with the client's problem. The lawyer must, with sensitivity, ask the client questions the client may be reluctant to discuss. However, though sympathetic to the client's situation, the lawyer must be objective about the advice. The client must remember that the lawyer is still on their side even though the client does not like the advice given.

WHAT THE LAWYER IS NOT

1. A THERAPIST: The client must remember that although his or her case may have a very emotional element, the lawyer did not take training to treat emotional problems. Just telling the lawyer their story will be therapeutic to many clients. If counseling is required, the client should seek a qualified health professional. The lawyer can help guide a client to the appropriate specialist. The cost of these professionals is usually covered by a drug plan or by OHIP.

2. A HIRED GUN: If the client's position is untenable, wholly unrealistic, and has no chance of success in negotiations or at Court, then the lawyer has the right to withdraw from the case. The lawyer is not a "hired gun." A lawyer is an officer of the Court and owes a duty to the system to be realistic. It also hurts the lawyer's credibility with colleagues and judges if the lawyer argues ridiculous positions. Some lawyers will disagree with this position. The client can then hire those lawyers if the client so wishes but the result is usually disastrous.

3. A MIRACLE WORKER: If the relief requested is not something the other party will accept, or a court would probably order, then it will just not be obtained. The law is not an exact science. It is vague and uncertain in many areas, and as there is a broad discretion with a judge, the range of possibilities is indeed wide. However, the probability range of what the result will be is usually much smaller.

Clients must understand that if the client and the other party cannot agree on a settlement, a judge must decide the case. Having no agreement means going to court to argue the case. The result is much higher costs; however, there is no alternative as there is no settlement.

THE ROLE OF THE CLIENT

1. TO PROVIDE INFORMATION: The result of any case depends on two factors - the facts and the law. It is the client's responsibility to provide all the facts that the lawyer requests. Providing all the facts may involve extensive work by the client. Old records will have to be found, time and energy will be needed to detail all of the assets in a marriage and their costs and to prepare a budget. A client may have to interview relatives and friends to confirm certain events. This work is essential for the success of the case.

2. TO GIVE INSTRUCTIONS: After the lawyer has given advice and has explained the alternatives, the client must tell the lawyer what to do. The client should not let the lawyer make the decisions.

3. TO PAY THE LAWYER: At the first interview, the lawyer will have discussed fees with the client. If the client cannot pay the cost in the manner requested, the client should say so. If the client, as the file progresses, does not live up to his or her obligation to pay the rendered bills, then the lawyer has the right to stop work on the file. However, discussing the matter with the lawyer will usually result in alternate arrangements being made if the facts warrant it.

CONDUCT THE LAWYER REQUIRES FROM THE CLIENT

1. TO SUPPLY TRUTHFUL INFORMATION: Lying to the lawyer has harmful consequences for the client. The other party and their lawyer almost always discover lies. When that discovery occurs, the client will lose credibility with the Court which might even suspect truthful assertions. The lying is often about irrelevant or minor matters, but the loss of credibility will apply to all the issues.

If the client tells the truth from the beginning, the lawyer can build the case and develop the strategy. However, when the lying is discovered, it may be too late to switch the plan. Besides perhaps destroying his or her case, the court may charge the lying client with the criminal offense of perjury. Holding back relevant information against one's case has the same consequences as lying. TELL THE LAWYER THE TRUTH AND LET THE LAWYER BUILD THE CASE BASED ON THE TRUTH.

2. TO PROVIDE THE FACTS IN AN ORDERLY FASHION AND ON A TIMELY BASIS: A lawyer cannot complete the file on a timely basis or file appropriate documents on behalf of the client if the client does not provide the facts when asked. It is also difficult to conduct the case if the client continually tells the lawyer of facts the client just remembered.

3. TO READ THE CORRESPONDENCE AND APPROPRIATE ARTICLES WRITTEN BY THE LAWYER: Though there will be many articles and reporting letters the lawyer will ask the client to read, the client must take the time to read them. Reporting letters will confirm what the lawyer and client discussed, so there are no misunderstandings

between them. Reading a reporting letter may catch a misunderstanding. Reading the articles will help the client understand their case better.

4. TO ACT RATIONALLY: Family law matters can be very emotional. Separation from one's spouse is one of the most challenging times in one's life and may result in a client's irrational behavior. The client must try to take the emotional aspect out of their behavior and decision-making process.

5. TO ADVISE THE LAWYER AS TO HOW THEY ARE HANDLING THE CASE: If the client is dissatisfied with any aspect of the way the lawyer is handling the case, the client must advise the lawyer. The lawyer will then be able to resolve the complaint. On the other hand, if the client waits until the case is over, it may be too late to fix it.

6. TO SHOW APPRECIATION: Lawyers are human beings and therefore like to be appreciated. If the lawyer did a good job, then the client should express this satisfaction. The lawyer's leading sources of business are usually from repeat clients and referrals from happy clients. A satisfied client can best show appreciation by referring relatives and friends to the lawyer.

WHAT THE CLIENT IS NOT EXPECTED TO DO

1. TO KNOW THE LAW: The client is not expected to know the law. If clients knew the law, lawyers would be out of business. Therefore, the client should not feel embarrassed to ask any question of the lawyer regarding the law.

CONCLUSION

This memorandum sets out my beliefs as to how lawyers and clients should conduct themselves. I try to adhere to my own rules as a lawyer and hope you can do your best to follow your rules. If you have any questions concerning this memorandum, please do not hesitate to discuss them with me.

A 5.12.5.2 Client Expectations Article

Client Expectations

Clients should have realistic expectations of their case's result, what it might cost, and how long it might take. Knowing this information will allow clients to try and plan their lives, reduce their stress and sometimes frustration during the process and be better able to accept the final result.

Unfortunately, it is tough for me to predict the results and timing though I try to do the best I can in each case. I think it is vital for my clients to keep in mind the following information to help manage their expectations.

Results

I base my opinions on the facts known to me at the time my opinions are rendered. Therefore, my opinion is based solely on what my clients have told me at the first client interview. Those facts might not be entirely correct, or they may not be proven or accepted by the court if contested by the other spouse. I have not heard the other side's story at that point. My clients may have held back facts damaging to their case or simply did not know all the facts. My opinion may change or even have to wait until I hear from the other side what they allege the facts to be. As the case progresses, new facts may emerge. A problem with family law is that the facts may change during the process, such as for custody and support issues. So my opinions on some issues will probably change with new and evolving facts and be subject to what I can prove are the facts.

Another problem is that the law is quite uncertain in some family law areas, and there may be different decisions on similar facts. And as the law allows a judge a lot of discretion for some issues, which judge hears the case might make a big difference in the outcome.

Costs

At the beginning of a case, when the clients have not yet agreed on an agreement's basic terms, they often ask what the final cost will be. It will be difficult for me to estimate the total legal fees and disbursements at that time. Until both sides confirm they have agreed on an agreement's basic terms, I cannot estimate the cost. This inability to predict the cost is because of the following reasons: I do not know how many issues are contested. I might not know what further work is needed to get the necessary evidence to deal with contested issues. I might not know the process that the parties will use to resolve the matter. I will not know whether the matter will go to court, and if it does, to what stage in the court process it will go before the parties come to a resolution. I might have a rough idea of costs and often suggest not pursuing an issue or issues very far because I can see the costs outweighing the likely result. Generally, I just do not know how much a contested matrimonial matter will cost. So, I simply do not try to estimate the cost.

A part of my job is to keep the costs down, which I try to do, but sometimes it cannot be done – unless my client wants to give in and accept their spouse's terms to settle.

Timing

I appreciate my clients want their file completed as soon as possible. Quickly completing a file is a part of providing good service, and doing so will produce a happy client, and I will be able to move on to other files. But the client must realize we are working with a slow court system. And often, I am dealing with an opposing side who may be slow to provide the information needed and slow to even negotiate on a timely basis. Often there is an advantage for one side not to settle quickly. Sometimes in matrimonial matters, one party can just not accept or deal with the separation. It is often more difficult dealing with a spouse who will not come to the table to negotiate than a spouse who comes to the table angrily.

And I may be the reason the file is not moving as quickly as a client wants. Generally not realized by my clients, at any one time, I have about seventy open files, of which about for thirty of them the ball is in my court, and I have work I do on them. The rest of my files are ones I am waiting for the other side or my client to do something, and at any time, they will join the thirty files I can work on. So I may not get to a client's file as fast as everyone wants (including me –I don't make money if I am not working on the file). At times when my caseload gets too high, I refuse new clients for a while to better serve the clients I have.

I have done some time studies on myself and found in the course of a day, besides administrative work (non-billable time), which takes up 1/3 of my time, I have measured at least 1/3 of the day, or more, is for planned appointments, 1/3 of the day or again more is doing completely unplanned work – such as answering phone calls and emails and matters requiring some urgency and the remaining 1/3 is spent on that planned work for the 30 files I have to work on. The planned work is the one that gets reduced the first and the most.

I try to do small things right after being given the task, but if I cannot, that work gets on the to-do planned list, and sometimes it takes time to get to it. I will handle real emergencies right away. I do return calls and emails by the next day. But for larger tasks, it just takes a while to get to them.

Please keep all these facts in mind when formulating the expectations of your file's results, costs, and timing.

A 5.12.7.1 Topics Discussed in Legal Fees in a Matrimonial File Article

Legal Fees in Matrimonial File

What are the Components of a Client's Account? What is a Retainer?

Why Money Retainers? When are Accounts Rendered?

Fees - How are they Determined?

How is the Hourly Rate Set?

Is the Hourly Rate a Fair Way to Determine Fees?

Why Not Set the Fee-Based on the Value to the Client?

Can the Lawyer Give an Estimate of the Fees? How Can Clients Help to Reduce their Fees? How Does the Legal System Try to Keep Fees Lower?

How Do I Try to Reduce Your Costs?

Are Lawyers' Fees Tax Deductible?

A 5.12.7.2 Memorandum on Understanding My Accounts

I have detailed my approach to legal fees and accounts in my article entitled Legal Fees in Matrimonial Matters. This article is found in my Family Law Manual. I would like to remind you of the following concerning my accounts.

The account is made up of three sections, generally on three pages. The first section contains your fee for this account, adds the disbursements that were not paid out from your trust account, adds any amount previously outstanding, and then subtracts the amount taken from your trust account to pay for the account. If there is no money or not enough money in your trust account, there will be an amount owing at the end of the account.

The second section lists the services I performed by date.

A brief description is shown with the amount of time I took. The time is in tenths of an hour. That means ".1" means 6 minutes, and ".5" means 30 minutes of 1/2 an hour. Unfortunately, my accounting program (the most popular legal accounting package in Canada) does not show the account's added up time. If you add it up manually and multiply it by the hourly rate in your retainer agreement, it will be the fee charged for this account.

The third section contains an accounting of all transactions in your trust account since the beginning of the file and not just this account. This trust accounting is a requirement of the Law Society. The other two sections do not go back to your first account. I will generally pay for disbursements for cash-flow purposes, except for photocopying, faxes, and postage, from the trust account.

To determine how much in total you have paid me when there is more than one account on your file, which is usually the case in matrimonial matters, add up all of the receipts from me in the trust account. I generally deposit all of your payments into my trust account and then transfer them to pay your invoice. That makes it easier to see the total you pay me. It is possible for a payment for an amount owing to go directly to settle your account and not be deposited into the trust account.

I suggest that you retain all your accounts in your manual.

A 5.13.2 Memorandum on Costs and Process for Uncontested Divorces

FEES, DISBURSEMENTS, PROCEDURE, AND TIMING FOR UNCONTESTED DIVORCES

DEFINITION OF UNCONTESTED DIVORCE:

An uncontested divorce is one in which the client is not seeking anything other than a divorce, or a Separation Agreement or Court Order has already settled the terms of the relief. There would also be no problem in locating and serving the spouse.

If the parties have agreed to settlement terms, but there are no written Separation Agreements or Court Orders, no issues as to property or financial disclosure, the case would be considered an uncontested divorce. In that case, however, there would be an extra charge to draft Minutes of Settlement, setting out the terms of the agreement between the parties.

SOLICITOR'S FEE:

$1,000.00 plus HST (Tax) of $130.00. This fee includes:

(a) advising the client as to their rights and obligations under the Divorce Act and the Family Law Act;

(b) drafting, signing, issuing, and serving the Application for Divorce;

(c) preparing documentation to obtain the Divorce Order;

(d) preparing the documentation to obtain a Certificate of Divorce;

(e) reporting to the client.

DISBURSEMENTS:

Issue Application for Divorce 167.00

Service of Application for Divorce (if required) 32.00

File Continuing Record to obtain Divorce Order 280.00

Certificate of Divorce 19.00

Court filing 67.80

Photocopying & postage 15.00

Marriage Certificate (if original not available) 22.00

602.80

Total fees, disbursements and HST(tax) (approx) $1,730.00

PAYMENT OF FEES AND DISBURSEMENTS:

A payment of $900.00 is required at the time of signing the Application for Divorce. The balance of the fees and disbursements is required when signing the Affidavit for the Divorce Order.

PROCEDURE & TIMING TO OBTAIN AN UNCONTESTED DIVORCE

1. Client phones the lawyer with information to draft the Application for Divorce (Day 1)
2. Client signs the Application for Divorce (Day 5)
3. Court issues the Application for Divorce (Day 6)
4. Spouse is served with the Continuing Record, which includes the Application for Divorce (Day 8)
5. Lawyer applies for Divorce Order (30 days after the spouse is served if served in Ontario, 50 days if outside of Ontario. (Day 38)
6. Client receives Divorce Order directly from Court (approximately 2 to 4 weeks after applying, provided there is a Central Divorce Registry Clearance Certificate). (Day 59)
7. Lawyer applies for Certificate of Divorce (31 days after judge signs Divorce Order which is approximately 1 to 2 weeks from the applying for Divorce Order). (Day 80)
8. Client receives Certificate of Divorce from the lawyer (about 1 week after the lawyer applies for the Certificate of Divorce)

If the stars are aligned, a client may obtain an uncontested divorce within three months after contacting the lawyer. This timeline is often delayed because the Central Divorce Registry Clearance Certificate is not received by the Court when the lawyer applies for the Divorce Order. The Court and not the lawyer controls this search time.

One should not set a wedding date until the Divorce Order is issued. The Court issues the Divorce Order only once the Central Divorce Registry Clearance Certificate is issued.

Appendix 6 Wills and Powers of Attorney

A 6.1.2.1 Wills and Powers of Attorney Manual Index

<u>WILLS and POWERS of ATTORNEY MANUAL INDEX</u>

1. Letters from Lawrence S. Pascoe
2. Copy of the Will of **X**
3. Copies of letters to Estate Trustee(s) and Attorney(s)
4. Memorandums:
   - (a) Lawrence S. Pascoe New Client Memorandum
   - (b) Storage of Wills and Powers of Attorney
   - (c) Retrieving of Wills and Powers of Attorney
5. Articles
   - a. The Purpose and Plain Meaning of Clauses Contained in a Will
   - b. Changing Your Will
   - c. Administering an Estate
   - d. Inheritances and Gifts to Children
   - e. Preparing for an Easier Administration of an Estate
   - f. When Death Occurs
   - g. Estate Planning for the Average Canadian
   - h. The Administration of a Simple Estate
6. Instructions from Client
   - a. Funeral and Burial Instructions
   - b. People to Notify
   - c. Personal Belongings
7. Information
   - a. List of Assets
   - b. Location of Documents
   - c. Personal Advisors
8. To-Do List
9. Retainer & Consent to Act Re-Conflict
10. Notes

A 6.1.2.2 Instruction and Information Forms for Wills and Powers of Attorney Manual

FUNERAL AND BURIAL INSTRUCTIONS

Though I realize the following is not binding on my Executor (Estate Trustee), the following are my wishes:

- Choice of the funeral home or memorial society:
- Location of burial plot:
- Open or closed coffin:
- Cremation or not:
- Where ashes are to be spread:
- Location of funeral:
- The wording of the obituary:
- Hymns or songs to be sung:
- Pallbearers:

PEOPLE TO NOTIFY INSTRUCTIONS

There should be a list with addresses (preferably emails) and telephone numbers of all executors, relatives. friends, clubs, and professional associations.

PERSONAL BELONGINGS INSTRUCTIONS

"Though I realize the following is not binding upon my Estate Trustee(s), after consultation with my beneficiaries, I would ask my Estate Trustee(s) to distribute the following personal belongings to the following people:"

LIST OF ASSETS AND DEBTS

Location of Will

Location of Safety Deposit Boxes

Bank Accounts - branch name and bank numbers

Stocks and Bonds - company names, number of shares, and where certificate located

Insurance Policies and Death Benefit - company name, policy numbers amount, beneficiary, and where the policy is located

Pensions - name of Pension Plan

RRSP's, RRIF's, TFSA name who with and amounts

Interest in Other Estates or Assets

Real Estate - address, mortgages

Debts - name of creditors, what kind, security given, amount due, terms

LOCATION OF DOCUMENTS
(A – Accountant's Office) (B – Stock Broker's Office) (H – Home) (L – Lawyer's Office) (O – Office) (S – Safety Deposit Box) (W – Will Manual)

LIST OF PASSWORDS FOR COMPUTERS
WHERE DOCUMENTS CAN BE FOUND
Use one of the locations above to identify where the following documents may be located:

Will:

Income Tax Returns:

Marriage Certificate:

Birth Certificate:

Bank Books:

Stocks:

Bonds:

Deeds to Property:

Life Insurance Policies:

Mortgage, Loan, Creditor Documents:

Funeral Arrangements:

Automobile Insurance Policies:

Property Insurance Policies:

PERSONAL ADVISORS

LAWYER:

Address:

Phone No.:

Reason to Notify: To Administer Estate

The same should be done for the following:
Life Insurance Agent:
Stock Broker:
Accountant:
Investment Counselor:
Spiritual Advisor:
Doctor:
Employer Personnel Department:

A 6.4 Wills and Powers of Attorney First Consultation Slideshow

A 6.4 The Wills and Powers of Attorney First Consultation Slideshow

WILLS AND POWERS OF ATTORNEY FIRST CONSULTATION Lawrence S. Pascoe
INTRODUCTION & IDENTIFICATION 1. Review information forms client has filled out for consultation, if not already sent in 2. Obtain and explain need for identification and obtain copy of driver's licence
PURPOSES OF CONSULTATION 1. To obtain client's instructions to draft Will and Powers of Attorney 2. To answer client's questions 3. To advise client with respect to Will, the Powers of Attorney and Estate Planning concepts 4. To finalize obtaining all necessary information 5. To confirm LSP process to finalize file 6. To review client's "To- Dos" and follow up checklist
WHAT A WILL DOES 1. Decides who gets what assets or what part of the estate 2. Decides at what age beneficiaries receive their bequests 3. Decided who looks after the estate and who looks after the trusts for minors 4. Suggest who would be the custodians of minor children 5. Suggest mode of burial

ASSET INFORMATION

1. Reasons to obtain asset information
   - To decide what beneficiaries receive
   - Starting point to help locate assets on death (explain assets not found problem)
   - Advice about forms in manual to keep up to date
2. Confirms Capacity
   - Explain law of competency to make a will
   - Ensure obtain values if competency might be an issue
3. Simple Probate Planning
   - Joint ownership, naming beneficiaries directly
   - Suggested changes
4. Decide whether more complex tax planning is needed
5. Finalize Asset Information Form
   - Review form and make sure it is complete

BENEFICIARIES

1. Review the client's suggested beneficiaries
   - Record beneficiaries and their bequests
2. Explain who would normally be the beneficiaries (if there was no Will)
3. If suggested and normal beneficiaries are different obtain from client the reasons why
4. Decide if medical competency report is needed for why beneficiaries are different than normal
5. Ensure there are alternate beneficiaries
   - Explain the need for alternates including Rule of Saunders v Vautier
   - Record alternate beneficiaries and their bequests
6. At what age are the children and grandchildren to receive their bequests
   - Explain how Trusts work for children
   - Record ages beneficiaries obtain their bequests outright
7. Are there children born outside of marriage?
   - Explain the law and the will clause

ESTATE TRUSTEES (EXECUTORS)

1. Explain duties of Estate Trustees
2. Review choices of Estate Trustees and alternates
3. Explain LSP theories on who should be Estate Trustees
   - Why more than one Estate Trustee
   - Who Estate Trustees should be
4. Record Estate Trustees and Alternates

ESTATE PLANNING 1. Review when appropriate 2. Testamentary Trusts • Explain how testamentary trusts work and how money can be saved • Explain appropriate situations • Explain whether their case is appropriate • Explain costs • Record whether need to be put in the Will 3. Multiple Wills • Explain how probate fees can be saved • Explain appropriate situations • Investigate whether their case is appropriate • Explain costs • Record if client wants multiple Wills
ESTATE PLANNING CONTINUED 4. Simple Estate Planning • Review again joint ownership and naming beneficiaries 5. Review what not to do • Joint ownership with children • Giving away assets
CUSTODIANS (GUARDIANS OF CHILDREN) 1. Explain duties of custodians 2. Explain the law of appointing custodians 3. Review choice of custodians and alternates
BURIAL INSTRUCTIONS 1. Explain law 2. Explain instruction page in Wills and Powers of Attorney Manual
SAFE KEEPING OF ORIGINAL WILL 1. Explain need for the Will to be kept in a safe place 2. Does client have their own safety deposit box 3. Explain process if Will kept in LSP safe 4. Decide where Will will be kept
LOCATION AND DESTRUCTION OF PREVIOUS WILLS 1. Where are previous Wills now being kept 2. Explain need for dealing with previous Wills 3. Obtain instructions for directions and letter to get and destroy previous Wills

ESTATE TRUSTEE LETTERS

1. Explain purpose of letters to estate trustees
2. Review what letters state
3. Obtain addresses of estate trustees

LEGAL CONSIDERATIONS

1. Discuss and record notes on testamentary capacity
2. Discuss need for capacity assessment
3. Discuss whether anyone is influencing the client
4. Discuss whether Will is being made in contemplation of marriage
5. Discuss whether there are any dependants
6. Is there a marriage contract/cohabitation agreement
7. Discuss property and multiple Wills in other jurisdictions
8. Discuss whether need for an international Will
9. Ensure no contravention of the Rule against Perpetuities
10. Ensure no contravention of the Rule against Accumulations
11. Ensure no contravention of the Rule in Saunders v. Vautier

WILL SUMMARY and SPECIAL CLAUSES

1. Review what Will states
2. Born Outside of Marriage clause
3. Family Law Act clause
4. Meaning of "per stirpes"
5. Technical clauses

LAWYER'S OBLIGATION WHEN JOINT INSTRUCTIONS

1. Explain a lawyer's obligation when advising and drafting Wills for a married or unmarried couple

CONTINUING POWER of ATTORNEY for PROPERTY

1. Explain purposes of this type of Power of Attorney
2. Explain how it takes effect immediately
3. Review choices of Attorneys and Alternates
4. Explain acting separately or together

POWER of ATTORNEY for PERSONAL CARE

1. Explain purposes of this type of Power of Attorney
2. Explain when it takes effect
3. Review choices of Attorneys and Alternates
4. Explain acting separately or together
5. Explain and decide about life support clause

LSP PROCESS TO FINALIZE 1. Explain process to execute the documents and complete the file 2. Follow Up Checklist • go through each item on the checklist • make an appointment date to sign the Will and Powers of Attorney
ANY OTHER QUESTIONS FROM CLIENT 1. Ask if there is anything not covered that the client wishes to know or anything the client does not understand
MANUAL & NEW CLIENT MEMORANDUM 1. Give client the Wills and Powers of Attorney Manual 2. Explain what is in the manual 3. Give and review LSP New Client Memorandum
REQUISITION TO OPEN FILE FORM 1. Complete the Requisition to Open File form 2. Give client LSP magnetic business card

A 6.9 Wills and Powers of Attorney Client Checklist

WILL and P of A CLIENT TO DO LIST	TO DO	DONE
Check deed states "as Joint Tenants and not as Tenants in Common"		
Check RRSP's, RRIF's have named beneficiaries		
Check TFSA's have named beneficiaries		
Check Life insurance has named beneficiaries		
Change Bank accounts to joint names		
Change Investments to joint names		
Confirm Estate Trustees, Attorneys will act		
Confirm Alternate Estate Trustees, Attorneys will act		
Confirm Custodians will act		
Confirm Alternate Custodians will act		
Finalize Asset Information Form		
E mail addresses for Estate Trustees & Attorneys		

WILL and P of A CLIENT TO DO LIST	TO DO	DONE
Complete Lawyer Performance Questionnaire		
Check former Will is destroyed after signing		
Appointment Time and Date to sign the Will		

A 6.12 Wills and Powers of Attorney Process Chart

WILLS & POWERS OF ATTORNEY ACTIONS	BRIEF EXPLANATIONS OF ACTIONS
1. Client Chooses a Lawyer. (Client).	Client asks relatives and friends for a referral. Clients check out referrals on lawyer's website as well as websites of other lawyers who practice Wills and Powers of Attorney Law.
2. Contact Lawyer for an appointment. (Client).	Client phones or emails lawyer's office requesting an appointment.
3. Intake form completed by lawyer and consultation scheduled. (Lawyer). *Takes 1-2 weeks to obtain appointment.*	Lawyer obtains contact details and information to ensure the lawyer can act for the client. Price of service is confirmed.
4. Confirmation letter sent to Client. (Lawyer). *Sent same or next day as appointment is made.*	Lawyer confirms date and time of appointment. Links to questionnaires are given to client to fill out prior to appointment.
5. Client completes questionnaires and sends back to lawyer. Client also makes copies of questionnaires as backup. (Client). *Done before appointment date.*	The questionnaires are found on the website and can be sent from the website but best to make a backup copy.
6. Lawyer reviews client's questionnaires. (Lawyer). *When received or done before appointment date.*	Lawyer looks for situations out of the ordinary to discuss with client.
7. Initial Consultation with client. (Lawyer and Client).	See first Wills and Powers Consultation Slide which shows in detail what is discussed at this consultation. Client signs retainer and arranges mode of payment.

WILLS & POWERS OF ATTORNEY ACTIONS	BRIEF EXPLANATIONS OF ACTIONS
8. Client gets back to lawyer with instructions if not completed at initial consultation. (Client). Lawyer drafts Wills and Powers of Attorney and send drafts to clients. (Lawyer). *Done within a few days of first appointment.*	Generally, the client does not need further time to think about instructions or to obtain information but if does, the lawyer will wait for that information before drafting.
9. Client starts on their To-Do List. (Client).	Most of the client To-Do lists can be done at this stage and some are necessary before signing the Will. Others can wait until even after Will signing.
10. Lawyer drafts Wills and Powers of Attorney and sends drafts to clients. (Lawyer). *Done within a few days of first appointment or receiving final instruction, well in time before signing appointment.*	Based on client's instructions drafts the Wills and Powers of Attorney and sends out to client for their review.
11. Client reviews documents and advises lawyer all is ok or asks lawyer questions about documents or requests changes. (Client). *Must be done at least two days before appointment to sign date.*	Client should ensure instructions were followed and names are correctly spelled. Client may have questions about clauses in the documents that were not understood at the consultation and of the articles. Client may have changed their mind on the instructions.
12. Lawyer answers questions and if changes, redrafts documents and sends them out. (Lawyer).	Generally, this step is not used as most drafts are accepted without changes.
13. Lawyer confirms appointment, and all is well the day or two before signing. (Lawyer).	Lawyer reminds client of their appointment and ensures there are no changes so documents can be prepared in final form for signing.
14. Signing Consultation and final report to client. (Lawyer and Client). *Same day as signing date.*	Client does one last review. Client then signs documents and takes Wills and Powers of Attorney Manual with them and perhaps original Will. Manual is discussed in more detail.

WILLS & POWERS OF ATTORNEY ACTIONS	BRIEF EXPLANATIONS OF ACTIONS
15. Original Will is put in safekeeping. (Lawyer or Client). *Same day as signing date.*	Either Lawyer keeps the Will in office safe or client takes their Will with them.
16. Letters sent to Estate Trustees and Alternates. (Lawyer). *Same day as signing date.*	These letters set out Estate Trustees' responsibilities by linking to articles and advises where original Will is located.
17. Letters sent to previous lawyer. (Lawyer). *Same day as signing date.*	After client signs direction to former lawyer, it is sent to ensure there are no other Wills in existence and allows the previous lawyer to no longer store the old Will.
18. Client finalizes To-Do list if not done already. (Client)	There may be some items on client To-Do list that client must still complete.
19. Client keeps up to date Instructions and Information in Wills and Powers of Attorney Manual. (Client). *Ongoing when changes made.*	To ensure an easier administration of the client's estate on death these forms should be kept up to date.
20. Client Reviews Will when there are changes in circumstances and wishes and consults lawyer to change Wills and Powers of Attorney. (Client). *Should review annually or when major changes.*	If there are changes to the client's life such as the children becoming adults so should be named as Estate Trustees or there is a falling out with a beneficiary, the client should contact the lawyer to redo their will.

A 6.13.6 Wills and Powers of Attorney Retainer and Consent to Act for Both Parties

1. We retain Lawrence S. Pascoe to advise us on all legal matters related to the drafting and execution of our Wills, Continuing Powers of Attorney for Property, and Personal Care Powers of Attorney.
2. We understand that Lawrence S. Pascoe is not responsible for any tax planning regarding our present financial situation or our Estate as he is not a tax specialist.
3. We understand that we are responsible for:
   a) providing accurate information on the ownership and value of our assets and debts;
   b) providing accurate spelling of the names of our estate trustee(s) and beneficiaries.
4. Lawrence S. Pascoe will be compensated based on his posted fee schedule, which in our case is $________ plus HST. We further agree that he will also be compensated if additional time is expended by him or his assistant above and beyond the usual time required because of unforeseen circumstances.
5. We will pay Lawrence Pascoe's fees after the first consultation. He will hold the money in trust until he performs the work. Or we will sign a credit card authorization at the first consultation to be charged when he completes the work, or he renders a partial account if we postpone the signing date.
6. We acknowledge that should we wish to hold onto our original Wills and Powers of Attorney, we are responsible for the important task of safeguarding these documents.
7. We acknowledge that Lawrence S. Pascoe will be retiring within the next few years. We further acknowledge that if our Wills are stored in Lawrence S. Pascoe's safe, but upon his retirement, our Wills (and Powers of Attorney, if applicable) will be transferred to the Law Firm of XXX and X. Upon signing the Wills & Powers of Attorney Retainer, we are providing our consent to the transfer of our Will file to XXX and X.

8. We also understand that our Wills are automatically revoked upon marriage, and Lawrence S. Pascoe has advised us that we should have new Wills if we are going to remarry. *Note Law has been changed in Ontario.
9. We acknowledge Lawrence S. Pascoe advised us that:
   a) he represents us jointly, and we expressly consent to him acting in this capacity;
   b) all information received in connection with this matter from either one of us cannot be treated as confidential where the other joint party is concerned, and that the rules of the Law Society of Ontario require that when law firms represent clients jointly, the lawyer must raise certain issues with each of the joint parties and obtain their consent on the course to be followed if a conflict arises;
   c) if a material conflict arises between us that we cannot resolve, Lawrence S. Pascoe will advise us thereof. It may be necessary for Lawrence S. Pascoe to discontinue acting for either party.

Dated this day of, 20__.

____________________	____________________
Print Name	Client Signature
____________________	____________________
Print Name	Client Signature

- The law on revocation and marriage has changed in Ontario now and may be different in each jurisdiction.

A 6.15.1 Executor and Powers of Attorney Letters

Date

VIA EMAIL TO:

Re: Wills and Powers of Attorney of X

I recently drafted the Wills for X. X named you as an Executor/Alternate Executor in his/her/their Will. You were also named Attorney/Alternate Attorney in his/her/their Personal Care Powers of Attorney and an Attorney/Alternate attorney in his/her/their Continuing Powers of Attorney for Property.

The original Wills and a set of original Powers of Attorney are being held in safekeeping at my office. A second original set of the Powers of Attorney is situated at my client's residence in his/her their "Wills and Powers of Attorney Manual," a three-ring binder. I have an electronic copy of each of the Wills and the Powers of Attorney. The manual also has information memoranda about my client's assets, burial wishes, and personal belongings directions. I have instructed my client/clients to keep this information current.

To help you better understand your duties of the important jobs you have taken on, I suggest you read the following articles I have written found on my website. The article entitled "Administration of Estates" generally sets out what must be done to administer an estate and can be found at http://thepascoedifference.com/administration-of-estates/ The Continuing Powers of Attorney for Property and Powers of Attorney for Personal Care articles discuss the purposes of Powers of Attorney as well as setting out the obligations and rights of an attorney and can be found at http://thepascoedifference.com/continuing-power-of-attorney-for-property-faq/ and http://thepascoedifference.com/personal-care-power-of-attorney/. I would also suggest you visit my website at www.thepascoedifference.com and review my comprehensive "Estate Administration Introductory Guide", which sets out the process of what must be done after a person passes away. It can be found at http://thepascoedifference.com/introduction-estate-administration/.

Yours very truly,

LAWRENCE S. PASCOE

A 6.18 Wills and Powers of Attorney Reporting Letter

DATE

Name

Address

Dear Sir/Madam:

Re: Your Wills and Powers of Attorney

On the XXX day of XXXX, 20xx, you attended at my office when you executed your Wills, Continuing Powers of Attorney for Property, and Personal Care Powers of Attorney. You signed your documents in the presence of the required witnesses. I gave you your Will Manual containing a copy of your Wills, an inventory list, certain memoranda and articles I have written.

On this date, **you took your original Wills with Affidavits of Execution with you, as well as your original Powers of Attorney. Or you advised me your Wills are in your safety deposit box at the Canadian Imperial Bank of Commerce on 123 Main Street, Ottawa.** I have kept an electronic copy of these signed documents. Please do not keep your original Powers of Attorney in a safety deposit box or a safe as your attorney may have difficulty accessing them when needed.

It is very important that if you move or sign a new Will or Powers of Attorney with another lawyer, you advise me. It would be best if you did so so that an old Will or Power of Attorney can be destroyed so that there is never any confusion about the most recent document.

Your Will was drafted, taking into account what you have done or will do concerning the designations of the beneficiaries for your insurance, TFSAs, RRSPs, RRIFs, and assets held in joint ownership. Please keep that in mind and do not deviate from your overall plan by changing these designations of beneficiaries or changing ownership. Your Will does not override these designations nor change the nature of the ownership of these assets.

I will be sending a letter to your estate trustees (executors) advising them of the location of the original Wills and the existence of the Wills and Powers of Attorney Manual. My letter will also include a link on my website and to obtain further information about the Administration of Estates.

I would remind you to attend your bank to discuss your Continuing Power of Attorney for Property. Unfortunately, some banks make their own rules for Powers of Attorney.

Your bank may at this time request copies of your Continuing Power of Attorney for Property and specimen signatures of your attorneys. The bank may also require you to sign their own forms. You may do this if their forms do not say that you have revoked the Power of Attorney that I have prepared for you. As the law is unclear whether a Power of Attorney allows the Attorney access to a safety deposit box, I would ask that you discuss this issue with your bank. Some banks have their own separate forms allowing access to a safety deposit box.

For my services in reviewing your personal matters with you and drafting your Wills and Powers of Attorney to your satisfaction, I enclose my statement of account, which I trust you will find satisfactory.

Wills and Powers of Attorney are prepared under the circumstances as they exist at the time of drafting. You should review them from time to time, keeping in mind changes of intention and circumstances. Changes in the law could affect your planning. Concerning planning, a common misconception is that creating joint accounts always means the account passes to the survivor and does not form part of your Estate. That is not always the case, so please do not set up joint accounts without clearly stating your intention of what should happen with that account on your death.

I would remind you that your Wills and Powers of Attorney are based on Ontario law so if you move to another province or country, you will have to consult with a lawyer in your new jurisdiction. That lawyer will determine the validity and appropriateness of the Wills and Powers of Attorney you have just signed with me.

I would also like to remind you that a Will is automatically revoked on marriage and partially revoked on Divorce (the sections dealing with your spouse); therefore, I suggest you contact me if either of these scenarios applies to you.

I encourage you to keep your Will Manual up to date with changes in accounts, assets, personal property, specific gifts, people to notify, personal particulars, etc. I created the Manual to help you stay organized and manage your affairs. It also makes for an easier administration of your Estate. Should you need additional forms for your manual, you may obtain them from my website at http://thepascoedifference.com/wptpd/wp-content/uploads/2017/07/Form-to-Update-Wills-Manual.pdf. I would also suggest that you save a copy of these forms to your computer so that in the future, when I have retired and my website is no longer active, you will have these forms for your use.

It is not my obligation to advise you and all my former clients of changes to the law that could affect your Wills and Powers of Attorney. Therefore, I suggest that if you hear of any changes through the regular media or my social media platforms that you believe affect you, please contact me, or if I am no longer in practice (I do not plan to work forever), another lawyer.

Finally, I would ask that you complete the questionnaire in your manual. The information from it will be of great use in ensuring the highest quality of service to all my clients. It will also give you another chance in my survey contest. I hope you will consider recommending our firm to your friends or associates to whom we might be of assistance. I deal in the legal areas of the Administration of Estates and in most aspects of family law.

Yours very truly,

LAWRENCE S. PASCOE

LSP*jm

Enclosure: Statement of Account

A 7.1.2.1 Administration of Estates Manual Index

ADMINISTRATION of ESTATE MANUAL

RE: The Estate of

1. Administration of Estates

   Article: *Grief Intelligence: A Primer*

   Lawrence S. Pascoe New Client Memorandum

   Tasks and Fee Schedule in Administration of an Estate

2. Estate Task & Fees Chart
3. Letters from L. S. Pascoe to Client
4. Copies of Other Correspondence
5. Copy of Will; Copy of Certificate of Appointment of Estate Trustee; Court Documents
6. Estate Accounts, Assets

   Debts and Benefits

7. Estate Bank Account Ledger
8. Sample Letters and Memoranda

   Letter to Service Ontario (Health Card)

   Letter to Subscription Company Name

   Letter to Passport Canada

   Letter to Service Ontario (SIN Card)

   Letter to Service Ontario (Driver's License)

   How to Transfer a Motor Vehicle to a Beneficiary With a Will

   How to Transfer a Motor Vehicle to a Surviving Spouse With a Will

   Unclaimed Balances – Bank of Canada – How to Claim

9. New Information for Estate Trustees

   Checklist of Information Required to Complete the Estate Information Return

   Guide to Completing the Estate Information Return

   Sample Estate Information Return

   The Life & Health Insurance Industry's Policy Search Service

10. Client To-Do List & Notes

A 7.3.2 Estate Asset and Debt Information Form

DESCRIPTION of ASSETS and DEBTS	TYPE & % of OWNERSHIP	BENEFICIARY or JOINT OWNER	DATE OF DEATH VALUE	PROBATE VALUE	DOCUMENTARY PROOF
Real Estate					
Bank Accounts					
Cash					
Registered Retirement Savings Plans					
Tax Free Savings Account					
Registered Retirement Income Funds					
Mutual Funds					
Stocks					
Life Insurance					
Employee Benefits					
Pension/Survivor's Benefits					
Canada Pension Plan Death Benefit					
Motor Vehicle					
Jewelry					

DESCRIPTION of ASSETS and DEBTS	TYPE & % of OWNERSHIP	BENEFICIARY or JOINT OWNER	DATE OF DEATH VALUE	PROBATE VALUE	DOCUMENTARY PROOF
Household Furniture					
Art Work					
Other					
Mortgage					
Loans					
Credit Cards					
Total Value of Estate					
Total Value of Assets for Probate					
Probate Fee					

A 7.4 First Administration of Estate Consultation Slideshow

ADMINISTRATION OF ESTATES INITIAL CONSULTATION

LAWRENCE S. PASCOE

IDENTIFICATION

3. Explain need and requirement for identification
4. Obtain copy of driver's license or photo identification

PURPOSE of CONSULTATION

1. To obtain information so to be able to advise as to what tasks have to be done to administer the estate
2. To explain the details of the tasks that must be done to complete the administration of the estate
3. To obtain instructions from the client as to what tasks the lawyer will do and at whatl cost and what tasks the client will do
4. To explain the court application of applying for probate and calculate the probate fees
5. To obtain client authorizations to discuss the assets with financial institutions
6. To provide the client with the notarial copy of the Will if necessary and discussed dealing with the bank to receive money and pay bills
7. To discuss the issues of advertising for creditors, income tax, executor's compensation and claims against the estate
8. To discuss the accounting and distribution of this estate
9. To provide an explain the Administration of Estates Manual
10. To explain the lawyer client process and timing
11. To provide client with client checklist of what to do and lawyer/staff to do checklist
12. To introduce the client to the legal assistant
13. To answer client's questions

REVIEW WILL AND QUESTIONNAIRES WITH CLIENT

1. Confirm client has authority to act as executor
2. If there is no Will, confirm client has right to be appointed the estate trustee
3. Review forms client filled out and note what information is still needed

ASSETS, DEBTS AN BENEFITS INFORMATION 1. Complete LSP asset, debt and benefits information form, and provide to client 2. Discuss what information about assets still needs to be obtained 3. Discuss whether probate is necessary based upon nature and value of assets 4. Calculate probate fee if necessary
TASKS NEEDED TO BE COMPLETED 1. Go through each task on the task form to explain what tasks need to be done 2. Decide who will do what task 3. Calculate legal fees associated with death and method of payment
APPLYING FOR PROBATE 1. Explain what probate is 2. Explain what is involved in obtaining probate 3. Explain obligations to beneficiaries 4. Ensure have all or will get all information needed to apply for probate
Authorizations 1. Explain and obtain authorizations to financial institutions to obtain information and to give instructions to pay probate and legal fees
ESTATE BANK ACCOUNT 1. Explain reasons for setting up an estate bank account 2. Provide notarial copy of the Will for establishment of a estate bank account 3. Explain bill paying by financial institutions
ADVERTISING FOR CREDITORS 1. Advise as to when advertising for creditors is necessary 2. Decide whether to advertise for creditors 3. Discuss where to advertise and the costs
INCOME TAX 1. Explain how the estate is taxed in year of death 2. Decide who will look after tax returns 3. Explain tax clearance certificates

EXECUTOR COMPENSATION 1. Explain general rules of executive compensation 2. Decide if compensation will be taken
ACCOUNTING AND DISTRIBUTION OF THE ESTATE 1. Explain the need and how to keep accounts 2. Decide who will keep the accounts 3. Discuss how and when the estate will be distributed 4. Discuss obtaining releases from beneficiaries
LSP ADMINISTRATION OF AN ESTATE MANUAL 1. Provide client with Administration of an Estates Manual 2. Explain what is in the manual and how to use it 3. Review New Client Memorandum
LSP PROCESS 1. Explain what further client appointments are necessary and when they will be 2. Explain reporting letters and fees
CHECKLISTS 1. Produce client to-do checklist 2. Produce lawyer/staff to do check list
ESTATE LEGAL ASSISTANT 1. Introduce client to the legal assistant
REQUISITIONED OPEN FILE FORM 3. Complete requisitioned open file form 4. Provide LSP magnet
QUESTIONS 2. Confirm client has no further questions at this time

A 7.6 Administration of Estates Retainer

- The undersigned retain(s) Lawrence S. Pascoe to advise on all legal matters related to the administration of this estate and to complete the tasks required to administer the estate as set out in the Administration of Estates Tasks List.
- It is understood that Lawrence S. Pascoe is not responsible for any tax planning regarding the estate, nor for filing any of the deceased personal or estate tax returns.
- It is understood that the undersigned are specifically responsible for these tasks in addition to those set out in the Administration of Estates Tasks List.
    - Making the funeral and burial arrangements.
    - Determining the identity of and locating the estate's beneficiaries and providing all information to complete an application for a Certificate of Appointment if necessary.
    - Determining the value and providing documentary proof of each asset and debt of the estate within a reasonable time.
    - Opening an estate bank account and keeping detailed records of all estate transactions.
    - Retaining a qualified person to complete all necessary tax returns for the deceased and the estate.
- It is specifically understood that if a Certificate of Appointment is obtained that the undersigned must by law file the Ontario Estate Information Return within 90 days of issuing the Certificate of Appointment (Probate). The undersigned as Estate Trustee(s) is responsible and liable for the statements and values reported to the court.
- Lawrence S. Pascoe will be compensated on a task basis as set out in the Administration of Estates Tasks List. It is further agreed that he will also be compensated if additional time is expended by either himself or his assistant to complete said tasks due to unforeseen events or if additional tasks are added.

- Though the estate is primarily liable for Lawrence S. Pascoe's fees, the undersigned acknowledges that the undersigned may be called upon to pay Lawrence S. Pascoe's fees in advance should the estate not do so on a timely or final basis. The undersigned, therefore, agrees to provide a credit authorization at the time of the initial consultation.

Dated this day of 202X.

______________________ ______________________

Print Name Client's Signature

______________________ ______________________

Print Name Client's Signature

A 7.9 Estate Client To-Do List

Estate Client To-Do List		
DOCUMENTS TO OBTAIN	**TO DO**	**DONE**
Will		
Death Certificate		
Birth Certificate		
Doctor's Report		
Date of Death Asset and Debt Statements		
Beneficiaries' Names and Addresses		
TASKS		
Set up Estate Bank Account		
Contact Life Insurance Agent		
Contact Accountant (re: taxes)		
Pay Funeral Home		
Apply for CPP Death Benefit		
Apply for CPP Survivor Benefits		
Write Employer about Benefits		
Transfer Vehicle Ownership		
Cancel Newspaper, Utilities		
Change Mailing Address		

A 7.10 Estate Tasks and Fees

#	TASK	LAWYER	CLIENT	FEE
1	Initial Contact & Consultation: Obtain information, answer questions and advise as to all the tasks that must be done to administer the estate and advise of compensation issues. Determine whether an application to the court is necessary (this might not be known at this time). Assign which tasks will be done by the client and which by the lawyer. Cost $475 but subject to increase if it takes more than an hour spent, then will be based upon time taken at $375 per hour. (lawyer only)	X		$475
	Extra lawyer time			
2	Obtain the probate and estate values of every asset and proof of those amounts. Best to be the task of the client but in rare cases the lawyer will do it on an hourly rate basis of the lawyer and the administrative time. (lawyer or client)			
3	Prepare a list of all assets and debts of the estate at time of death and when redeemed with binder of documentary proof (administrative task). Will charge only when time is excessive because of many assets or documents not complete and must calculate date of death value manually. (legal assistant)			
4	Setting up the Estate Bank Account: Either changing an existing bank account to an estate bank account or setting up a new one to receive estate assets and pay estate bills. The estate trustee, not the lawyer, will be the person controlling the payment of all estate monies. Lawyer will provide notarial copy of Will. (client only)		X	

#	TASK	LAWYER	CLIENT	FEE
5	Application for Appointment of Estate Trustee: Involves making a list of assets and their values that are subject to the probate fee; preparing the documents to apply for appointment; preparing and sending the notices required by law to the beneficiaries. Cost $1000 but subject to increase if there are more than five beneficiaries or estate trustees to deal with, if a guarantee bond needs to be obtained or dispensed with, or there are changes to the estate trustees originally appointed. There will be a charge of $75 for each beneficiary over 5. If there is no Will, the cost of applying is $1100 because of the extra work involved. Hourly rate of $375 applies if unusual problems obtaining the appointment or more time than usual is taken by lawyer or legal assistant. (lawyer only)			
	Extra legal assistant time			
6	Letters to Government Departments: To ensure that there is no possibility for identity theft, a number of government departments should be advised of the testator's death. They include the Ministry of Health, Passport Canada, Social Insurance registration, and Ministry of Transportation. The Administration of Estates Manual provides samples of these letters with addresses. The estate trustee usually performs this task, but if the estate trustee wants the lawyer to do it, the lawyer will, but at a charge of $30 per letter. (lawyer or client)			
7	Application for Canada Pension Plan Benefits: Complete the forms with required documents to obtain CPP Death benefit and survivor's benefit. Cost $100. The Department of Human Resources responsible for CPP will help client complete the application. (lawyer or client)			

#	TASK	LAWYER	CLIENT	FEE
8	Transfer of Monetary Assets: Write banks, financial institutions, to obtain procedure to transfer the asset to the estate or beneficiary. Arrange to transfer the assets. Cost $250 per institution. $25.00 for each notarial copy made if client is dealing with bank (Lawyer's or client's task though some forms to transfer may need to be done by the lawyer.)			
	Extra legal assistant time			
9	Transfer of Motor Vehicle: Advise client as to how to transfer the registration of an automobile. No charge except $25.00 for each notarial copy made if client is dealing with automobile transfer (Client's task to attend at Motor Vehicle Licence Bureau.)			
10	Arrange for Payment of Life Insurance: Write insurance companies advising of death and prepare documentation to obtain payment of life insurance: Cost $250 per institution. (Lawyer's or client's task). Some Insurance companies' agents will help the client with the application.			
11	Arrange for Transfer of RRSP's: Write financial institutions to obtain procedure and documents to transfer the funds and complete the transfer. Cost $250 per institution. (lawyer or client)			
12	Arrange for Receipt of Pensions and Annuities: Write institutions to obtain the pension or annuity procedure and complete documentation to obtain pension or annuity. Cost $250 per institution. Most employers and institutions will help the client with the application and provide a letter explaining all the benefits. (lawyer or client)			

#	TASK	LAWYER	CLIENT	FEE
13	Transfer of Property: Legal Fees of $200 with disbursements of approximately $200.(lawyer only)			
14	Advertise for Creditors: Arrange for the creditor's notice to be placed in a local newspaper. This is generally necessary only when the estate trustee is concerned there are unknown debts and wants to protect him or herself from being personally liable. Cost $150 for lawyer $600 - $1200 for newspaper. (lawyer)			
15	Payment of Debts: Write all financial institutions and persons to whom money is owed to ascertain amount owed and whether debt was life insured and then arrange to pay the debt. Cost $100 per institution. (lawyer or client)			
16	Defending a Claim against the Estate: If the estate is sued by a person claiming to be a dependant under the Succession Law Reform Act, a spouse under the Family law Act or anyone contesting the validity of the Will, the cost would be based upon the normal costs of a litigation lawyer defending a law suit. (lawyer only)			
17	Income Tax: Arranging and providing accountant with information to prepare the terminal tax return, and if required, a trust tax return. Cost $100. (lawyer or client)			
18	Obtaining Final Tax Clearance Certificate: Preparing documentation to be used to obtain a final tax clearance certificate. Cost $150 (lawyer, accountant or client)			
19	Keeping the Accounts of the Estate: Recording all the transactions of the estate in proper court form. Calculating the amounts payable to beneficiaries. Cost $300 for the interim distribution to the beneficiaries (if there is one) and $300 for the final distribution to the beneficiaries, subject to an increase, if complicated. (lawyer or client)			

#	TASK	LAWYER	CLIENT	FEE
20	Extra legal assistant time			
21	Prepare Ontario Government Form required within 90 days of obtaining the Certificate of Appointment stating the value of the estate. (lawyer or client) Cost $150.			
	Reporting and Obtaining Releases from the Beneficiaries: Advising the beneficiaries of the accounting and distribution of the estate, drafting and obtaining from the beneficiaries a Release of the Estate Trustee and indemnification in case of further income tax. Cost $100 per beneficiary. Extra on a time basis if must deal with a beneficiary contesting the amount of their payment. There will also be an extra charge if there is an interim distribution of $100 per beneficiary. (lawyer)			
22	Passing The Accounts Before the Court: If a beneficiary requests the estate trustee to have the estates accounts approved by the court, a "passing of accounts" must take place. Cost is charged on a regular hourly basis. (lawyer)			
23	Value of Estate If the estate's value is greater than $500,000 fees will be increased because of extra liability by charging ½ % of value over $500,000. Negotiable for larger estates			
24	Reporting to the Client: Confirming with the client in writing after the first consultation as to what has to be done to administer the estate and who will do it. Advising the client in writing at various stages of the administration of the estate of the results of all the tasks performed. $150 (except if only initial consultation or transferring property. (lawyer)	X		$150
	TOTAL LEGAL FEES			625

A 11.1 Lawyer's Chart of Applications

PRACTICE AREA				**Value** 1. **Little importance but useful** 2. **Important; should have** 3. **Very important; definitely have**
APPLICATIONS	**Chapter In Book**	**Should use it? Yes/No**	**Value 1-3**	**Time to create and implement; No time; Less than an hour; A few hours; Many hours**
Client Manuals	4.1			
Manual purpose	4.1.1			
Manual sections	4.1.2			
Keeping the Manual up to date	4.1.3			
Importance of the Manual	4.1.4			
Website	**4.2**			
Importance	4.2.1			
Organized	4.2.4			
Content	4.2.5			
Questionnaires	4.2.6			
Videos	4.2.7			
Resources	4.2.8			
Third period use	4.2.9			
Making appointments	4.2.10			
Promoting clients	4.2.11			
Legal Quiz	4..2.12			
Monitor	**4.3**			
1st Consultation Slideshow	4.4			

Questionnaires, Forms	**4.5**			
Intake Form	4.5.1			
General Information Questionnaire	4.5.2			
Specific Info Questionnaire	4.5.2			
Client Preference Questionnaire	4.5.3			
Performance Questionnaire	4.5.4			
Marketing Questionnaire	4.5.5			
Survey Contest	4.5.6			
Change of Info Form	4.5.7			
1st Appointment Confirmation	**4.6**			
Subsequent Appointment Letter	**4.7**			
Lawyer Notes	**4.8**			
To-Do List	**4.9**			
Document List	**4.9**			
Calculation of Fees	**4.10**			
Client-Helpful Word Processing Features	**4.11**			
ARTICLES FOR CLIENTS	**4.12**			
Substantive Law	4.12.1			
Definitions Annotations	4.12.2			
Legal Process Articles	4.12.3			
New Client Memorandum	4.12.4			
Expectations, Client-Lawyer Relationship	4.12.5			
How-to Articles	4.12.6			
Legal Fees and Bills	4.12.7			

Articles by Others	4.12.8			
Third Period Articles	4.12.9			
Why Use a Lawyer	4.12.10			
LEGAL FEES	**4.13**			
Method of Determining Fees	4.13.1			
Estimate of Fees	4.13.2			
Discussing Fees	4.13.3			
Ensure Getting Paid	4.13.4			
Tax Deductibility	4.13.5			
Retainer	4.13.6			
Unbundled Fees	4.13.7			
FOLLOW UP LEGAL SERVICES	**4.14**			
REDUCED RATE FEES	**4.14**			
LETTERS TO NONCLIENTS	**4.15**			
FOLLOWING UP WITH CLIENTS	**4.16**			
PROVIDING RESOURCE INFORMATION	**4.17**			
REPORTING LETTERS	**4.18**			
SOCIAL MEDIA	**4.19**			
CLIENT NEWSLETTER	**4.20**			
RADIO, TV, NEWSPAPER ADVERTISING	**4.21**			
RADIO, TV, PUBLIC APPEARANCES	**4.22**			
PHYSICAL APPLICATIONS	**4.23**			

Three-Hole Punch				
Business Cards				
PROPER THANK YOUS	**4.24**			
SPECIFIC LEGAL SOFTWARE	**4.25**			
DECISION MAKING FORMULA	**4.26**			
COMMUNICATIONS	**4.27**			
Checking In With Clients	4.27.1			
Automatically Sending Copies to Client	4.27.2			
Providing Court Arguments	4.27.3			
Detailed Voice Message	4.27.4			
Virtual Phone Calls and Virtual Consultations	4.27.5			
Telephone Policy	4.27.6			
Dictating in Front of Client	4.27.7			
Client Portal on the Cloud	4.27.8			
FLOWCHARTS	**4.28**			
INVENTING NEW PROCESS	**4.29**			
OTHER APPLICATIONS	**4.30**			
Safekeeping Client Documents	4.30.1			
Storing Completed File	4.30.2			
Discounts to Local Business	4.30.3			
Hours of Service	4.30.4			
Sales	4.30.5			

A 11.2 Application Elements and Their Importance

Appendix 11.2 Application Elements and Their Importance

CLIENT NEEDS	IMPORTANCE
Clients Want to be Confident Their Lawyers Are Very Competent	
Clients Want Their Lawyers to Be Empathetic	
Clients Want Good, Timely and Understandable Communications with Their Lawyers	
Clients Want to Know What Their Costs Will Be	
Clients Want to Know the Timing of Their Matter and Want It Completed Quickly	
Clients Want Their Tasks to Be Easy to Do	
Clients Want to Understand the Substantive Law and Legal Process	
Clients Want Their File Personalized Based on Their Preferences	
Clients Want to Participate in the Process	
RECOMMENDED LAWYER ACTIONS	
Lawyers Should Recognize What is Important to Lawyers May Not Be Important to Clients and What is Important to Clients May Not Be Important to Clients	
Lawyers Should Use All Three Time Periods (Before, During, and After Being Retained) to Provide Service	
Lawyers Should Utilize Available Legal Software	
Lawyers Should Utilize General Software	
Lawyers Should Indulge Clients but Give Realistic Expectations	
Lawyers Should Provide Information About Related Resources	
Lawyers Should Create Moments of Exceptional Service	

CLIENT NEEDS	IMPORTANCE
Lawyers Should Have Some Physical Aspects in Their Applications	
Lawyers Should Use Humor to Put Clients at Ease	
Lawyers Should Recognize Most Clients Are First Time Users of Legal Services	
Lawyers Should Show Appreciation to Clients and Others Who Refer Clients to Them	
Lawyers Should Always Remember What Business They Are In	

3-very important; 2- important; 1– a little important 0 - not important

A 13.1 List of Referral Sources

Friend, Previous Client, Drafted Deceased's Will, Another Lawyer Referral, Business Referral, Website, Referral from Friend, Referral from Client, E's Referral (a lawyer in my firm), P's referral (a lawyer in my firm), Location, Telephone Book Ad, Speaking Engagement, Article in Nepean Clarion, Advertisement in Nepean Clarion, Radio Advertisement, Collaborative Law Network Referral.

If the particulars, such as the name of a person referring, are known, lawyers should also note the person. For example, if one person, such as a doctor, is directing a lot of business to the lawyer, then that person might get their own category.

Acknowledgments

There are many people to thank for helping me write this book. I must start by thanking my wife, Carol, who spent many hours editing my writing and often saved me from myself. She cleaned up my many misplaced modifiers along with other grammatical mistakes and made this book much more readable. She stopped me from writing things that should not have been in the book. She also told me some stories were not that funny, and so I reduced some, but not all, of my humor. She gave me a lot of moral support.

I thank my friend, Aaron Caplan, who gave me weekly feedback and encouragement about what I had written during the many months it took to write this book.

I thank the few lawyers who read some of this book and gave me feedback: Norm Carroll, Jon Snipper, Norm Bowley, Bjorn Christenson, and my son, Byron Pascoe.

I thank my son, Noah Pascoe, who encouraged me to get a better book title, and those lawyers who tried valiantly without success to come up with a better title.

I thank the many people in the legal world, a few clients and relatives who I interviewed for the book or who helped with the writing of it: Paul Bregman, Carmen Baru, Norm Bowley, Leigh Lampert, Lynn Harnden, Jeffrey Goldberg, Noah Potechin, Douglas Livingstone, Norm Carroll, Jack Newton, David Bolton, Barbra Francey, Allan Brass, Shira Brass, Richard Shanbaum, David Lyman, Kristen Cinnamon, Mitch Besner, Thomas McMurtry, Colin McCorriston, Marta Siemiarczuk, Cecil Lyon, Barb Cohen, James Jeffcott, Margaret Matheson, Elizabeth Swarbrick, Lynn Bessoudo, David Jung, and my sister, Robin Pascoe.

I thank the American Bar Association, especially Lorraine Murray, for giving me the opportunity to have this book published so I can pass on what I hope are some words of wisdom about the practice of law to other lawyers.

Since an Acknowledgment section can be like an Academy Awards speech where one can thank everyone who helped them in their career, I would like to thank the following:

I thank those law partners or associates with whom I enjoyed practicing for several years: Bill Honeywell, Bill Garay, Doug Stel, Peter Mirsky, Howard Lithwick, and Elise Hallewick.

I thank my secretarial/administrative staff, who lasted more than a few years putting up with me: Jenny Mirsky, Sherry Fortune, Tara Bassett, and Ella Turner.

I thank the many court staff I dealt with over the years on the Family Law and Estates desks, with a special shout out to Penelope Mylonakos and Marie St-Clair at the Ottawa Estates office.

I thank the many local Ottawa and Eastern Ontario Judges and Masters I appeared before in Ottawa, Perth, Pembroke, Brockville, Kingston, Cornwall, Toronto, and L'Orignal. I did not always agree with them, but they (for the most part) gave me fair hearings and treated my clients and myself with respect. I had only a few bad experiences with judges over the years. I had many more exceptional "moment" experiences with judges than bad ones. And sometimes, though not often, when they disagreed with me, they had good reasons why they might be right.

I thank the Court of Appeal judges I appeared before, who gave me some of my most memorable moments as a lawyer.

I thank the many lawyers I have dealt with over the years, those who generously gave me advice, and the many lawyers I had files with, most of whom were Family Law lawyers.

And lastly, I would like to thank all my clients. In addition to providing me with a livelihood, they allowed me to have a rewarding and meaningful legal career.

Index